Contemporary Art and the Display of Ancient Egypt

Contemporary Art and the Display of Ancient Egypt

Alice Stevenson

UCLPRESS

First published in 2025 by
UCL Press
University College London
Gower Street
London WC1E 6BT

Available to download free: www.uclpress.co.uk

A CIP catalogue record for this book is available from The British Library.

ISBN: 978-1-80008-755-2 (Hbk.)
ISBN: 978-1-80008-756-9 (Pbk.)
ISBN: 978-1-80008-757-6 (PDF)
ISBN: 978-1-80008-761-3 (epub)
DOI: https://doi.org/10.14324/111.9781800087576

Contents

List of figures

List of tables

Acknowledgements

I undertook the research for this book during a sabbatical from the UCL Institute of Archaeology in 2023, funded by a British Academy Mid-Career Fellowship (MCFSS22\220026). I am hugely grateful to Rachel Mairs and Christina Riggs for supporting my application. Two PhD students provided paid research assistance on the project, supported by the grant: Ellen Pavey, who checked interview transcriptions, and Elaine Charwat, who collated German language newspaper resources and reviewed German translations. I also extend my great appreciation to Rafie Cecilia, who kindly helped to source Italian language sources.

Contemporary art represents a new area of research for me, as does the study of art history and Egyptian art. They are topics in which I have had no prior education but to which I was drawn by my interest in the interpretation of material culture and mediations between past and present. Consequently, I have approached the project with some trepidation. I am therefore especially thankful to several people for helping me to navigate this new body of literature. For advice on defining contemporary art, I am indebted to Evi Baniotopoulou, and I have drawn upon her expertise in my introduction. I would also like to thank the following for suggesting sources or providing access to relevant archives: Summer Austin, John Baines, Jan Dahms, Vanessa Davies, Patrick De Soete, Stuart Frost, Corrine Kratz, Robert Kuhn, Laura Osorio Sunnucks, Alessandro Pezzati, Daniela Picchi, Melanie Pitkin, Sophie Pretorius, Patricia Usick and Elizabeth Wood. The Egypt Exploration Society kindly hosted a panel discussion on this topic in June 2023. I am similarly thankful to the Musées royaux d'art et d'histoire in Brussels for the invitation to chair a conversation on contemporary art and Egyptology in September 2023.

I owe a particular debt of gratitude to James Putnam for his openness and generosity in sharing his personal archive relating to *Time Machine*, and indeed to all the curators and artists who graciously gave their time to speak with me on this topic and to review chapters. All interviews for this study were conducted in compliance with UCL Ethics Research Committee guidance (approval number 2022.013) and all quotes from interviews are used with permission. In the final stages of preparation, three anonymous peer reviewers pushed me in helpful directions to tighten the arguments presented here. At UCL Press I would especially like to thank Pat Gordon-Smith, Lara Speicher, Jaimee Biggins and Elliot Beck for their guidance. Michele Greenbank oversaw the final production of the volume and I am enormously grateful for her attention to detail and editorial suggestions.

Beyond the immediate thanks related directly to the project, I must acknowledge a longer-standing debt to Colin Renfrew, whose undergraduate module at the University of Cambridge in 2000, Art and Archaeology, sowed the first seeds for the ideas in this book. It was through his class that I was first introduced to contemporary art and architecture, as well as the potential for cross-fertilisation of concepts from those disciplines and their histories of thought and practice. I must confess that I was bemused by the module at the time, seeing it initially as being well beyond the scope of archaeological training and my interest in human antiquity. But those classes have stayed with me for more than 20 years, fostering a confidence to visit art galleries and explore material beyond my comfort zones.

Finally, my deepest gratitude goes to my husband Paul for being so supportive during 2023 as we juggled between the two of us a challenging year of childcare.

Introduction

On a warm summer's day in July 2017, I was attending a workshop at Blythe House, a massive Edwardian baroque building in South Kensington, London. Its labyrinthine interiors had been repurposed from a Post Office Savings Bank to a museum store in 1979 and its vast storeys, attics and sub-basements were stacked high with collections from the British Museum, Science Museum and Victoria and Albert Museum (V&A). That morning, however, I found myself peering out from the reception at the one artefact not kept in the building: *Tsuki-No-Hikari* (*Moonlight*), a three-metre-tall bronze sculpture created by the Polish artist Igor Mitoraj (Figure 0.1). An A4 piece of stained, curling white paper lay on the windowsill, bearing a quote from the artist:

> While making my sculpture for this exhibition I felt lost like a grain of sand in the desert of Egypt. What do the immense eyes of the statues see, looking inside their soul and gazing for centuries at their shadows in the light of the sun and the moon?

The sculpture had originally welcomed more than a million visitors to the British Museum during the 1994 *Time Machine: Ancient Egypt and Contemporary Art* exhibition but now, more than 20 years later, it was gazing rather forlornly at the concrete forecourt of the museum's storage facility. Its tenure in the public eye had been brief, its relationship to existing collections ambiguous.

From the 1980s, contemporary artists were increasingly being invited by museums to provide their own unique interventions in gallery spaces, in all manner of forms. Juxtaposing historic archaeological collections with contemporary art is a practice that has continued with regularity ever since (Roberts 2013; Settis 2018, 10; Shaya 2021, 647–51; Kiilerich 2021). By the 2010s, museums of all types were 'awash with artists' (Stephens 2012, 22), who remain today a popular addition to academic programmes and museological projects. Outside of the 'white cube' of the modern art gallery, these 'bricoleurs' (Malbert 1995, 25) have, as artist–curator James Putnam suggests, 'offered individual museums an opportunity to take an objective look at their traditional approaches to the display and presentation of their collections and thus learn more about themselves and their audiences' (Putnam 2009, 202). But have museums really embraced this opportunity? And might these exhibitions offer more than a rethink of display and presentation? Could they alter interpretive approaches and perceptions of the subject matter itself? Or are they merely appropriations of 'non-European' artefacts in pursuit of creative artistic experiment, new audiences and relevance? To what extent do they provide dialogues between the past and present? What do these interventions *do*?

These are questions that I want to explore through Egyptology collections since, as a discipline, Egyptology is frequently chastised for its academic insularity and its narrow, self-referential discourses. However, the interface of contemporary art, Egyptian material culture and museums discussed in this book reveals mutually reinforcing modes of cultural production. It serves too as a broader demonstration of the ways in which contemporary art interventions are themselves not ahistorical but share with other representational practices ways of looking and knowing that are influenced by wider intellectual, political and cultural milieus. This supports my allied conviction that in trying to understand the ancient past, it is just as important to examine how that past has been understood and to consider the conditions that have shaped those understandings (Bahrani 2003; Riggs 2017). I concur, therefore, with archaeologist Colin Renfrew (2003, 83) that there is much to be gained from taking a more introspective look at how the display of both contemporary art and archaeology affects our interpretation of the past.

This is not to say that Egyptology has ignored the contemporary. The influence of ancient Egypt on more recent art practice is well-charted territory, addressed most frequently under the guise of 'Egyptomania' or as part of reception studies (Moser 2015a), a burgeoning subfield of academic enquiry that examines the impact of ancient Egypt historically as well as in popular culture today. But such work tends to describe the products of Egyptomania, including modern art, as self-contained, esoteric cultural and historical phenomena that have limited repercussions for the scholarly study of the Egyptian past itself.

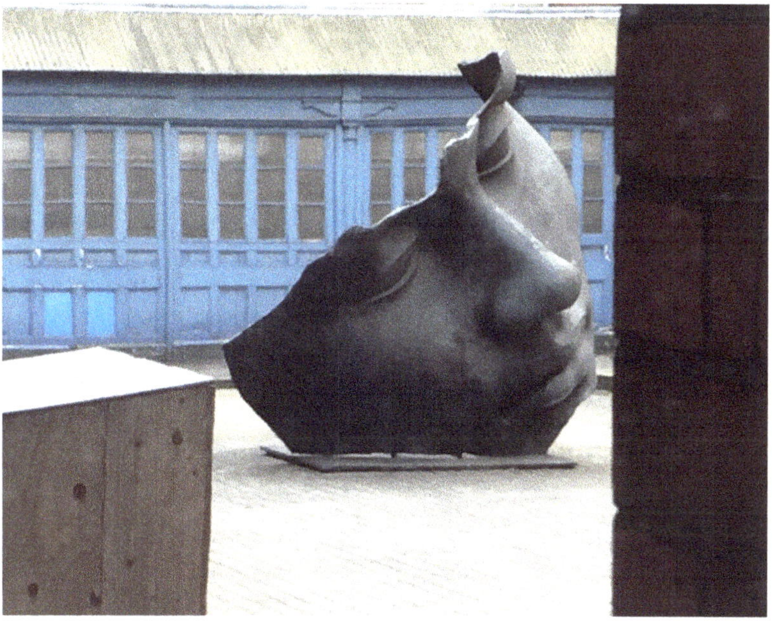

Figure 0.1 Igor Mitoraj's *Moonlight* sculpture lying on the forecourt of the British Museum's then storage facility at Blythe House in 2017. Photograph by Alice Stevenson.

In contrast, related subjects to Egyptology have explored the role of contemporary art as a means of communicating the results of academic work to the public and colleagues (e.g. Cochrane and Russell 2007), and moreover, to produce relevant disciplinary knowledge (Renfrew 2003). This is most notably the case in anthropology, where contemporary art as a methodology or as knowledge representation has been explored in a range of fieldwork and research contexts (Deliss 2012; Geismar 2015). Classical Studies has a similarly flourishing field of scholarship on the intersections of classical and contemporary art (e.g. Gallo and Storini 2018; Kiilerich 2021; Squire et al. 2018). Archaeological fieldsites, meanwhile, have been subject to artistic involvement from the phenomenologically informed exploration of the Leskernick landscape in Cornwall, UK (Bender et al. 2007), through to Dragos Gheorghiu's *Artchaeology* (2009) at the site of Vadastra, Romania. As a body of scholarship these examples provide some valuable prompts for this study, but my focus is the museum as a site of knowledge practice – a site that both Egyptological and contemporary art collections have long occupied – rather than active archaeological surveys or ethnographic endeavours more generally.

This book therefore sits within a scholarly tradition of examining museum cultures not for how they are consumed, but for how they are produced. It responds to calls for Egyptologists to confront the legacies of Egyptian art and how it shapes the contemporary world (Meskell 2005; Moser 2015b; Riggs 2014a). In this vein, while a popular refrain when ancient and modern are juxtaposed is that they are 'in dialogue', I argue that in practice the contemporary and the ancient do not necessarily inform each other but are both mediated by and mediations on the frame that produces them. Following Jacques Rancière (2013, x), this is not about reception, but about the 'fabric of experience within which they are produced ... performance and exhibition spaces, forms of circulation, and reproduction – but also modes of perception and regimes of emotion, categories that identify them, thought patterns that categorize and interpret them'.

As a more museological than art-historical study, then, this book is an exercise in exploring museum agencies that shape exhibitionary practice. It is all too easy when discussing artists' interventions to fall into the vernacular of referring to 'the museum' as if it has its own institutional agency. Artists, however, do not work with museums per se, but with specific people and departments within them. Such projects are comprised of competing sets of expertise and authority, different disciplinary knowledge and alternative functional duties from front of house and marketing to curatorial and collections management. Who takes responsibility for facilitating, mediating and promoting the work of contemporary artists amidst a museum's collection? Curators? Educationalists? Designers? A further consideration is an external area of display practice – the art market – which shares with museums and Egyptology a history of exhibitionary strategies, classificatory language and intellectual exchange that has informed how antiquities are understood and how contemporary art relates to them. Scholarship has only quite recently begun to critically understand the role of dealers and their impact upon histories of collections (Westgarth 2020; Biro et al. 2023): Chapter 1 takes up these currents to demonstrate how the agency of dealers shaped academic conceptions of Egyptian art. Dealers formed part of a wide network of archaeologists, scholars, curators, critics and contemporary artists who collectively laid the foundations for the museum displays of later decades that are the subject of this study.

To answer some of the above questions, my chapters employ three extended case studies of institutions in which contemporary artists' work has been introduced alongside the Egyptological collections they curate: London's British Museum (Chapter 3), Turin's Museo Egizio (Chapter 4) and Munich's Staatliches Museum Ägyptischer Kunst (Chapter 5). Each holds substantial collections first founded centuries ago: Sir Hans Sloane's (1660–1753) private collection, which became the nucleus of the British Museum in 1753; items collected during Vitaliano Donati's royal commission to Egypt that same year, which became the core of the Turin Museum when it opened in 1824; and Duke Albrecht V of Bavaria's Kunstkammer, founded in Munich in 1565. Asking shared questions of these museums permits a comparative approach, although each example speaks more strongly to some themes than others. This is not surprising given the different buildings, histories and policies of these institutions, but is also due to the variable 'cultural armature' and the influence of place upon them (Levitt 2015).

The contemporary exhibitions that have been staged in these museums have been largely analysed previously either from the perspective of visitor experience and education (Robins 2013; Roberts 2013; Larceneux et al. 2016) or from the purview of art practice (Putnam 2009). They have never been fully evaluated with reference to museological practice and knowledge production as they relate to archaeology or Egyptology (but see Tully 2010). Thus, while it is rightly asked what these displays offer to visitors, the issue of what they offer to the museum and its staff, as well as to specialist audiences, is more rarely broached. How might those invested in researching and documenting Egyptian material take such interventions seriously as a mode of enquiry or, at the very least, as a means of shifting perception and productively disrupting received wisdom? Like the public, academics are not a homogeneous group and thus I prefer to avoid the tendency in much of museum writing to assume that there is a singular experience of space, art or the construction of knowledge in this dynamic. It is, for instance, common for writers to make reductive proclamations regarding 'the visitor' and what they may take away from exhibitions. The field of visitor studies, however, has produced a substantive body of evidence concerning the range of messages that museum-goers take away from their visits, often contrary to the intention of curators or artists and framed by variable lived experiences and social circumstances (e.g. Falk and Dierking 2013).

My aim is not only to collate and document for the first time these examples of transient artistic interventions in Egyptian collections from the late twentieth century onwards – many of which have left little archival trace in the institutions in which they resided – but also to historicise them. To this end I consider their social and political contexts and the modalities of engagement between art and antiquity, and argue that there is potential in these experiments for providing benefit to artists, curators and the public through a more interdisciplinary process. In one sense it is an attempt to continue these experiments, by reviving the dialogue with those who were involved in their production and dissemination. A key part of the research design has therefore involved 25 semi-structured interviews, supplemented by public panel discussions, with artists and curators. Such dialogues were invaluable not only to redress gaps in the archive, but also because they exposed disciplinary and professional antagonisms between art history, archaeology, Egyptology and museology, as well as tensions between museum departments. These dialogues were complemented, where possible, by a survey of available exhibition plans, the surfaces and detailing of architectural interiors and the wider museum ecosystem of the cities in which the exhibitions took place. Archival correspondence, visitor comments and media reviews were additionally consulted to chart some of the varied responses to the staging of these exhibitions.

What is contemporary art?

At its most prosaic, contemporary art is the art of the present (Geismar 2015, 183). In art-historical terms, contemporary art has been temporally separated from modern art, the latter generally belonging to Euro-American trends of the late nineteenth and early twentieth centuries, the former emerging in the 1960s and being produced by still living artists. These terms involve not only temporal separation, but also conceptual differences. Although both types of art are deemed quite radical and abstract, contemporary art tends to be produced in a much wider range of forms than modern art. The chronological distinctions between them, and the primacy given to the abstracted form, however, do not hold true in all times and places. Different countries locate the line between 'modern' and 'contemporary' at other temporal junctures (Lorente 2011, 7). Likewise, it is valid to question the deep-rooted assumptions as to what 'art' should be (Weibel and Buddensieg 2007, 7; Geismar 2015). It has been argued, for instance, that in locations outside of Europe and America, contemporary art is a liberation from modernism's heritage, drawing instead from more recent local art currents (Belting 2012, 20).

As the variety of media in which contemporary art is produced diversifies – including all manner of technological tools, artists' own and others' bodies, space, combined arts and, recently, virtual reality (VR), artificial intelligence (AI) and non-fungible tokens (NFTs) – and as the range of spaces in which it is located expands and the speed of communications increases, it becomes harder to establish hard-and-fast definitions. Definitive movements within art today, such as cubism or surrealism, are more difficult to identify, with many artists working independently rather than as part of a collective seeking the same ideals. More critical readings of what contemporary art entails, therefore, have found generalisations wanting (Smith 2006). For these reasons, I have heeded the advice of my colleague Evi Baniotopoulou to localise analysis of artists' practices rather than try to place them within a general framework of 'contemporary art' that is almost impossible to contain. Significantly for this study and its focus on what happens in museums, Gell's (1998, 12) observation that 'to discuss "works of art" is to discuss entities which have been given a prior *institutional* definition as such' is helpful in this attempt to localise practice and set it within broader historical and institutional conditions.

Five modalities of engagement

The engagement of artists with Egyptian collections is not a unitary or shared general practice, in either purpose, process or outcome. In examining the intersections of contemporary art and collections from ancient Egypt, I therefore propose that it is useful to distinguish five general modalities of relationship: inspiration, insertion, intervention, interdisciplinarity and invention. As with any such classification, the boundaries between these categories are not always clear cut nor mutually exclusive. They do, however, provide a heuristic means to characterise different motivations and processes, as well as to draw into relief themes and issues.

Inspiration refers to instances where ancient heritage becomes a stimulus for artistic creations, for which archaeology has provided a rich set of references (Renfrew 2003; Roelstraete 2013), ancient Egypt especially (Kholeif 2014; Brown 2022). This is the mode that has been most intensively explored for the intersection of Egyptology and modern or contemporary art, with numerous temporary exhibitions on the theme of inspiration having been hosted over the decades. Amongst these are ensemble enterprises that showcase a diversity of artistic responses to Egypt: *The Inspiration of Egypt: Its Influence on British Artists* (at the Royal Pavilion, Brighton Museum and Art Gallery, and Manchester City Art Gallery in 1983), *Ägyptische und moderne Skulptur* (see Herzer et al. 1986), *Egyptomania: Egypt in Western Art, 1730–1930* (see Humbert et al. 1994), *Egyptian Echoes – Contemporary Art Inspired by Ancient*

Monuments (see Wilkinson 1993) and *Visions of Egypt* (see Ferrari and Hinson 2022). Wider-ranging, but still encompassing Egypt, are shows such as the Getty Villa's *Modern Antiquity: Picasso, de Chirico, Léger, and Picabia in the Presence of the Antique* (2011–12). Additionally, there have been several exhibitions that have taken a single artist's oeuvre as their focus, such as *Alberto Giacometti et L'Égypte Antique* (at the Giacometti Institute in 2021; see also Klemm and Wildung 2008), *Paul Klee: Die Reisen ach Ägypten 1928/29* (Staatliche Kunstsammlungen Dresden 2014) and *Rêve D'Égypte* (at Musée Rodin in 2022–3). What is surprising about all these appraisals of modern and contemporary art is how infrequently the art-historical milieu in which these artists worked is recognised as being equally relevant for how it shaped Egyptological practice of the time, a lacuna that Chapter 1 addresses. And rarer still is for those who specialise in the interpretation of the past to take inspiration from artistic productions in turn, as Chapter 2 onwards evaluate.

While works that are inspired by ancient Egypt in general are not my primary focus, there is a relevant legacy that draws them into the frame: relatively few sculptors and painters who were inspired by ancient Egypt visited the country (Ferrari 2022, 123). This is mostly the case for European-based modernists – Alberto Giacometti, Pablo Picasso, Francis Bacon, Henry Moore, Jacob Epstein, Henri Gaudier-Brzeska or Roland Moody – as well as for African-American artists in the Harlem Renaissance like Aaron Douglas and Meta Vaux Warrick Fuller. Their encounter with Egypt was largely a museological, collections-based and artefact-focused one. More specifically, it was an association with the national and colonial collections of the Louvre and the British Museum that shaped their imaginations (Clifford 1988; Ferrari 2022; Moore 1982), and for those in the USA, The Metropolitan Museum of Art or the Boston Museum of Fine Arts. Many even established their own private antiquities collections, including Cy Twombly, Pablo Picasso, Henry Matisse, Jacob Epstein, Jacques Lipchitz and Auguste Rodin. For more recent artists, museums and collections are similarly a primary point of reference, with the bust of Nefertiti held in Berlin's Neues Museum a prominent example (Brown 2022).

There are exceptions. For David Hockney, Egypt was 'one of the most thrilling countries' he had ever visited, although his obsession with Egypt is well documented to have been nurtured originally through encounters at the British Museum (Hockney and Stangos 1993, 36). Paul Klee's lifelong interest in Egypt also culminated in a visit to the country in 1928 (Staatliche Kunstsammlungen Dresden 2014). French cubist painter and teacher André Lhote spent considerable time in Egypt with one of his students, Mohamed Naghi (Khalil 2020), while American conceptual and performance artist Lorraine O'Grady's visit to Egypt in 1963 inspired key works exploring diaspora, hybridity and Black female subjectivity. Nevertheless, there is still critical work to be undertaken to contextualise such encounters which, as for the Romantics of the previous century, might also be seen in an Orientalist frame, as has been shown to be the case for Bridget Riley (Johns 2022) and Paul Klee (McGavran 2013).

Works inspired by ancient Egypt have additional relevance for this study as they have often subsequently been inserted into Egyptology galleries, primarily informed by aesthetics and form rather than ancient meanings or archaeological context. Here insertion and intervention exist on a spectrum, since the extent to which the modern artworks act back on the interpretation of ancient material is questionable. For instance, an artistic addition may serve simply to complement or enhance standard interpretive strategies, whereas others are more disruptive and challenge institutional framing. Insertions are usually preconceived artworks that are not produced to speak to a specific museum collection or holding but may latterly have a general relevance that justifies their placement alongside ancient materials. In contrast, interventions are more often created for a specific museum space, collection or theme, with creative processes and performances integral to the site-specific encounter and often emerging from historical research within institutional archives and stores. Interventions include the genre of institutional critique (see Chapter 1), a shorthand for the variety of conceptual art practices that seek to expose the ideologies and power structures upon which museums and galleries are founded (Alberro 2009).

As will be demonstrated in Chapter 1, by the 1990s there existed an array of diverse artist involvement with museums (Putnam 2009; Pearce 1999, 21–5), linked by their site-based engagements with collections, their buildings or their social histories (McShine 1999). All are in a sense disruptive of norms and expectations of display in these contexts, but the level of critique brought to bear upon those spaces and practices varies. Robins (2013) has argued for a distinction between more benign insertions that 'brighten up' museum spaces and those interventions that are more radical or critical in intention. Similarly, Marshall (2012) identifies a more poetic, less overtly political type of intervention originating in Western Europe, in contrast to the more politically engaged examples of institutional critique that emerged in North America. Merriman (2004, 98) has questioned 'how far such questioning and subversion extend beyond the highly culturally literate core museum audience'. These differences have led some to restrict the term 'intervention' only to those projects that are deliberately and effectively provocative, a term that 'signifies the act of interceding to create change' (Marstine 2017, 4). Yet this distinction risks devaluing the power of affective, aesthetic experiences for creating and challenging knowledge and expectations (Barrett and Millner 2014). I will argue that it is these sensorial dimensions of artworks that are of particular value to archaeological and Egyptological interpretation. The contrast between ahistorical, aesthetic-led approaches, on the one hand, and contextual-led strategies of interpretation and representation, on the other, also highlights ongoing tensions between the worlds of museums, Egyptology and art. It is a common polarity of debate in the arts sector, one that curators such as Clémentine Deliss (2020) have found wearisome. Nevertheless, this question of the contexts for cultural heritage has significant import for archaeologists, descendant groups and communities of implication ('those who may be affected by tangible or intangible cultural products in ethical terms': Lehrer 2020, 304) that is not so easily dismissed and demands to be confronted.

Throughout the following chapters, these two modalities of engagement – insertion and intervention – between art and antiquity are the primary focus of my enquiry. Both terms are arguably overused in the museum sector and literature, foregrounding the agency of contemporary art and the artist which are parachuted in to mediate between museum and artwork, drawing museum visitors into the artistic project (La 2017, 217). What is often missing in accounts of insertions or interventions is the sense of process behind them, with the primary assumption being (especially with institutional critique) that displays are inherently flawed and art provides a solution, rather than an opportunity and invitation for what is frequently a negotiation of meaning, authority and space. And this is where interdisciplinarity might come in. As Bertola and Rich (2020, 159) describe, within academia the notion of 'interdisciplinarity' is generally considered to involve two or more cognate disciplines, in contrast to work with non-academic partners like artists which is regarded variously as 'knowledge exchange' or 'partnerships' rather than 'interdisciplinarity'. However, as is explored in the following case studies, there are examples of artists who are historically and archaeologically minded, whose creations blur neat distinctions. Their work reveals a shift from a focus on the outcomes of interdisciplinary practice towards its processes, including the generation of research questions, identification of sources, choice of methodologies and direction of discourse. Interdisciplinarity in this context of exhibition practice can be usefully defined, then, as 'looking for overlaps, shared interests, and reciprocal collaboration between disciplines but without disturbing their individual boundaries and practices' (Bencard et al. 2019, 143).

In these ways, artworks can potentially penetrate disciplinary knowledge more deeply, in providing a prompt not just to see or think differently, but also to alter practice, particularly where artists and academics actively collaborate. In anthropology, for instance, Geismar (2015) notes that art and anthropology share methods and practices of observational techniques, such as photography and film-making, potentially allowing for complementary approaches to undertaking and analysing research that may be of mutual benefit to artists, curators and scholars. Such efforts have also been cast in terms of 'experiment', in which the museum can generate fresh perspectives (Macdonald and Basu 2007; Hansen et al. 2019; Bjerregaard 2019). There are very few examples of such interdisciplinarity where Egyptian archaeology or Egyptology is concerned, but the review of the case studies leads me to advocate for this modality as a means for art to be productive rather than merely representative of knowledge and practice.

Invention refers to initiatives that 'move beyond the boundaries of archaeological practice and archaeological interpretation as well as of art history and practice' (Bailey 2017, 694). This art/archaeology is a radical call to directly utilise the material produced by archaeologists as raw materials in the creation of original work with potential for political action. Such an argument is not a critique of more standard approaches to the past but rather has been promoted as an additional way to treat the remains of the past, one that is neither art nor archaeology and sits outside of the confines of scholarly expectations or professional associations. An example is the 2020 exhibition *Ineligible* at the International Museum of Contemporary Sculpture in Santo Tirso, Portugal. The show utilised surplus archaeological material from commercial archaeological projects in the USA as the raw material for new artwork. In so doing, it presented a novel way to transcend the 'curation crisis' (Childs 2022) of storing material deemed to have little cultural or historic value at a time when space and financial resources are limited. The political and cultural context of archaeological work in Egypt makes such a proposition ethically problematic, and the form of such practice would equally be untenable in the space of museums outside of Egypt which have stewardship over heritage largely procured in colonial contexts.

Whichever modality is employed or represented in a display, it might not always be received as intended. Art might be introduced to diversify a museum's audiences, yet it may equally prove alienating; an ineffective intervention may only be accessible to those with an existing confidence within the art world. Artists might be brought in to 'change up' traditional displays that are otherwise hard to update, but their intercessions are often only temporary, with galleries reverting to standard modes of representation thereafter. Creative works may provide emotional and sensory environments for static objects overly dependent upon specialist terms, although the greater degree of subjectivity brought into archaeological interpretation may depart so significantly from historical sources as to obscure them and raise ethical questions regarding interpretive framing. To what extent insertion and intervention bridge a divide between past and present for the mutual benefit of understanding both, or simply overlay the past with contemporary relevance, varies considerably. One thing to note here is that while I am a museum archaeologist principally interested in how contemporary art interventions can inform how specialists gain insight into the ancient past, I also do not offer these modalities as a classificatory hierarchy of good or bad practice. Ultimately, the use of contemporary art within museums will serve different purposes, moments, audiences and spaces.

Chapter overviews

Chapter 1 explores the histories of these modalities in the museum sector and their relationship to Egyptology from the late nineteenth century to the present day. It charts how modernist art practices of the early twentieth century not only entailed artists finding inspiration from Egyptian art, but also influenced how Egyptologists interpreted the past. It argues that the legacy of diverse modernist juxtapositions of the ancient and modern led to an over-emphasis on ahistorical descriptions and aesthetic presentations of Egyptian material. Divorced from the times and spaces in which these objects had originally been given meaning, this has in turn profoundly shaped Egyptological discourse regarding 'ancient art'. In contrast, towards the end of the twentieth century, more critical, contemporary art practices emerged, some rooted in historical research itself. These have the potential to work back upon trends that have decontextualised Egyptian material culture in favour of revealing the frames that inform how we talk about the past and the references we use to do so. These more recent artworks can highlight aspects that are silenced by museum display, but which are vital for archaeological interpretation. Chapter 2 then outlines illustrative examples of modalities seen in artists' work with Egyptology collections in the twenty-first century, together with some of the challenges and opportunities they offer for the interpretation of the past in the present, for both the public and academics.

Chapters 3 to 5 present the extended case studies, beginning with one of the first examples of a full-scale contemporary intervention in a permanent Egyptology gallery, at the British Museum in 1994 (Chapter 3), and a reappraisal of its legacy and significance for archaeological interpretation. This first exhibition at the British Museum, *Time Machine: Ancient Egypt and Contemporary Art*, was reimagined the following year in Turin, Italy, at the Museo Egizio. This museum is the subject of Chapter 4, where I argue that a different set of local historical pressures has facilitated a city-wide embrace of contemporary art in the service of urban regeneration. More recently, the Museo Egizio has taken a more proactive institutional reappraisal of the role of contemporary art as not just a transient source of inspiration and intervention, but also as part of the permanent collection. Chapter 5 shifts the focus to Germany and the Staatliches Museum Ägyptischer Kunst in Munich, where there has been a long-term institutional commitment to contemporary art as a communication and engagement strategy, albeit one that has been unidirectional in terms of how the past influences the present, but not vice versa.

Throughout these case studies, the mutual implications of contemporary art, Egyptian material culture, the art market and museum practice are foregrounded, together with their shared historical, sociocultural and sensorial contexts of production and consumption. Equally relevant are the agencies that are responsible for promoting and implicating modern with ancient works, whether curators, exhibition designers, educationalists, dealers, artists or academics, as well as the broader dynamics of installing works within wider institutional contexts and physical settings. In all these activities, the question of which times are being evoked – ancient pasts, more recent historical constructions or contemporaneity – is touched upon, to see what the possibilities are for interdisciplinarity and whether relationships between artists and Egyptologists might be mutually beneficial. The final chapter draws together a comparative analysis of the case studies to make suggestions for what might form shared ground for fostering a shift from inspiration and intervention to interdisciplinarity, so that art might inform rather than just sit alongside collections.

1
Juxtapositions: a historical perspective

Exhibitions that mix antiquities with contemporary art appear on the surface to be novel, often being described in the media as 'surprising', 'quirky', 'innovative' or 'fresh'. Following Geismar (2015, 185), however, I contend that contemporary art's relationship with museums and other disciplines needs to be understood in a longer-term perspective as this has repercussions for more recent practice and politics of representation. Experimental juxtaposition of contemporary artistic creations with objects of antiquity is an activity that has been undertaken for more than a hundred years. Thus, while Egyptologist Moreno García (2015) has rightly brought attention to the social and political worlds which forged a myth of eternal Egypt at the end of the nineteenth and in the early twentieth centuries, leading beautiful objects and monuments to have a disproportionate weight in Egyptology, I argue that this 'preferential attention devoted to works of art' (Moreno García 2015, 52) is equally a product of developments in the early twentieth-century modern art market and its institutionalisation within museums. As a result, many museums prioritised in their displays of ancient Egyptian aesthetic over contextual information about where artefacts were found and originally used, as the language and perspectives of scholars, curators and artists were recursively transformed.

In contrast, later twentieth-century social, political and cultural worlds catalysed alternative types of artistic intervention within traditional museum spaces. More conceptual installations that challenged earlier modernist views of ancient material emerged alongside those continuing to work in a more ahistorical vein. Included amongst the former are various forms of what has been called 'institutional critique' (Alberro 2009), in which artists, rather than simply taking inspiration from objects themselves, explicitly sought to recontextualise museum artefacts, their histories and their framings, by provocatively addressing the structures of cultural organisations. This mode of engagement became popular in the museum sector in the early 2000s. As the twenty-first century progressed, a range of modalities came to operate within museums, each with a different degree of artistic engagement with historical sources. Some concerned the acquisition and display conditions of the previous two centuries; others examined sources of evidence for past meanings in antiquity. All sought to bring a new relevance of ancient material to the present day, but, arguably, few changed how the past itself was understood.

Art and archaeology in the nineteenth and early twentieth centuries

Archaeology has a long-standing association with art-historical traditions, 'sharing conventions and vocabularies for visualising the world' (Russell and Cochrane 2013, 1). Archaeologist Stephanie Moser (2020) has recognised a movement which flourished in Britain from the late 1850s that she describes as 'archaeological genre painting'. Her detailed study focused on the classical revival paintings of Lawrence Alma-Tadema, Edward Poynter and Edwin Long, identifying how archaeology was used by these artists in their depictions of ancient life and how these artists influenced archaeology in turn. All three paid close attention to details of Egyptian artefacts in museum collections, engaged deeply with Egyptological publications and were well acquainted with leading archaeologists and Egyptologists of the day. Indeed, Alma-Tadema, like his French contemporary Gustave Moreau, was often considered to have such expertise as to be identified as an archaeologist himself.

The famous archaeologist Flinders Petrie's social circle included a significant number of artists, including Alma-Tadema and Poynter, in addition to Henry Wallis, George F. Watts and Henry Holiday (Garnett 2021). They variously visited Petrie on his digs, funded fieldwork through donations to the Egypt Exploration Fund or actively participated in preservation campaigns, such as the Society for the Preservation of Monuments of Ancient Egypt (Drower 1985; Gange 2015). In these interactions, developing ideas of what constituted the focus for archaeological enquiry became mutually reinforced (Moser 2020). On the one hand, Petrie had extolled the importance of small, fragmentary and mundane things for archaeological interpretation; on the other, Alma-Tadema and colleagues revered minor antiquities through meticulous renderings of materials, textures and ancient uses of objects on their canvases. Notably, Petrie is also lionised in histories of archaeology for emphasising the importance of making a record of the circumstances of an archaeological find (Petrie 1904), something more readily recognised in professional archaeology and Egyptology today as archaeological context. This refers to the location of a find in physical space, together with associated material. It is a vital part of archaeological inference, not only permitting the dating of finds, but also providing evidence for how material was used and made meaningful by past peoples.

Egyptologist Dominic Montserrat (2000, 68–9) has similarly demonstrated the impact of modern-day art on archaeology in Petrie's effusive 1892 descriptions of the painted pavement from Akhenaten and Nefertiti's Great Palace at Amarna, which were suffused with references to the Art Nouveau movement: the 'naturalistic grace of the plants' and 'the new style of art'. The resonance between ancient and modern times was not simply a casual or convenient point of reference, but implied a comparable ideology: 'Amarna art, he [Petrie] implies, is somehow more democratic' (Montserrat 2000, 69). These phrases in Petrie's writing further betray the political relationship between art and archaeology. Petrie's tastes for the Pre-Raphaelite and Art Nouveau were aligned with his definition of culture and civilisation. In keeping with the cultural evolutionary ideology that had informed his earlier studies of Egyptian prehistory, he contended that civilisation was cyclical, interspersed with phases of barbarism (Petrie 1911). Accordingly, he situated art periods relative to their position in this cycle and appraised sculpture relative to it (Petrie 1911; 1931). These attitudes were made explicit in his public attack on modernist sculptor Jacob Epstein's *Day* and *Night* statues erected on the building above St James's Park underground station in 1928 (Figure 1.1). Epstein himself had spent hours admiring the Egyptian art in the galleries of the Louvre and the British Museum. Like Petrie, he was struck by Amarna art, with a limestone bust of Akhenaten in the Louvre particularly catching his eye (Arrowsmith 2010, Ch. 1). In 1929 Petrie denounced Epstein's sculptures in a letter to the *Manchester Guardian* as 'part of the modern system of Jazz' and a 'primitive product of a race' (Challis and Romain 2014).

Epstein was just one of numerous modernist artists inspired by their time spent in museums, with London's museum network one of the most important centres of global aesthetic exchange in the early twentieth century (Arrowsmith 2010). James Nash, Roland Moody and Francis Bacon are further good examples. The latter held Egyptian sculpture in

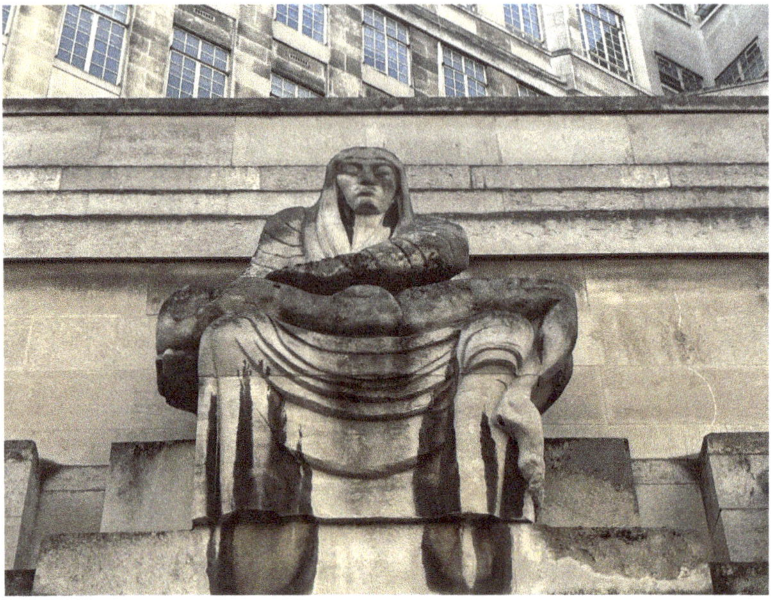

Figure 1.1 Jacob Epstein's sculpture *Night* on the north side of the east wing of 55 Broadway (above St James's Park underground station), London. Photograph by Alice Stevenson.

high regard (Bragg 2013) and was well acquainted with Egyptologists: Guy Brunton, one of Petrie's students who had led excavations in Middle Egypt throughout the 1920s, made regular social visits to Bacon's home, with at least four occasions recorded for 1929 (Pipe 2020). While the modernist art movement was not homogeneous, encompassing many different styles, these artists shared an interest in the radical shift in artistic discourse away from the pre-eminence of classical modes of representation and a tendency towards abstraction. For many, this meant embracing 'pre-Greek' visual imagery, appropriating the art of ancient cultures and remote colonies as a source of transgressive artistic inspiration (Force 2023). In so doing, the decontextualisation of material culture was prioritised, bringing attention to the formal qualities and direct aesthetic experience of sculpture and form, rather than being drawn into historical narration. Concurrently, the genre of 'history painting' was to 'plummet even further in the twentieth century' (Tate n.d.), disappearing almost entirely from art circles following the post-World War Two break-up of empire.

Parallel developments in art theory saw a move away from self-contained accounts of stylistic progression towards studies of visual phenomena with a view to accessing broader spiritual and cultural insights into human experience. Publications such as art dealer and collector Paul Guillaume's 1926 *Primitive Negro Sculpture* combined the aestheticisation of art with the evolutionary psychology of scholars like philosopher and ethnographer Georges-Henri Luquet or psychoanalyst Sigmund Freud. Such work sought a universal unconscious, and a continuous 'will to art' identified as a primal instinct to produce art shared by children, the mentally ill and 'primitive peoples'. These sorts of wider cultural attitudes and dispositions underpin what is considered to be one of the fundamental treatises on representation in Egyptian art: Heinrich Schäfer's *Principles of Art*, first published in 1919 (Baines 1985), which also included attempts to understand Egyptian art through the study of children's drawings. Schäfer's interest in modern art remained a subtext in this 1919 volume but it is the explicit focus of his 1928 publication *Ägyptische und heutige Kunst*, written for a cultured lay public. Throughout, Schäfer made comparisons between Egyptian art, on the one hand, and impressionism and expressionism, on the other, with cubism considered the closest parallel in terms of its emphasis upon geometrical forms. He also undertook a characterisation of the art of different 'pre-Greek' civilisations, comparing them to various ancient Egypt periods, accompanied by figures depicting the work of Pablo Picasso, Erich Heckel and Marc Chagall. Here, as in Jean Capart's (1905) treatment of Predynastic art (art from Egyptian prehistory of the fourth millennium BC), the spectre of 'primitivism' casts a long shadow over Egyptological visual culture discourse in its language and assumptions about the origin, function and nature of art.

Schäfer's 1928 treatise on Egyptian art quoted directly from Carl Einstein, an influential German Jewish writer, art historian and critic who had penned *Negerplastik* (1915), a publication that became a major catalyst for Western avant-garde imaginations. Einstein is often credited with creating the problematic category of 'African art', which, alongside material from Oceania, became the core focus for the study of 'primitive art'. Notably, Einstein had a decades-long friendship with Hedwig Fechheimer (Peuckert 2014), a German Jewish Egyptologist and art historian, with whom he visited Egypt in the spring of 1910. She had published *Die Plastik der Aegypter* the year before Einstein's *Negerplastik*, extolling the value of cubism as an aesthetic means to comprehend Egyptian visual culture, work that also informed Schäfer's thinking.

Fechheimer sought to establish a grammar for ancient Egyptian art that aligned with its formal language of artistic expression, heeding Paul Cézanne's call to treat nature according to the cylinder, the sphere and the cone. Similar arguments can be found in Henri Frankfort's (1932, 40) appraisal of the 'aesthetic significance of the cubism of Egyptian art', in which he also invoked comparisons with the art of the Congo, Mexico and the Gold Coast, inflecting elements of primitivist tropes alongside explicit references to the work of modern artists such as Eric Gill. Frankfort's interest in the affinities between ancient and modern art is further demonstrated by the excursions he arranged for his students of Egyptian art at the Oriental Institute of Chicago, such as to a Picasso exhibition held in the city in 1940 (Evans 2012, 6). Like Brunton, he was acquainted with the modernist artists living in London, notably Barbara Hepworth, whose studio near Frankfort's 1930s home in Hampstead was the centre of the abstract art movement in the UK. Frankfort reviewed her artworks for *Axis: A Quarterly Review of Contemporary Art* (Frankfort 1935) and even acquired one of her sculptures, *Two Forms* (1933), which is now in the collection of the Tate (registration no. TO7123).

It was not just in the frameworks for comparison and language that these Egyptologists echoed modernist sensibilities, but also in the presentation of their scholarship. Fechheimer's discussions of form and style were influenced by her intensive use of black and white photographs of museum artefacts, which were 'framed in peculiar and unusual ways' informed by the avant-garde movements of Berlin (Étienne 2021, 33). Fechheimer's impact upon modern artists is clear, with her book being one of the primary sources for sculptor Alberto Giacometti's Egyptian-inspired works (Étienne 2021; Bru 2024) and appreciated by modern artist Paul Klee (Mahler 2019). Her work was also admired by André Breton, leader of a group of poets and artists in Paris who came together under his 1924 *Surrealist Manifesto* to challenge norms, embrace the uncanny and unexpected, and revolutionise human experience by imagining alternative realities. A dialectic space that combined modern art, anthropology and archaeology was similarly created through the pages of lavishly illustrated periodicals such as the one founded in 1926 by Picasso's publisher, Christian Zervos, *Cahiers d'art*, where 'archaic' objects were subject to sumptuous black and white camerawork in full-paged reproductions (Kosmadaki 2017). Other publications of the time, amongst them the short-lived dissident surrealist magazine *Documents* (1929–30), intermixed photographic collages of ancient material culture, ethnographic objects and modern art, alongside scholarly articles on archaeology, ethnography and museums, including contributions by Fechheimer.[1] The journal was, as anthropologist James Clifford (1988, 132) observes, 'a kind of ethnographic display of images, texts, objects, labels, a playful museum that simultaneously collects and reclassifies its specimens'.

This 'surrealist archaeology' was firmly situated within museums, not within archaeological sites, landscapes or excavations, only with their products (Evans 2004, 105). Such an object focus was reflected too in the personal collections of ancient, ethnographic and modern art that were amassed by several participants in movements like surrealism. These most famously include Breton's collection, now partially immortalised as 'the wall from 42 rue Fontaine' in the Centre Pompidou Musée national d'art moderne which incorporates ancient Egyptian artefacts within an ensemble of world cultures and contemporary artworks. Many collectors sourced these artefacts from Parisian dealers like Joseph Brummer and Paul Guillaume (Tythacott 2003). Joseph Brummer established his gallery in Paris in 1909 and was joined by his brothers Ernest and Iman in the business in 1911. They, like antiquities dealer and collector Sydney Bernard Burney in 1920s London, developed reputations for promoting material previously not considered central to the Western art canon by intermixing in their galleries the arts of Africa with those of medieval Europe, the classical world, the Americas, the Near East and Egypt, alongside the creations of contemporary artists – Cézanne, Monet, Rousseau and Picasso, amongst others. Brummer's Parisian gallery (Figure 1.2) has been regarded as responsible for valorising African works as art, which was considered through 'a purely formalist standpoint that ignored their original meaning and function' (Biro 2023, 157). This approach extended to their antiquities sales. As Hardwick reports (2023, 277), the Brummers' stock books rarely used Egyptological terminologies, preferring instead to employ universal artistic terms, in turn implicitly emphasising their relationship with material from other cultures, while creating self-referential artworks that stood apart from their original context.

The galleries of dealers like the Brummers therefore blurred the boundaries between collecting fields, an approach that became increasingly common in the 1920s and the 1930s (e.g. Fry 1920). This included shows such as *Sculpture Considered Apart from Time and Place* (Burney and Underwood 1932) which 'stressed the aesthetic continuity between different traditions and cultures' (Bierbrier 2019, 80). The Brummers were the source of many Egyptian artefacts now held in major museums worldwide, including The Metropolitan Museum of Art and the British Museum (Hardwick 2023). Notably, Joseph Brummer systematically photographed all the artworks in his possession in order to use them for advertising, but he also made them available to avant-garde journals like *Cahiers d'art* and to authors like Carl Einstein (Biro 2015; 2023).[2]

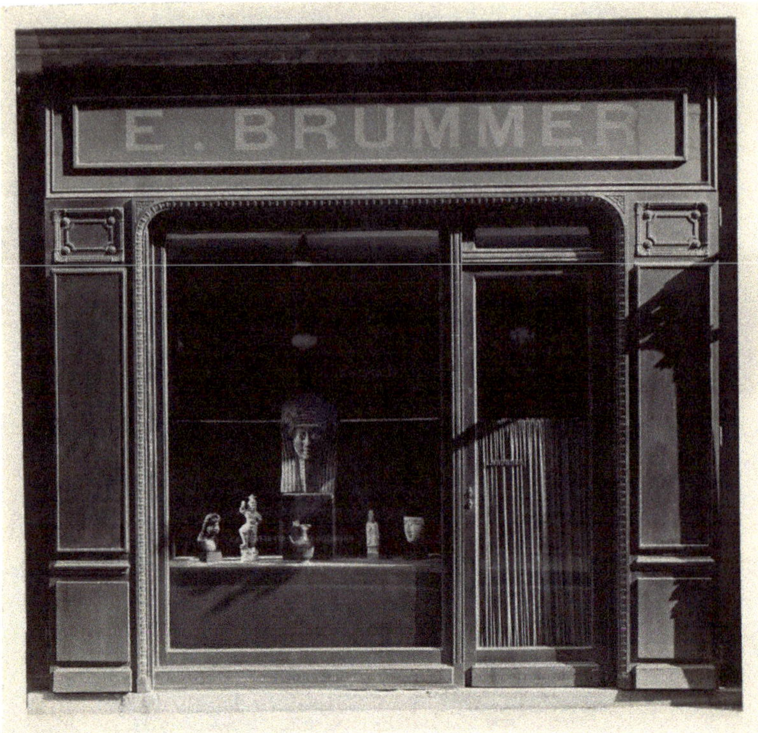

Figure 1.2 Ernest Brummer Gallery, Paris, 1921. Donated to The Metropolitan Museum of Art in 2016, by John Laszlo, nephew of Ella Baché Brummer, wife of Ernest Brummer. Located in The Cloisters Archives. Image in the public domain.

They were also vital for his sales pitches to museums, as letters sent to curators demonstrate.[3] In other words, it is likely that the same sets of photographs were circulated through the Egyptology departments of major museums, through the hands of scholars and through editorial meetings of surrealist magazines for their publication, homogenising ways of seeing and appraising ancient Egyptian artefacts.

Photography and the presentation of collections therefore brought mutually reinforcing modes of aesthetic attention to objects. This point is further underscored by a presentation given by Flinders Petrie at the UK's Museums Association conference in 1910:

> The first qualification for the designing of a gallery should be a familiarity with the requirements of photographing objects. Without proper lighting a successful photograph cannot be obtained; and what will photograph well will exhibit well (Petrie 1910, 55).

The role of photography as central to the viewing of Egyptian art, enacted in museums, became a primary tool for the art-historical work of Hans-Wolfgang Müller and Bernard V. Bothmer (1978), who like Schäfer, dominated scholarship on ancient Egyptian art for much of the twentieth century. Significantly, this interrelationship between photography and museum display further contributed to severing artefacts from their original contexts, facilitating their transformation into *l'art pour l'art* (cf. Malraux 1947; Kosmadaki 2017, 102). In the museum and in the photograph, objects were dislocated from their previous settings, erasing scale, colour and location as variables of meaning-making, creating in its place a space for the abstract concept of style. These processes themselves modernised archaeological remains, which had been extricated from their contexts and held up for aesthetic consumption in the museum, years before they enticed modern artists.

Further interrogation of these histories reveals that Egypt was not just one inspiration for modern artists, nor was it simply a generalised Egyptomania that prompted aesthetic engagement. Contrary to assertions that modernists took little interest in ancient Egypt or that Egypt played no role in the artistic movement of 'primitivism' (e.g. Cohen 1994; Wildung 2021), the idea of ancient Egypt was intimately implicated within the project to create the very category of primitive art and modern art itself. In the melting pot of post-war Paris, dealers trading in an eclectic melange of contemporary art, ethnology and antiquities leveraged their reputations as connoisseurs of contemporary art to recast the ethnological as 'high art', by asserting a 'very clear relation to Egyptian aesthetics' (Apollinaire and Guillaume 1972 [1917], 2). Art critics such as André Warnod, for instance, set up highly symbolic juxtapositions, such as the triptych of a sixteenth- to seventeenth-century Madagascar ritual post set between an ancient Egyptian bas-relief and a sculpture by Matisse (Warnod 1911; Biro 2023, 167). By these means, unprovenanced African sculptures could be given an air of historicity as part of their 'aesthetic impact' (Monroe 2018, 58). Some even went as far as to suggest that certain African 'wooden fetishes' were perhaps contemporaneous with, or even predated, Pharaonic antiquities, while those that were more recent were so similar to ancient ones that they were deemed to constitute authentic representations of ancient forms (Apollinaire and Guillaume 1972 [1917]). This sleight of hand assimilated African sculptures into the category of 'antiquity', drawing on the concept of the 'primitive mind' of nineteenth-century ethnographic traditions (Monroe 2018). Such rhetoric promoted comparison of diverse cultures and catalysed academic discourse in a collective vocabulary of objects unencumbered by their context (Evans 2012, 69).

There was never, of course, a complete homogenisation of tastes, and other parts of the art market remained circumspect about the value of a modernist framing for Egyptian art, such as has been noted for the summer 1921 Burlington Fine Arts Club exhibition of Egyptian art (Hardwick 2023, 289). Nevertheless, the modernist language used became deeply embedded in art criticism, with tenuous ancient Egyptian parallels continuing to be brought into dialogue with African art throughout the twentieth century and beyond – suggesting, for example, how 'these pieces [of tribal art] echo the dignity of Ancient Egypt' (Lucie-Smith 1964, 5), or that pairing them 'reveals interesting formal and stylistic analogies from both cultural circles' (Jung and Wildung 2008, 14; see also Cummings 2016). This extended right through to 2021, when The Metropolitan Museum of Art opened the temporary exhibition *The African Origin of Civilization* that paired 21 artefacts from ancient Egypt with 21 objects from sub-Saharan Africa based on superficial similarities of form. The art market thus fuelled the formalist language of taste and connoisseurship in its mixing of antiquities, ethnographically framed artefacts and modern art, language that survives today entrenched within Egyptological literature and museum catalogues (Riggs 2017; Hardwick 2011).

Early twentieth-century museum reforms

The various ideologies of visual creation and consumption that emerged in early twentieth-century art networks equally worked back on contemporary museum reformers and educators. This was particularly the case in Germany, where a new generation of curators sought, within the German tradition of *Bildung*, radical change in the design of public museums to privilege a formal-aesthetic perception of art. In explicit contrast to the cluttered and dense displays that had been the mainstay of natural history exhibits and classification, reformers sought to separate study collections for the specialists (*Depotsammlung*) from pleasing displays for the general public (*Schausammlung*). They argued in the pages of *Museumskunde* (founded in 1905) that the task of the museum was to create visual tableaus that permitted visitors to hone their aesthetic sensibility and encouraged them to have an empathetic engagement with artworks (Noordegraaf 2004, 91–3). Carl Einstein equally championed museums as the centre of aesthetic and intellectual innovation, taking his mixing of cultural forms, ancient and modern, as one that should continue in the museum space through swapping collections back and forth between the research store and public displays (Deliss 2012, 19). In developing new visual modes of display, German art museums followed the lead of commercial galleries with their bright, stylish spaces, together with the design ethos of the famous German art school Bauhaus, established in Weimar in 1919. Such interiors were comprised of clean lines, simple shapes and minimal decoration, and used modern materials like glass, steel and concrete. Despite some disagreements on how reform should be implemented, this fresh aesthetic was adopted throughout Germany in the 1920s and 1930s (Sheehan 2000, 180–2).

These trends are evident in the radical interior design shift at the Neues Museum in Berlin. In the mid-nineteenth century the director, Karl Lepsius, had implemented his museum vision in which the visitor would be immersed in ancient Egyptian surroundings through the use of mural paintings and architectural embellishments like richly coloured pillars. Seventy years later, the new director, Heinrich Schäfer, wrote of how such features were now looked upon with 'horror by a later generation, which naturally believed itself to have entered more deeply into the Egyptian spirit' (cited in Savoy and Wildung 2011, 65). Murals were painted over, while the former Greek Courtyard was roofed to form the Amarna Courtyard, providing a plain background with limited labelling for the finds from the fourteenth-century BC workshop of the sculptor Thutmose. These included the bust of Nefertiti, isolated on an individual plinth and framed primarily as an artwork for visual contemplation rather than for evaluation as historical artefact (Figure 1.3).

Several European and North American museums similarly adopted a modernist aesthetic display from the 1920s onwards (Konijn 1993, 24; Noordegraaf 2004), most famously in 1929, when Alfred Barr, director of the newly established Museum of Modern Art in New York, organised the exhibition *Cézanne, Gaugin, Seurat, van Gogh* according to what was later referred to as the 'white cube' principle (O'Doherty 1986). Works were widely spaced, set against a neutral white emulsion background to focus on individual pieces – aestheticised and autonomous – curated for an ideal (elitist) audience. Such sterilised environs contributed to a 'Musée imaginaire', where works of art could be freely arranged regardless of date or culture, based simply upon combinations of shapes and colours (Malraux 1947). In parallel developments in the USA, Albert Barnes (who bought numerous examples of African sculpture from Guillaume

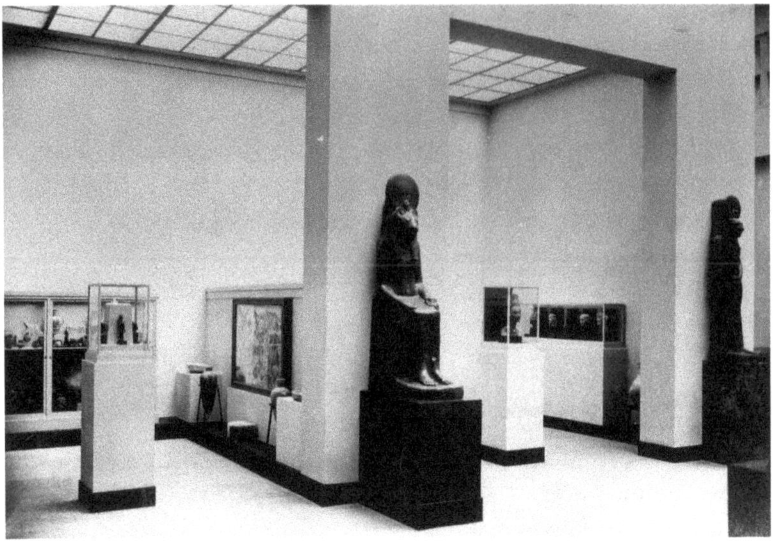

Figure 1.3 View of the Amarna Courtyard at the Neues Museum after the conversion of the Greek Courtyard, with the Nefertiti bust on the right, *c.*1924.

in Paris) developed from the 1920s 'wall ensembles' in his Philadelphian foundation. These formed a pedagogical experiment in the systematic study of art through mixing antiquities (including Egyptian material; Walsh 2021), contemporary artworks, metalwork and even furniture, in order to develop students' sense of 'plastic form' in aspects such as line, colour, light and space.

It was within these sorts of wider discourses that antiquities and modern art coexisted, developing further in the post-war era into exhibitions explicitly aligning past and present, as with *40,000 Years of Modern Art*, held in London at the Institute of Contemporary Arts in the winter of 1948–9, and *Moderne kunst nieuw + oud* ('Modern Art New + Old') at Amsterdam's Stedelijk Museum in 1955. The broad rationale for each was to demonstrate the 'universality of art' and the recurrence of particular forms and styles. Thus, while infamous exhibitions such as curator William Rubin's colonialist *Primitivism in 20th Century Art: Affinity of the Tribal and the Modern* at the Museum of Modern Art (1984) occupy a central position in canons of scholarly criticism, such shows have deeper historical precedents that deserve closer scrutiny if their repercussions are to be fully addressed.

Mid-twentieth-century challenges: institutional critique

Implicated within the aesthetic currents of early twentieth-century art were works underpinned by more political and social commentaries, such as in the activist artistic practice of Dadaists and surrealists. The most famous is the 'ready-made' urinal *Fountain* (1917), usually but disputably attributed to Marcel Duchamp.[4] Later artistic practices that emerged in the late 1960s and 1970s owed considerable debt to these earlier experiments as museums became not just sites for artistic inspiration, but also spaces of critical practice, most visibly in North American institutions amidst the civil rights movements of those decades. These initially antagonistic events were staged in art galleries by artists challenging institutional power and highlighting elitist attitudes in museums – their racism, classism and sexism. In revealing the network of relations that is required for art to exist, meaning was shifted from what were considered by modernists as autonomous art objects to art as being contingent on institutional context.

Amongst the earliest and most high-profile artist-led events were those of the Guerrilla Art Action Group. In November 1969 they staged a protest in the entrance lobby of the New York Museum of Modern Art against the Rockefeller family's role on the museum's Board of Trustees, as they were alleged to have considerable investments in the manufacture of weapons destined for Vietnam. Other examples include the work of Mierle Laderman Ukeles, whose feminist performance piece *Maintenance Art* (1973) saw her cleaning public spaces over two days at the Wadsworth Athenaeum in Hartford, Connecticut, to highlight the invisible labour that maintains institutional displays of art. The latter project included a performance piece called *Transfer: The Maintenance of the Art Object* in which Ukeles focused her attention on a display of an Egyptian mummified woman on loan from The Metropolitan Museum of Art encased in a glass vitrine. Once the maintenance worker had completed his regular dusting of the case, Ukeles repeated the process herself, subsequently date-stamping it as a *Maintenance Art Original*, thereby legitimising it as an artwork to shift responsibility for its care from the janitorial to the conservation staff (Figure 1.4). In this, her *Maintenance Art* is indicative of the shift in artistic practices of the 1970s, away from aesthetic concerns to discursive ones, opening dialogue on issues of social concern (Desai 2002).

Retrospectively, these activities have come under the umbrella of 'institutional critique', an artistic practice that can address museum conventions and policies, whether they regard collections, boards of

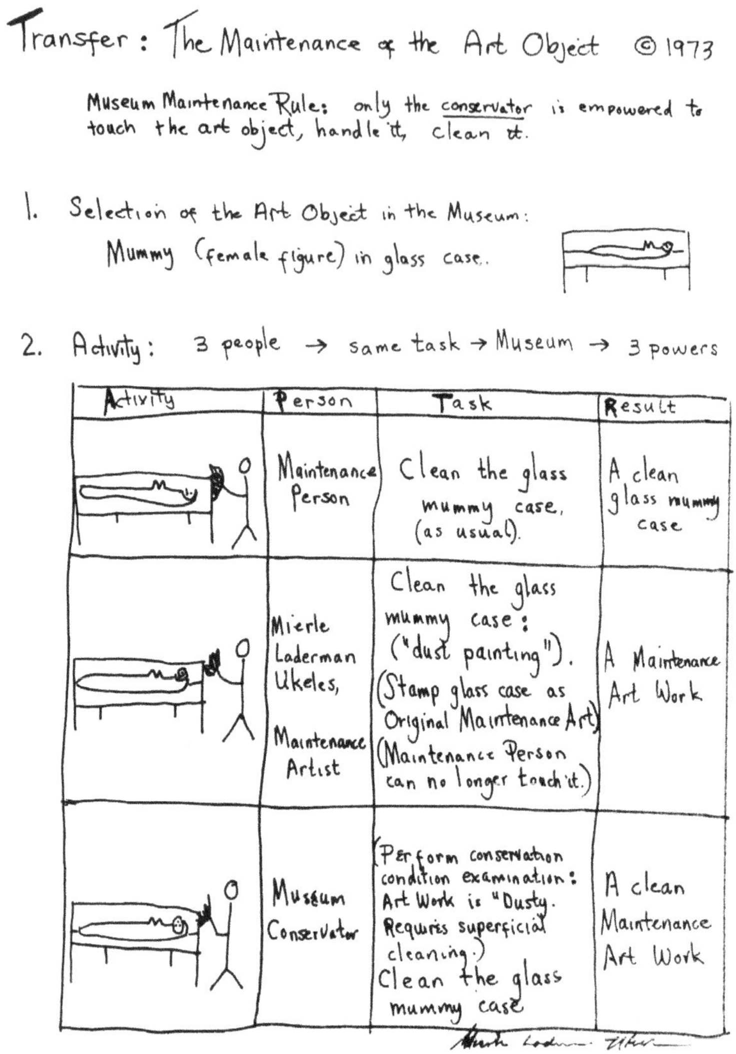

Transfer : The Maintenance of the Art Object © 1973

Museum Maintenance Rule: only the conservator is empowered to touch the art object, handle it, clean it.

1. Selection of the Art Object in the Museum: Mummy (female figure) in glass case.

2. Activity: 3 people → same task → Museum → 3 powers

Activity	Person	Task	Result
	Maintenance Person	Clean the glass mummy case, (as usual).	A clean glass mummy case
	Mierle Laderman Ukeles, Maintenance Artist	Clean the glass mummy case: ("dust painting"). (Stamp glass case as Original Maintenance Art) (Maintenance Person can no longer touch it.)	A Maintenance Art Work
	Museum Conservator	(Perform conservation condition examination: Art Work is "Dusty. Requires superficial cleaning.) Clean the glass mummy case	A clean Maintenance Art Work

Mierle Laderman Ukeles

Figure 1.4 *Transfer: The Maintenance of the Art Object: Mummy Maintenance: With the Maintenance Man, the Maintenance Artist, and the Museum Conservator*, Mierle Laderman Ukeles, 20 July 1973. Eleven 16 × 20 in. photographs, three 20 × 16 in. and three 11 × 8½ in. handwritten texts. © Mierle Laderman Ukeles. Courtesy of the artist and the Ronald Feldman Gallery, New York.

trustees, corporate sponsorship, building projects or public programmes (Fraser 2005, 18; Buchloh 1990; Alberro 2009; Raunig and Ray 2009; Welchman 2006). By the mid-1970s, some museums had begun to proactively welcome artists in to critically examine their holdings, interrogate the canons in which those collections had been categorised and highlight the curatorial biases of representation. Andy Warhol's *Raid the Icebox 1* exhibition at the Rhode Island School of Design in 1970, in which the artist created an exhibition displaying collections as he found them in storage, is frequently referenced as this kind of intervention (Marshall 2012).

The majority of these early interventionist exhibitions were staged in modern or contemporary art venues. Placing such works within other types of institutions with permanent collections of natural history, anthropology, fine art or archaeology did not really feature with any regularity until the mid-1980s, when funding by artist residency programmes became more readily available to museums (Stephens 2001). In the UK, one of the earliest was at London's Imperial War Museum in 1984, when Angela Weight, Keeper of the Department of Art at the museum, championed artists to work alongside the collections and archives. Her explicit aim was to reveal a little-known collection, with the rationale that if you bring in contemporary art, 'you are bringing in a new public' (Moriarty and Weight 2008). In 1985, Eduardo Paolozzi's *Lost Magic Kingdoms and Six Paper Moons from Nahuatl* opened at the Museum of Mankind (McLeod 1985). It is acknowledged to be the UK's first invited exhibition by a contemporary artist within an ethnographic museum context (McLeod 1985; Shelton 2001; Schneider 2006). In a move reminiscent of Warhol's *Raid the Icebox*, the Keeper of Ethnography, Malcolm McLeod, invited Paolozzi to select objects from the British Museum's store, which Paolozzi then exhibited alongside examples of his own work. The show itself was considered innovative but problematic as Paolozzi's work was crammed into vitrines beside the collection without explanatory panels (Schneider 2006, 31). Ethnographic museums have been especially receptive to artistic interlocutors ever since, in part because these institutions have been subject to considerable disciplinary introspection, with the 'critical artist' seen as an alternative to the 'neutral curator' (Shelton 2013). Shelton thus recognises a distinctive museology, a 'praxiological criticism', developed by artists to subvert orthodox exhibitions and confront the political and cultural positions of museums and galleries. He acknowledges, however, that rarely did this form of museology impinge upon critical museum studies or the more operational aspects that underpin museum practice.

The year after Paolozzi's exhibition, Oxford's Pitt Rivers Museum Annexe on Banbury Road hosted its first mixed exhibition, with a series of experimental interventions initiated by the Ruskin Head of Sculpture, Chris Dorsett. From 1990, with Arts Council funding, these artistic projects moved to the main museum site, where they were held under the umbrella of *Divers Memories: The Company of Things*[5] (Dorsett 1995), welcoming nearly a hundred artists over the course of several years (La Rue 1995, 33). Although his work at the Pitt Rivers Museum arose rather organically, Dorsett recalled that the seeds of the idea that non-art museums had the power to provide a productive space of artistic practice had been sown a decade previously at Philip Rawson's *Tantric* exhibition at London's pre-eminent 'white cube' space, the Hayward Gallery, in 1971.[6] Rawson had rejected the featureless space as a condition for encountering art, instead creating nine brightly coloured rooms within the gallery and including loans from the V&A collections to produce quite dense displays. Here the non-art museum and its collections intervened in the contemporary art gallery space as a refusal of the over-conventionalised, bleached environment.

In our interview, Dorsett described his work at the Pitt Rivers as generally being 'under the surface': subtle, unannounced intercessions supported by ethnomusicologist Hélène La Rue, and some that the director of the museum, Schuyler Jones, was frequently unaware of. Dorsett's roles as lecturer at several contemporary art schools in the UK, along with invitations to share his work, introduced generations of students to possibilities for 'sculpture in the expanded field' of museums (cf. Krauss 1979). Other institutions in the UK and abroad invited Dorsett to facilitate interventions. Amongst them was the Manchester Museum, which hosted a version of *Divers Memories* in its permanent galleries in 1996, containing the installation of artist Katie Maverick McNeel, *Mummified Headphones*, which had been submitted by the artist in the post with no gallery location in mind. It was eventually placed beside a gilded mummified body of a child (Bracewell 1996). Hers was one of more than 40 artworks that were introduced throughout, signalled only by a small transparent sticker to indicate that a display had somehow been altered.

Awash with artists: museums in the 1990s

By the 1990s artist interventions were commonplace and the museum as a focus for practice in the art world was well established, a trend confirmed by the major survey exhibition *The Museum as Muse: Artists Reflect* at New York's Museum of Modern Art (McShine 1999). In 1995 the UK Museum Association's *Museums Journal* devoted its May issue to artists as curators, showcasing the wide variety of initiatives active in museums across the UK, Europe and the USA. So pervasive was the practice now that by the end of the decade Dorsett stepped back from the programme he had developed at the Pitt Rivers Museum, seeing contemporary art as having been instrumentalised by museums. For him all sense of subversion had been lost.

Museologically, the work of mixed-background American artist Fred Wilson (see also Chapter 3), specifically *Mining the Museum* (1992) at the Maryland Historical Society, is the most prominent example of the type of critical practice addressing the politics of display that museums became keen to emulate (Corrin 1993; Globus 2011). Wilson drew from the society's collection to disrupt the museum's authoritative voice and centre the Black narrative in America's history. Works like *Metalwork* saw Baltimore repoussé silverware set beside a pair of rusted slave shackles, while *Modes of Transport* featured a Ku Klux Klan hood in an antique stroller. The exhibition is now *the* textbook example of institutional critique cited extensively in museum studies literature. It highlights two very different motivations that condition the practice. On the one hand, the project had come about due to the museum director's desire to attract a more diverse audience to what was a very conservative museum, while on the other hand, there had been the interest of an alternative arts organisation, The Contemporary, in finding projects through which it could actively question museum practices.

The success and fame of Wilson's installations was partly due to the exhibition's coincidence with the American Association of Museums' Conference in Baltimore (Robins 2013, 178), where the audience was deeply engaged in contemporary discussions regarding the future of museums. This was a time of critical change in the Anglo-American museum world, often identified as being prompted by the 'new museology', a discourse concerned with museums' social and political roles rather than collections-method-focused models (Vergo 1989).[7] This new museology primed the sector to challenge its normative thinking around audiences, shifting the focus of museum literature, in the English-speaking world at least, from methods to purpose, with museums becoming more reflective with regard to the politics of display, acquisition, conservation and community engagement. In other words, museum theory and practice began to more actively engage with many of the themes that institutional critique had explored decades before (Barrett and Millner 2014, 19). In their review of artist interventions in Australia, Barrett and Millner (2014) credit the new museology as it was conceived in the UK as a key facilitator for the willingness of Australian museums to open up to artists. Consequently, it catalysed a less oppositional form of artistic practice in museums, allowing it to develop in multiple directions.

The number, frequency and diversity of artist interventions during the 1990s was not just ideologically motivated. It was also enabled by transformations in the wider world, including major post-Cold War geopolitical shifts, widespread internet use, economic deregulation and open markets, all of which fuelled a new world order (Stallabrass 2020, 8). The postmodern critique – manifest in archaeology and anthropology in a 'crisis of representation' – challenged the white male domination of the art world. From the Guerrilla Girls campaigns to the rise of multicultural exhibitions, the art world was conceptually prepared for the neoliberal opportunities offered by the 1990s and the rampant globalisation that ensued. Large international exhibitions (biennials) were founded across the globe, themselves stimulating a profound reshaping of the contemporary art world (Niemojewski 2021). Their origin in the mid-1980s sought to challenge the Western-centred art capitals, with one of the earliest being established in Cairo in 1984, although as Niemojewski (2021) highlights, most post-1989 biennials were more interested in expanding the Western art world than in challenging it. Jean-Hubert Martin's exhibition *Les Magiciens de la Terre* (1989), held at Centre Georges Pompidou and the Grande halle de la Villette, and itself inspired by Martin's visit to the studio of André Breton and seeing his collection (Piggott 2017, 150), is considered one example of this 'global turn'. Its explicit aim was to foster a global art discourse with 50 per cent Western and 50 per cent non-Western artists to deconstruct the dominance of European-American art. Although criticised for being a '*laissez faire* form of postcolonialism' (Kapur 1994, 43), inflected in this exhibition was a broader concern for what was termed a 'new internationalism' in institutional representation that would characterise contemporary art exhibitions of the 1990s (Fisher 1994) and the wider ethos of cosmopolitanism that underpinned scholarship in that decade. This new internationalism is especially evident in the British Museum case study (Chapter 3).

Throughout the 1990s and early 2000s, new museums of contemporary art proliferated in tandem with more commercial museum activities, branded through corporate ideals. City planners, hoping for the 'Bilbao effect' brought about by the Guggenheim's contribution to the arts-led urban regeneration of Bilbao in Spain (Plaza 2000), invested enthusiastically in such institutions. These were considered popular and popularising destinations promoting tourism and revitalising post-industrial cityscapes and waterfronts with extraordinary buildings designed by 'star-architects' (Lorente 2011). Even museums not traditionally conceived as housing contemporary art – such as those of natural history – began to use art and art-inspired elements in recently designed museum spaces to enhance 'a more experiential and evocative form of communications message that seeks to escape the dead hand of a too overt and traditionally didactic display' (Marshall 2005, 173). The emphasis upon experience fitted with a widespread shift in the late twentieth century to an 'experience economy' (Pine and Gilmore 1999) in which businesses were expected to provide experiences, not just products. For museums, that meant that objects alone were deemed unable to inspire or entertain – they had to be staged in spectacular or attractive arrangements (Noordegraaf 2004, 233).

These initiatives benefited from an increase in public spending on museums and galleries in Northern Europe in the 1990s, such as the UK Heritage Lottery Fund and EU cultural funding (a policy since the Maastricht Treaty of 1992). A partial symbiotic dependency between artists and museums then began to emerge, with museums reliant on seemingly fresh external perspectives to enliven their displays and artists more dependent upon non-art museums as funders and venues for their work. Further encouraging the collage of ancient and modern in museums was the looming presence of the millennium, ushering in an intensified interest in concepts of time. Historical and archaeological museums became potent sites for artistic contemplation, providing fertile ground for exhibition themes relating to temporality, as well as overt future-orientated contrasts of past and present. In this context, 'the contemporary' could be understood as a multiplicity of ways of being in time, an awareness of what it is to be in the present while also being cognisant of other sorts of time (Smith 2011, 5).

Contemporary artists and museums in the 2000s

While twentieth-century modernists eschewed the sort of historical detail or narration that characterised paintings and sculptures of previous centuries, from the 1990s a younger generation of artists embraced narratives and documentary modes of art-making as they navigated the politics of difference and identity. Their styles of storytelling leveraged mundane objects and materials together with their cultural associations, interleaving them with personal memories or experiences. In preparation for these works, many practitioners employ types of research and scholarship that have more conventionally been considered the domain of anthropologists, archaeologists or historians (see, for example, the work of Ala Younis, discussed in Chapter 5, and Sara Sallam, discussed in Chapters 2 and 4). Notably, the visual arts that developed here and in the early 2000s paralleled the nature of collections interpretation itself, marshalling the wider archival ecosystem within which museum artefacts reside – such as accession records, photographic objects, labels and miscellaneous historical documents – to inform their art. This 'archival impulse' in much of twenty-first-century contemporary art (Foster 2004; Callahan 2022), in which the 'artist as historian' acts (Godfrey 2007), challenges who has authority in the assembly of historical narratives. Such approaches offer considerable scope for interdisciplinarity since museum staff can play an active part in the process, exploring alongside artists archival traces and absences. The archival impulse and documentary mode of artistic practice may also account for the continuing ascendancy of contemporary art in institutions worldwide as artists revel in the memory practices that museums administrate.

In parallel, the 1990s saw the emergence of an explicitly collaborative, and potentially emancipatory, contemporary art practice that privileged dialogue and conversation (Kester 2005). In these projects, rather than a finished artwork being the focus for reflection or prompt for change, active and generative conversation is integral to the work itself. Usually this is practised with publics outside of the museum, but as museums in the 2000s started to uphold collaboration as a best practice ideal (Lonetree 2012; Simon 2010), participatory art projects (variously referred to in the literature as 'collaborative', 'community-based', 'conversational art' or 'dialogic art') have appealed more to curators (Hegenbart 2024, 11–12). The problem is that curators too often set themselves outside of these projects as facilitators rather than participants (Chapter 6).

The infrastructure necessary to support these sorts of practices strengthened throughout the 2000s, and in the 2010s specialist organisations devoted to facilitating interventions emerged. In the UK, for instance, Arts&Heritage[8] and Trust New Art[9] offer training and consultancies to facilitate collaborations between heritage sites and artists. Meanwhile, arts commissioning in heritage became a strategic investment embraced by major heritage organisations, such as Arts Council England, the National Trust and English Heritage, and many other British cultural bodies (Black et al. 2020). This is complemented by a wide range of other less centralised collaborations that continue to expand the scope and scale of these practices.

'Louvre, the great bastion of comme il faut art history, has succumbed to contemporary art' was an *Apollo* headline in 2004, underscoring the proliferation of artists' interventions in early 2000s museums (Spanier 2004). The *Contrepoint: l'Art contemporain au Louvre* programme first ran in 2003, consisting of a set of contemporary works placed within the permanent collection, designed by 11 artists to create dialogue with antiquities or spaces across the whole museum (Larceneux et al. 2016). For the Egyptian section specifically, in 2010, South African artist William Kentridge extended his artistic exploration of Egyptian iconography in the project *Carnets d'Egypte*. The show was an opportunity for Kentridge to ponder his experiences – his internal geography of Egypt (Versluys 2018) – in relation to the Louvre's collection, a process he documented through film, accompanied by an original music score, to create 'chapters' of a book with drawings made on miscellaneous pieces of paper or directly on books (Kentridge 2010). Continuing with the broader socioeconomic rationale for such innovations, in the case of the Louvre, although framed as being 'designed to "reopen" the meaning of the Beaux-Arts and archaeological collections', the underlying drivers for providing comparisons between old and new were to 'challenge the perspective of visitors ... as well as to rejuvenate our audience' (Coblence and Sabatier 2014, 19). This 'strategy of exhibitions is part of a broader corporate strategy, as the Louvre is now run and managed under a cultural industrial logic' (Wolf 2005, 4).

This more cynical co-option of artistic practice for corporate gain has unfortunately inflected a pessimism towards the more recent reliance upon artists to address critically the 'imperial encasing of the world' by museums (Sieg 2021, 207). Such histories were drawn into relief by activist campaigns of the 2010s such as #Museumsarenotneutral and the African Fallism movement, which together catalysed efforts to ensure that people of colour and minoritised communities see themselves reflected in museums – in their displays, collections and staff – while the repatriation efforts for African cultural heritage gained significant momentum and public visibility across European nations (Sieg 2021). The artist intervention in this age of museum contemplation and public scrutiny may be seen as a relatively simple and inexpensive means of presenting a direct museum response to these historical injustices, one that is not necessarily dependent upon adding more didactic content. For Mirjam Shatanawi (2011) of the Tropenmuseum, for instance, presenting and collecting contemporary art enables the museum to showcase diverse views, as well as to challenge the museum and its intellectual foundations. Cultural officials and curators have therefore championed artists as having the imaginative capacity to produce different forms of knowledge and ways of seeing, transforming museum spaces into sites of 'experiment' (Macdonald and Basu 2007; Bjerregaard 2019).

Museum director Deliss (2012) has been one such sector leader advocating these strategies. She spearheaded a series of artist residencies at Frankfurt's Museum of World Cultures under the *Object Atlas* project, critiquing institutional history by transforming the museum into a laboratory. In so doing, she tried to foster 'experimentation *inside* the museum by developing dialogues with artists, writers, and historians from the *outside*' (Deliss 2021, 27). Whether delegating this challenging work of providing museum counter-narratives to artists meaningfully effects long-term change in museums has been rightly questioned (Geismar 2015). Moreover, whether this inside/outside dichotomy between curator and artist is as straightforward as might be implied is something I question through the case studies of the following chapters, arguing that the museum has often already shaped artists' imaginations.

The turn to contemporary art within the cultural sector was mirrored by an intensified interest in its role in a cross-section of academic disciplines throughout the early 2000s, from geography (e.g. Hawkins 2011) to environmental science (e.g. Marsching and Polli 2012). In archaeology, the post-processual critique of the positivist, scientific approach that characterised post-World War Two archaeology cleaved open a creative space of theoretical reflection, some of which thought with, against and through modern art (e.g. Shanks 1992). The theoretical discourses that developed in archaeology out of this 1990s paradigm shift – around questions of agency, materiality, the senses and memory – further facilitated a variety of engagements with contemporary art and artists.

Renfrew (2003) was at the forefront of this trend and amongst the first archaeologists to highlight the value of collaborations between artists and archaeologists in exploring how meaning is made through human entanglements with material culture. Renfrew's focus was mainly limited to visual arts practice, and indeed this was central to his own definition of the contemporary art he considered most important – sculpture and painting, and to a lesser extent performance-based art (Renfrew 2004, 8). Other archaeologists, however, have extended these ideas to give more consideration to the processes that result in objects, the interactions between materials and practitioners, and the fuller panorama of sensory experiences that are involved (Renfrew et al. 2004; Russell and Cochrane 2013; Knappett 2006; Vilches 2007; Smith 2016;

Janik 2020; Valdez-Tullet and Chittock 2016). Degree programmes have even been established, such as the MA programme in Contemporary Art and Archaeology which was introduced at the University of the Highlands and Islands. Meanwhile, the requirement from the 2010s that all UK publicly funded research should have some form of demonstrable impact beyond academia has resulted in more projects bringing together scholars with museum professionals and artists. Rarely, however, have any of these initiatives engaged with Egyptologists, even as artist interventions in Egyptian collections became more commonplace in the 2000s (Chapter 2). Yet the archival turn in contemporary art, with its commonalities with curation in collections-based research, as I will argue across the following chapters, offers an even stronger basis for interdisciplinary engagement for archaeology and Egyptology, and challenges the visual bias of much of art production and consumption.

*

Scholars are not immune to how public perceptions are constructed in museums and the art market, as they share with museum professionals and publics a 'museal consciousness' (Crane 2000, 7; Moser 2010). Academics are equally susceptible to the 'museum effect' (Alpers 1991) whereby artefacts are transformed into artworks and held up for attentive looking. Such processes, in turn, have shaped Egyptological interpretations (Stevenson 2022a; Stevenson and Del Vesco 2024). It is important, then, to recognise how looking at Egyptian material culture has been mutually conditioned by shifts in art history and practice, as well as by developments in museum display strategies. These are not recent phenomena, but have been implicated in the construction of Egyptology, contemporary art, the art market and museology for more than a century, culminating in a swathe of artist engagements with Egyptian collections in the early 2000s, as discussed in the next chapter. For most of this time, however, although approaches to contemporary artworks and to antiquities have dialectically refashioned each other, this has largely been restricted to Western preconceptions regarding quality and taste.

Given the histories traced in this chapter, inspiration as a modality of engagement between art and archaeology should be extended from simply the ancient to the modern. The modern has equally informed ways of perceiving material from the past, with contemporary art (in all its diversity of forms and intentions) inserted into the world of Egyptian antiquity. These connections are not always direct, as various fields intersect at certain historical moments, subtly shaping their individual discursive character and cultural roles. Consequently, there is often a hidden reception of ideas, ones that are not overtly referenced in formal scholarship but more diffusely threaded through tacit understandings of the nature and affect of visual culture. But the connections are there, as are the historical assumptions that are bound to them, always sitting below individualistic artistic claims and celebratory accounts of innovation, or claims for dialogues between antiquity and contemporary art.

Notes

1 Fechheimer reviewed an exhibition of Chinese art that was organised in Berlin by the Society of East Asian Art and the Prussian Academy for the Arts between January and April 1929 (Mahler 2019).
2 The majority of images in Einstein's *Negerplastik* were provided by Brummer.
3 For example, the archives of the Penn Museum include several letters from Joseph Brummer in which he approached the director, G. B. Gordon, with offers of Egyptian antiquities: 'Knowing that you are interested in Egyptian things, I am sending you with this a photograph of an Egyptian false door of the 5th dynasty with the royal Cartouche on it ... Should you not be interested will you kindly return the photo' (Letter from Joseph Brummer to G. B. Gordon, 18 March 1925, Penn Museum archives). As this example highlights, many of these photos were not retained by the museum but recirculated by Brummer to other clients. The one exception shows that Brummer brought in a professional photographer, Carl Klein, to produce shots.
4 More recent art-historical research has suggested that the German Dada artist Elsa von Freytag-Loringhoven was the person who conceived of the installation, although this is not wholly accepted by everyone (see Spalding 2023).
5 'Divers' here meaning 'many'.
6 Dorsett, C. 2023. 9 Rooms: Philip Rawson and the exhibiting of tantra. Lecture given at the Oxford Centre for Hindu Studies, 16 February 2023. Available at: https://www.youtube.com/watch?v=2p9CKcDQAk4 [Accessed 22 June 2024].
7 I am careful here not to overgeneralise the significance of the 'new museology' for the international sector as it is clear that the discourse that occurred in the English-speaking world was of a kind that had already been underway in the Francophone world, was well developed in the Latin American context and had characterised literature in Eastern Europe.
8 Launched in 2009; see https://www.artsandheritage.org.uk/ [Accessed 23 July 2024].
9 https://www.nationaltrust.org.uk/visit/whats-on/trust-new-art-exhibitions-and-events [Accessed 23 July 2024].

2
Artists in twenty-first-century galleries of ancient Egypt

By the 2000s artist interventions and residencies were a relatively common occurrence in the museum sector in many countries. Chapters 3 to 5 will explore three museums' experiments in their Egyptian galleries with contemporary art in more critical depth. Below, I examine examples of individual interventions to give a flavour of the different modalities more widely at play in the early twenty-first century and what they potentially offer in the way of redefining their source materials and institutional display. Many are insertions of single works of art, rather than full exhibitions, and they traverse engagements with a range of materials including mummified remains, textiles and portable material culture, rather than just monumental or large figurative pieces as in the case studies, across a panorama of museum types inclusive of university collections, regional art galleries and national institutions.

The theme of audience diversification underpins many of these initiatives, rather than a concerted effort to experiment with meaning-making within museum contexts and the archaeological interpretation of collections. The more critical motive of institutional critique that developed in the latter part of the twentieth century, and which is increasingly sought after by museums, confronted the display of ancient Egypt quite early on through Fred Wilson's work, but this has largely been overlooked in the discipline of Egyptology itself. However, the turn to the question of decolonisation in the late 2010s and early 2020s, together with the spread throughout the museum sector of an interest in collections' histories (Delley and Schlanger 2022), has prompted a greater receptiveness amongst Egyptology curators to creative programming. This is notably the case with Egyptian artist Sara Sallam, whose work was embraced at several European institutions from

2022 onwards. Her interventions within the 2023 *Expéditions d'Égypte* exhibition at the Musées royaux d'art et d'histoire are the subject of an extended discussion at the end of this chapter, raising questions about the role of artists' research in curatorial programming.

Refreshing gallery spaces

One of the last artefacts that visitors encounter when making their way through the chronological story of ancient Egypt at the Ashmolean Museum, Oxford, is a representation of a small boy's body, created by Angela Palmer, a Scottish sculptor. Palmer has worked with permanent collections across the UK, Europe and the USA, using magnetic resonance imaging and computerised tomography (CT) scans to create glass-plate, multilayered 3-D images that appear to float within transparent cubes. In *Unravelled*, Palmer (2008) took as her subject the mummified remains of a child who had died of pneumonia during the Roman occupation of Egypt, in around 80 AD. His remains had been excavated by Flinders Petrie's teams at Hawara in 1888. At Palmer's instigation, the tightly wrapped remains were taken out of the Ashmolean and CT-scanned at the nearby John Radcliffe Hospital. The results were used to construct an ethereal sculpture across 111 glass sheets, each bearing a black-inked outline of the scan's cross-sections, collectively producing a life-sized image of the boy's corpse.

Palmer's artwork was first exhibited at a private London gallery in 2008, together with documentation of her visit to the site in Egypt from which the boy's body was taken, where she gathered sand and filmed local boys from the village. These associated pieces were intended to provide stronger linkages between the remains and the Egyptian landscape, but when the sculpture was installed in the renovated Egyptian galleries at the Ashmolean in 2017, none of the accompanying pieces of Palmer's research visit to Hawara were included beside it. They had only briefly been present in the cast gallery as a temporary exhibition. In the absence of these contextualising efforts, the artwork's fuller significance and potential as an intervention is arguably muted, with the aesthetic element emphasised instead. At a time when the ethics and morality of displaying the ancient Egyptian dead are being so intently debated (Abd el-Gawad and Stevenson 2023; Lytton 2023; Schoske 2019), alternative artistic representations may provide important mediations (as in the case of Sara Sallam's work discussed below and in Chapter 4). But divorced from the contextualising efforts, Palmer's *Unravelled*, simply sitting parallel to the child's body, potentially renders the experience of both more voyeuristic than poignant.

University museums, such as the Ashmolean at the University of Oxford, often lend themselves more easily to experimentation than other types of institution in the sector, on account of their advocacy of academic freedom, multidisciplinary perspectives and research environments (Challis 2013, 17; Reid 2016). UCL's Petrie Museum of Egyptian and Sudanese Archaeology is a case in point and has been the venue for a number of artists' work over the years, from the annual Central Saint Martins art college student show and one-off interventions to months-long artist residencies and practice-based research projects. All these projects have been low-key, fitted into and around the cramped accommodation provided to the collection by the university, with displays in decades-old wooden vitrines, a display environment that has itself appealed to many artists. An early example was the playful insertion of two antique-style viewfinders in 2001, produced by curator James Putnam (see Chapter 3) and Museum of Jurassic Technology (LA) initiator David Wilson amidst the densely packed shelves of artefacts. The viewfinders provided an audiovisual narration of the exploration of the geometry of the Great Pyramid by archaeologist Flinders Petrie and royal astronomer Charles Piazzi Smyth.

In March 2006 an academically funded programme by ceramic artist and lecturer Christie Brown resulted in *Collective Traces*, an exhibition of seated clay figures and modern-day amuletic grave goods alongside the ancient artefacts, responding to 'their worn condition, their incomplete narrative and their fragmented state' (Brown 2006, 4). For Brown, rather than setting her creations high on a pedestal, the museum and its collection provided a 'connectedness between things' (Brown 2006, 10). Her clay figures – expressionless and doll-like – have an uncanny quality, but as ceramic productions they faded into the terracotta hues of the busy pottery collection, so much so that one figure remained poised on the display shelf for some 15 years after the initial placement, rarely questioned by staff or visitors (Figure 2.1). This highlights that the power of interventions is often the very fact of their transience. Over time they may lose their interventionist character, merging into the permanent exhibition and becoming 'established' within the institution.

Artist-in-residence programmes have also featured at the Petrie Museum. One example involved Cathy Haynes, a London-based artist, curator and educator, whose period as 'timekeeper in residence' at the museum resulted in the installation *A Storm is Blowing* between 12 June and 2 August 2013. In work largely facilitated by the museum's public

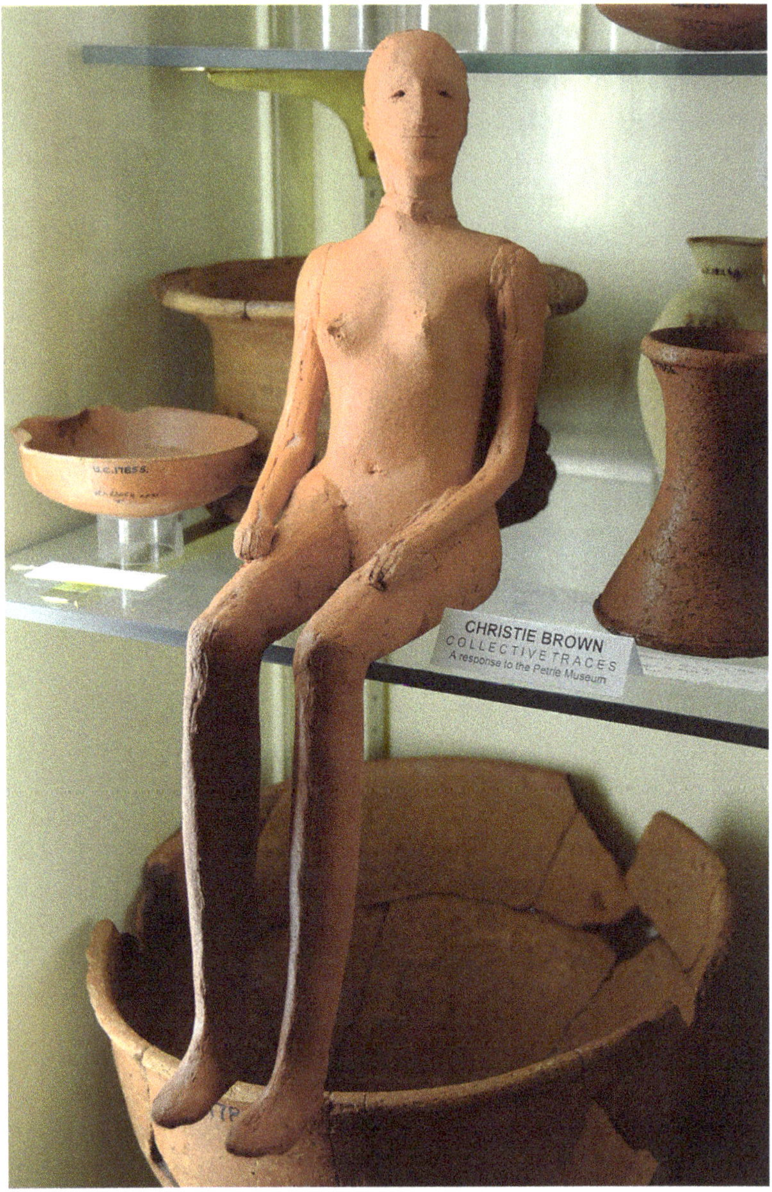

Figure 2.1 Photograph of Christie Brown's installation in the pottery gallery of the Petrie Museum, *c.*2010. Photograph by Graham Black, courtesy of the Petrie Museum of Egyptian and Sudanese Archaeology.

programming staff, Hayes explored how time is modelled, mapped and measured by speaking with the public and academics from a range of fields. The centrepiece of the exhibit was composed of a dense quantity of data about the historical understanding of time, visualised as maps and timelines. It conveyed a compactness that resonated with, but did not speak back to, the cluttered displays of the small gallery. These residency programmes were principally of benefit to the artists' practice and provided novel programming opportunities for the outreach team, but did not ultimately change how the Egyptian material might be seen. More recently, the Petrie Museum – along with the V&A and Manchester Museum – hosted the faience creations of Syrian ceramic artist Zahed Taj-Eddin, whose 'nu-shabtis' (based on ancient Egyptian funerary figurines called shabtis) made an appearance amidst gallery displays between 2014 and 2017 in *Shabtis: Suspended Truth*. These 'nu-shabtis' were said to have awoken in the twenty-first century where, on discovering that there was no afterlife, they were liberated to find new activities to engage in, including navigating present-day human issues like the European refugee crisis. As part of his artistic practice, Taj-Eddin investigated the process of creating Egyptian faience, examining recipes and production techniques with curator and Egyptologist Stephen Quirke, highlighting the potential for more interdisciplinary work between artists and scholars. Notably, the attention brought to these funerary figurines by Taj-Eddin has intellectually engaged Egyptologists seeking to gain insights into the material significance of ancient figures and the emotive efficacy of miniaturised forms (e.g. Howley 2020).

At University of Wales Trinity Saint David, Egyptologist Katharina Zinn's (2019) *Museum of Lies* project arose not from research per se, but from teaching with a completely unprovenanced collection of ancient Egyptian material held in Cyfarthfa Castle Museum and Art Gallery, Merthyr Tydfil, Wales. Most of the artefacts once formed the private collection of Harry Hartley Southey (1871–1917) and were bequeathed to the museum in the early twentieth century. As part of a swathe of experiments in storytelling around this material, artist Julie Davis was commissioned to respond to the collection as part of a broader communication strategy enlivening an otherwise 'unloved' collection and to make connections between unprovenanced ancient objects and modern identities, where she picked up on the aesthetics of avian imagery. This kind of engagement of an artist with ancient Egypt, although not necessarily contributing to understanding the past per se, still constitutes a research effort to question how such collections may come to have meaning and relevance.

Elsewhere in Europe, the copresence of Egyptian antiquities with contemporary art is not as well established as in the UK. There have been only occasional, more recent experiments, such as *Faïence-Faenza: From Ancient Egypt to Contemporary Art* inside the Archaeology Museum of Bologna in Italy[1] (see also Avanzo and Mimmo 2014, and my discussion of the Museo Egizio in Chapter 4 and the Louvre in Chapter 1). Egyptian collections in Germany are another exception, with a strong engagement with artists of the twentieth and twenty-first centuries evident, particularly in Berlin and Munich from the 1980s onwards (Chapter 5). More recently the Museum für Byzantinische Kunst (housed in the Bode-Museum, Berlin) has worked with Gail Rothschild, whose creativity has been inspired by Egyptian linen from prehistoric through to late Byzantine times, a materiality that has been a particular focus for artists (see also Devey 2007). In 2022–3 Egyptian tapestries from the museum were juxtaposed with a series of Rothschild's monumental paintings as part of her show *Think Big!* Despite criticisms that contemporary intercessions detract focus from older works (Marshall 2005), it has been suggested that the enlarged scale of Rothschild's reproductions of the originals does have the power to mediate between the object and audience, as it 'urges the viewer to return to the textile with a keener eye' (Walker 2019, 319).

Meanwhile, the Ägyptisches Museum of the Rheinische Friedrich-Wilhelms-Universität Bonn has hosted several artists since 2015 in what they have termed a 'laboratory of appropriation', including installations by German artists Anja Schindler (Förster 2017a) and Ruth Tauchert (Förster 2017b). *Re:animation: Aegyptiaca im Dialog mit Zeichnungen und Skulpturen von Ruth Tauchert,* as the title suggests, focused on movement, using primarily drawings, plaster and bronze figures. The aim was to enliven the Egyptian displays of static representations of Isis and Horus bronzes, figures of wrestlers and faience shabtis with dynamic complementary images in active poses. The exhibition's catalogue emphasised how the insertion of modern work 'breathes new life' into the galleries, giving 'the viewer a refreshingly new, even (re)invigorating look' at the displays (Förster 2017b, 4–5). The narratives accompanying each artwork projected ancient Egyptian concepts onto the modern art, acting as a communicative strategy for standard Egyptological interpretation, rather than disrupting those perceptions. But the purpose of the exhibition was never to challenge the source material. Rather, these were opportunistic projects initiated by the artists rather than the museum, and regarded by museum staff who were interviewed as a valuable means of bringing a 'changed/expanded "clientele"' into the galleries.

At least one curator interviewed was sceptical that such interventions constituted a dialogue between past and present. Instead, they characterised such installations as appropriations, not in the negative sense but more positively for 'making things alive'.

That being said, Anja Schindler's interest in displaying her art alongside Egyptian objects in *Der Tod ist Himmelblau* ('Death is Sky Blue') in 2016 was slightly different. Although initially seen by the museum curator at the time, Egyptologist Andreas Dorn, as helping the museum by appealing 'to people other than those interested in Egypt' and 'introducing new visitors', he came to realise that the interventions had more potential from a research point of view – 'a mutual exchange, communication'.[2] Over the course of two years, Schindler spent considerable time working through the collection and with the curator, even making a trip to Egypt to further inform the exhibition. Her installations included sky-blue lotus blossoms suspended from the ceiling, as well as small blue wax-sealed bottles of oil containing grains, scarabs and lotus flowers placed within the vitrines (Figure 2.2). The introduction of such a vivid colour is an especially effective strategy in pottery galleries, where the terracotta hues of multitudes of vessels saturate the view, potentially dulling and skewing perceptions of the ancient world. Similarly, the pairing of dried lotus blossoms preserved in oil next to an Egyptian stela depicting the deceased grasping such a flower lends a haptic quality to the display that arguably could prompt some viewers to perceive the relief afresh. In these ways Schindler challenges dominant European assumptions that death is black – the night, the grave, the earth. Her intercessions can instead give space for the appreciation of a different cultural cosmology. Because of her interests being divergent from the curator's, Dorn argued, she brought attention to 'easily overlooked but important' aspects of ancient Egyptian practices, such as the significance of 'the floral splendour that occupied a much larger place in ancient Egypt than we are aware of',[3] which she stressed by introducing botanical specimens from present-day Egypt into the displays. These had an impact on the curator and visitors, not just visually, but also reportedly in raising awareness of the possible lived realities of past life, inclusive of the aromatic environments of the ancient Egyptians, flows of substance and affective interactions.

For many of the large, encyclopaedic museums in the UK and USA, contemporary art programmes have expanded across the full range of their holdings, drawing Egypt into the frame, although not exclusively. The Boston Museum of Fine Arts, for instance, opened the Linde Family Wing for Contemporary Art in 2011, incentivising new activities

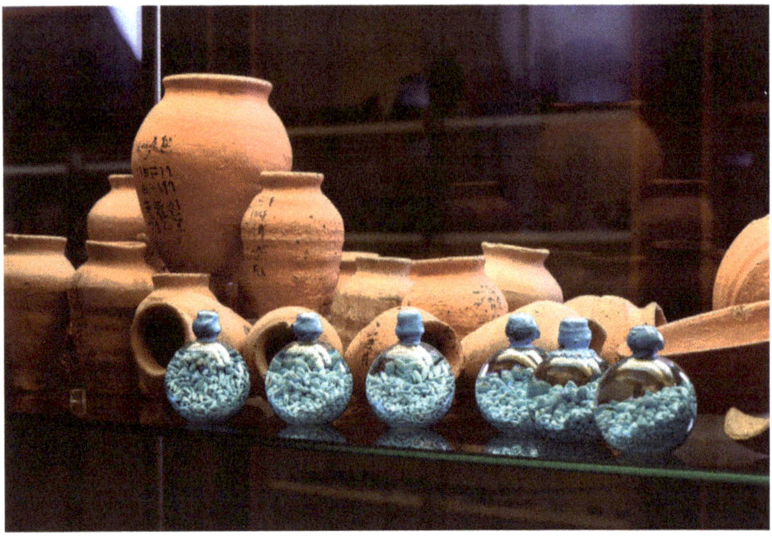

Figure 2.2 Installation in Anja Schindler's *Der Tod ist Himmelblau* at the Ägyptisches Museum of the Rheinische Friedrich-Wilhelms-Universität Bonn in 2016. © Anja-Schindler.com / Photograph by Jiri Hampl.

elsewhere in the institution and integrating performance art into its events programme. In May 2013 a series of artists' interventions under the umbrella title *Odd Spaces* saw a durational performance by Marilyn Arsem in the Egyptian galleries. The 'odd space' she selected was an area under a bench in a dimly lit gallery, surrounded by mummified human bodies. Wrapped in a black blanket with only her feet protruding, Arsem spent nearly seven hours lying still while the public ambled around the displays, frequently oblivious to her presence. More noticeable was the scent of jasmine that she infused into the space, 'an "animalic" scent, one that hovers between a piercingly sweet fragrance and the smell of flesh', as she put it.[4] The radicality of the performance for such an encyclopaedic museum has been said to reside in her invisibility in an institution otherwise predicated upon looking, offering instead another sense of presence through olfactory means, but not one of permanence (Schaefer 2020; see also the discussion of Rita Keegan's work in Chapter 3).

The famous purveyor of institutional critique Fred Wilson has engaged extensively with the topic of Egyptian antiquity in US institutions. Best known is a series he made for the Whitney Biennial in New York, *Grey Area* (1993), encompassing five differently coloured plaster replicas of the bust of Nefertiti, from white through to three shades of darkening grey to black.[5] It was related to a larger installation, *Re-claiming Egypt*, produced the previous year for the Fourth International Cairo Biennial, partly as a response to Martin Bernal's (1987) book *Black Athena*. This included staged displays of ancient artefacts and modern tourist souvenirs, a Metropolitan Museum video on ancient Egypt collaged with a Michael Jackson video and a reproduction of the figure of Pharaoh Akhenaten that on approach would speak 'What race am I?' After a short pause, the voice would utter 'Wrong. What race are you?' and finally 'What is race?' The theme is also featured in his installation *Panta Rhei: A Gallery of Ancient Classical Art* at Metro Pictures (1992). This time the installation featured canonical antiquities transformed into Egyptian art, such as *Artemis/Bast*, a sculpture combining a white neoclassical body of the Greek goddess Artemis with a dark grey cat-head of the ancient Egyptian goddess Bast (González 2011, 339). These hybrids were staged as violent grafts, as implied by the shattered plaster around them. By these means Wilson tried to question aesthetic and cultural ties between Egyptian and Greek antiquity, and by extension their African origin. In form, the broken plaster fragments memorialise the extraction and dislocation of material from Africa, while in substance, the use of plaster referenced nineteenth-century modalities of museum representation.

These works sat independently of displays of ancient Egypt, but Wilson has also collaborated with the Seattle Museum of Art, where a traditional museum layout led visitors from Egypt, Greece and Rome, through to medieval art and the European Renaissance, then to European and American culture of the nineteenth and early twentieth centuries. His *The Museum: Mixed Metaphors* (1993) disrupted this linear history, with one key element of the exhibition remapping Egyptian material through other parts of the museum: juxtaposing a stone Egyptian bird next to a painting of the Christ child holding a bird, situating an ancient Egyptian sarcophagus lid amongst African masks in the African galleries and placing Egyptian headrests alongside those belonging to the Masai and Samburu (Wilson 1994).

Someone employing a simplistic Egyptological reading might bristle at the implication of applying the modern idea of race to ancient artefacts. But as González (2011) argues, Wilson's work is not anachronistic but of contemporary framing, bringing attention to systems of representation that racialise material through its location, use, presentation or affiliation, just as he famously demonstrated in *Mining the Museum*. Art historian, archaeologist and Near East specialist Irene Winter (1996) has similarly appraised the value of Wilson's Egyptian reframings as a means of highlighting the ethnocentric and Eurocentric nature of archaeological interpretation. She too emphasises that Wilson's work is not intended as a revisionist reading that attempts to claim a different truth, but rather that it seeks a destabilisation of monolithic and exclusionary claims upon history.

In Egypt itself, there has been some minor precedence for contemporary artists sharing spaces otherwise occupied by ancient Egyptian heritage. At the end of March 1994, Munich-based artist Marlies Poss set up an exhibition at the Center of Arts in Zamalek, Cairo, showcasing her striking, sometimes disturbing, translucent latex, insect-like figures inspired in part by Egyptian iconography, prior to their exhibition in Munich (see Chapter 5). She experimented with having them photographed around local areas and heritage sites in Egypt, including setting up figures in niches around the step pyramid in Saqqara (Poss 1995). It was not until 2017, however, that *Eternal Light: Something Old, Something New* represented a first foray into installations within Egyptian museums, albeit only for four days and a single evening event at the Egyptian Museum in Tahrir Square. Here the museum was largely just a backdrop for 16 artworks by contemporary Egyptian artists, one that was hoped 'imbues the contemporary works with deeper resonance and enhances their ability to build the next layer of the Egyptian story'.[6] Going further, it was claimed that 'the presence of contemporary Egyptian artwork in this setting will stimulate the audience to question long-held interpretations of ancient Egyptian culture'.[7] Since these were insertions of works inspired by past visual cultures generically rather than by specific pieces, which interpretations it might have challenged and how it would challenge them remained vague:

> As such, in the context of the exhibition, it doesn't matter what the artwork actually portrays, what style it encompasses, whether it is a pastiche work or an innovative form or a conceptual provocation. The only thing that matters is its 'contemporaneity,' which is singularly utilized as a device to highlight or 'recontextualize' a specific site (Elnozahy 2021).

The initiative was supported by Art d'Égypte, a privately owned consultancy firm which, despite its Western name, claims its mission is to support Egyptian and international arts and cultural initiatives. Attendance of the evening event was by invited ticket only and was almost exclusively for the ultra-rich Egyptian elite, unfortunately bolstering a perception of contemporary art as a luxury of little relevance beyond a small circle in society. The curators and programming teams of the museum itself were not included in the design or development of the exhibition, nor were they invited to contribute, isolating the exhibition from existing heritage professionals. Later iterations sought to be more accessible through placement of works in public spaces, as with *Forever is Now*, which saw 10 works of art installed around the Giza Plateau in 2020 and 2022. Both iterations were supported by the Egyptian Ministry of Antiquities and Tourism and the United Nations Educational, Scientific and Cultural Organization (UNESCO), the latter extolling the exhibition as a manifestation of the 2005 UNESCO Convention on the Protection and Promotion of the Diversity of Cultural Expressions, which Egypt had joined in 2007.[8] Moreover, it had the support of Egyptian archaeologist Zahi Hawass, who was formerly Minister of State for Antiquities Affairs and who sits on the board of Art d'Égypte. The situation underscores Winegar's observation (2006, 294) that artists in Egypt are 'pulled betwixt and between' two operations of power: Egyptian state apparatus, on the one hand, and Western curators, on the other.

Despite the good intentions to raise global awareness of the contemporary art world in Egypt, these projects have not been without controversy. Concerns have been raised in the local Cairo art scene that such programmes have been at the expense of existing communities of practice and obscure the erosion of heritage across Cairo, a form of 'artwashing' (Proctor 2022). Much of the artwork presented is of non-Egyptian artists, often reifying an exoticised Egypt for an international audience. At the same time, it can be recognised that local challenges in Egypt – of navigating museum hierarchies, tight state control of antiquities and their public presentation, and the economic inequalities faced in the country – make interventions of any sort a very tricky proposition. Therefore, activities like those prepared by Art d'Égypte could be argued to have a role in cleaving open future possibilities for wider participation. However, at present that participation is orientated towards a homogenised global market rather than bringing or enfranchising local creativity grounded in Egyptian experience to a global audience. Regardless, the normalisation of such visual arts practice in the museum sector internationally, together with the prominence of contemporary art within economic and touristic strategies worldwide, suggests that more such interventions in Egypt are likely to be developed in future.

In these examples, the modalities of intervention have largely been insertions, either generally inspired by the Egyptian collections and their display, or else complementing their themes and drawing them towards issues of contemporary relevance. Notwithstanding the creativity and skill that many artworks embody, most of the practices ultimately pull ancient Egypt more closely into the present than the past and they primarily focus on Western experience of that material. This is not to say that these are not valid intercessions, but their production is culturally contingent, an observation that challenges general assumptions that contemporary artistic practice is somehow an external, diversifying agent made from a neutral creative ether.

That few exhibitions constitute what might be regarded as 'institutional critique' is a missed opportunity given that museum and Egyptological ways of looking have historically been so intertwined, as Chapter 1 demonstrated. Consequently, institutional critique has the potential not just to address the museum and its framing of ancient Egypt, but additionally to speak to and challenge the discipline of Egyptology's frames of reference and gaze. However, as I argue here and in the subsequent chapters, even the blunt introduction of institutional critique is not a sufficient basis for institutional or disciplinary change. Rather, finding a common ground, a focus for dialogue and cross-disciplinary exchange of ideas, may be a more productive means of sustained engagement between artists, curators and scholars.

Towards a more critical remit

In 2013 Saffron Walden Museum – a local government-run institution in a small market town in Essex, southeast England – hosted contemporary Egyptian artist Khaled Hafez. His work draws upon pop language, collage and colour to provide framing for the palimpsest of Egypt's identities and histories, challenging such binaries as East/West and ancient/modern. Curated with Gemma Tully, the museum's Visitor Services and Learning Officer, their *Reimagining Egypt* showcased a diverse array of Egyptian artefacts from prehistory to the present day alongside new artworks produced by Hafez and local schoolchildren (Tully 2017). These were interventions explicitly produced with the collection to challenge visitor perceptions of ancient Egypt and integrate voices from the modern country. This, it was hoped, would provide a more nuanced view of Egypt's heritage than had previously been presented in the small, dimly lit room in the museum, where 20 Egyptian antiquities had been traditionally set around an Egyptian coffin.

In the temporary exhibition space set apart from this permanent exhibit, objects from Saffron Walden's collection were arranged thematically, focusing on artefacts from daily life. Quotes from Egyptians, drawn from Tully's (2010) PhD research, were displayed around the walls alongside the artworks produced by Hafez and the local schoolchildren. As it involved a young researcher in a small local authority museum, the exhibition garnered limited national press and no Egyptological interest, despite the originality of the project and the positive response from visitors and staff, pleased to see an expanded, more diverse audience interested in the institution. At the end of the exhibition, the museum did refresh its ancient Egypt display to focus more on daily life than on the narrative of death and the afterlife, but it did not include the more recent artworks. The museum has retained a strong history of working with contemporary artists and regularly hosts temporary exhibitions which are co-curated in similar ways. These, however, are always in the temporary gallery space. Tully promoted the idea of contemporary art interventions at several conferences thereafter, but recalled in our interview considerable resistance amongst older members of the Egyptological community to the premise and a lack of traction for the ideas.

As contemporary art's media continue to expand, the realm of the digital has provided novel opportunities for institutional critique, as in the case of the now infamous *The Other Nefertiti* by German-Iraqi artist Nora Al-Badri and German artist Jan Nikolai Nelles. In 2015 they claimed to have covertly scanned the bust of Nefertiti in the Neues Museum to produce a replica that was then displayed in downtown Cairo, prior to making the data freely available online (Geismar 2018; Elias 2019).[9] The project subsequently narrated the experience of the bust utilising a simple AI chatbot system, allowing the object to 'speak for itself'. This *Nefertiti Hack* attracted substantial media scrutiny because it was unclear where such high-quality data originated from, as the claimed scanning technique would have been unable to elicit data of the resolution released. It has been suggested that the scan was, in fact, hacked from the museum's own data. Regardless of the source, the display of the replica and release of the data formed a powerful intervention in the long-running controversy regarding where the bust belongs, while also challenging museums not just on the ownership of cultural heritage, but also on their possession of associated data.

Egyptian artist Sara Sallam also makes use of multimedia and digital styles of art production. She became interested in ancient Egypt only once she had left her home country to live in the Netherlands, where she projected her feelings of homesickness onto the antiquities she encountered in European museums (Sallam 2022, 61). Working with photography, film and writing – often reappropriating archival material, materialising personal memories and self-publishing handmade books – her artworks critique colonial attitudes embedded in archaeology, museum practices and photographic archives. Through these documentary and archival activities, Sallam creates counternarratives, becoming not just a museum interlocutor but also a museum subject. In November 2022 she held a residency at the Sainsbury Centre, an art gallery belonging to the University of East Anglia in Norwich, UK, based on the collection of businessman Robert Sainsbury and his wife Lisa. Numbering several thousand works of art, the collection typifies early twentieth-century modernist tastes, with examples of creations by Henry Moore, Francis Bacon, Jacob Epstein and Alberto Giacometti held alongside visual culture from across the world, amongst which are 70 ancient Egyptian artefacts. Since the collection opened to the public in 1978, the modernist displays of artefacts, each reverentially set on individual pedestals in a large open-plan area dubbed the 'living area', have remained largely the same. The design was a deliberate response to its founders' ambition to provide a space in which visitors could have an informal aesthetic experience, just as they themselves had had when the collection filled their own home. Labelling is discreet and minimal. Lounge chairs are provided throughout, enticing visitors to sit back and browse some of the many coffee table books laid out between displays.

For her intervention, Sallam selected three ancient Egyptian funerary objects of different dates from the collection in order to question what it means to see artefacts that had been so closely connected with the ancient dead in an art museum such as this: a fragment of a sunk relief of a mourner ripped from a tomb wall, a pectoral extracted from mummified remains and a portrait of a boy prised from his embalmed body. In response to the displacement of these artefacts, Sallam created the mixed-media installation *Come to Your House*, as a means to perform a funeral, focused on the image of her own linen-shrouded body lying in British reed beds. Despite the different time periods that the objects belonged to, she imagined all three as having agency in this scene: the mourner reciting lamentations of the ancient Egyptian goddesses Isis and Nephthys, the embossed gods on the pectoral singing a spell of protection for the deceased's heart and the portrait calling the soul to return to the body. The voice-over provided by Sallam carried across the vast exhibition hall as part of the audio element of the installation, thereby transcending their specific Egyptian references and sending disruptive ripples across the space. With these as the only artworks to 'speak' in the gallery, it was as if 'the whole collection around them is growing restless' (Tychy 2023).

Come to Your House coincided with the 2022 temporary *Visions of Egypt* exhibition held in the basement of the Sainsbury Centre, which looked at the legacy of ancient Egypt in art and design from ancient Rome to the present day (Ferrari and Hinson 2022). Sallam was invited to contribute two works: *The Fourth Pyramid Belongs to Her* (2016–18) and an excerpt from her film essay *You Died Again on Screen* (2018–20). In different ways, both document alternate ways of experiencing an Egyptian tomb and the dissonance between ancient Egyptians as archaeological artefacts, on the one hand, and ancestors, on the other. In the *Fourth Pyramid Belongs to Her*, this manifested as a collage elevating the memory of her grandmother by portraying her as an ancient Egyptian. In *You Died Again on Screen*, 10 scenes from films depicting Egyptian mummified remains were spliced together, accompanied by a voice-over inviting viewers to identify with them in order to problematise their dehumanisation. The Sainsbury residency was Sallam's first, launching her profile in Egyptology, with subsequent invitations to include work at the Museo Egizio in Turin (Chapter 4), at Leiden's Rijksmuseum van Ouheden[10] and in a major collaboration with Egyptian collections of the Musées royaux d'art et d'histoire in Brussels, where a dialogue with Egyptological narratives was set up in 2023.

Brussels: telling histories of collections

Belgium's national museums – the recipients of direct federal funding – have historically faced inertia on account of the complex political regionalism in the multilingual country, a lack of funding and an 'unease' in the Belgian academic and heritage sectors over how to address its colonial histories (Van Bockhaven 2019). One consequence is that their museography has been described as 'dusty' (Bodenstein 2011, 47). However, pressures to more actively address colonial histories in the country's museums have been growing in recent years, most visibly around the Royal Museum for Central Africa in Tervuren (the Africa Museum), which houses one of the largest collections of heritage from Belgium's former colony in what is now the Democratic Republic of the Congo. It reopened in 2018 with the promise of decolonisation and an explicit engagement with more recent museological scholarship (Van Bockhaven 2019). To this end, one major emphasis was the role of commissioned contemporary Congolese art interventions throughout the museum (Sullivan 2020).

The Musées royaux d'art et d'histoire in Brussels, where the Egyptian collection is housed, was founded as a princely collection and expanded by private collectors in the mid-nineteenth century before its adoption by the state where today it is under the authority of the Federal Science Policy Department. It had been developed as a universal collection encompassing the art and history of the world from prehistoric to present times, amongst which is the rich and extensive collection of ancient Egyptian material. While funding has been made available in recent years for in-depth research on the collection and its archives, investment in the galleries themselves has notably, and visibly, lagged. The museum's displays of ancient Egypt for much of the early 2000s sat within white mid-twentieth-century vitrines with mustard-coloured, fraying fabric backing, set on tan-coloured, peeling vinyl flooring and informed by a mix of professional and makeshift labels in a variety of fonts.[11] Yet the institution itself has more progressive aspirations. Its mission statement, as it was in 2023, had adopted the language of the proposed (albeit ultimately rejected) new International Council of Museums' aspirational definition of museums of 2020, with the museum committing to 'provide spaces for democratisation, inclusion and polyphony, enabling critical dialogue about pasts and futures'.[12] It is in this institutional context that a more dynamic exhibitionary offering, *Expéditions d'Égypte*, was set up in the temporary exhibition area of the museum between 31 March and 1 October 2023. The show chronologically presented the history of Belgian Egyptology and the museum, using almost 200 objects from the collection, throughout which Sallam's work was strategically placed, including new work responding to the collection.

The exhibition was considered the 'capstone' of the four-year research project *Pyramids and Progress, Belgian Expansionism and the Making of Egyptology 1830–1952*, and was curated by one of the project's team members, the curator of the museum's Egyptian collection, Egyptologist Luc Delvaux. The museum's director, Bruno Verbergt, was keen that the exhibition be of immediate present-day relevance and, like the Africa Museum, include contemporary art. Delvaux was therefore joined by a temporary curator to assist with exhibition production, Elisabeth Van Caelenberge, an Egyptologist with 12 years' experience of installing contemporary art in commercial galleries. It was her suggestion to include Sallam's creations. The idea was initially received by museum staff with some scepticism and anxiety that any artistic response might distract attention from the historical narrative of the exhibition and that interventions might potentially be haphazard in presentation. However, Sallam is quick to note that her art practice is not confrontational, but fostered on empathy as a mode of questioning, and her seven sensitive, immersive installations were eventually enthusiastically endorsed by the museum. So much so, that Delvaux suggested that one further artwork by Sallam, *I Prayed for the Resin not to Melt* (see Chapter 4), be placed in the permanent exhibition beside the recently redisplayed human remains. In November 2023 the museum director and staff agreed to formally acquire the artwork. It is the first contemporary artwork in the Egyptian collection.

The museum had previously had some limited experience of working with contemporary artists, once for an exhibition on Aboriginal art in 2021–2, *Before Time Began*,[13] and then for another on *Shin hanga* Japanese material culture in 2022. In both cases the most recently produced works were included in the final room of the exhibition as a continuation of the chronological story. In contrast, for *Expéditions d'Égypte* the exhibition design deliberately sought to make Sallam's contributions an integral, rather than secondary, part of the exhibition throughout. One strategy to this end was to place Sallam's work at both the opening and closing of the exhibition, as well as in each of its sections. Another method was to vary the works' materiality and therefore make them stand out. Previously created pieces were reimagined to fit the space and bring movement and colour to the less vibrant, static ancient remains. *A Tourist Handbook for Egypt Outside of Egypt*, for instance, formerly realised as a small, hand-sewn softcover book, was reinvented as a wall projection, overlaying black and white photographs of French streets with coloured collages of Napoleon in Egypt (see also Chapter 4). The four digital photographic collage series *Playing in the Fields* meanwhile animated aspects of the images, while *The Fourth Pyramid Belongs to Her*, previously presented simply as printed panels, was refabricated as fluttering cloth banners, hung at different angles from the ceiling for visitors to walk through (Figure 2.3).

Three new pieces produced for the museum were featured, based on research Sallam conducted at the museum, where according to curators she 'had access to everything, no censorship'. One was an addition to Sallam's *Home Outside of Home* series begun in 2016, which collaged ancient Egyptian objects outside of Egypt with the monuments and landscape of Egypt, now extended to include Belgium and the greyscale image of a vitrine containing a pair of funerary statues layered against the coloured background of a tomb and its false door. *A Layer of Salt for My Oblivion*, meanwhile, was a response to a series of archival photographs depicting newly cleared decorated blocks at Saqqara of Neferirtenef's tomb superstructure (mastaba), before their transportation to Brussels in

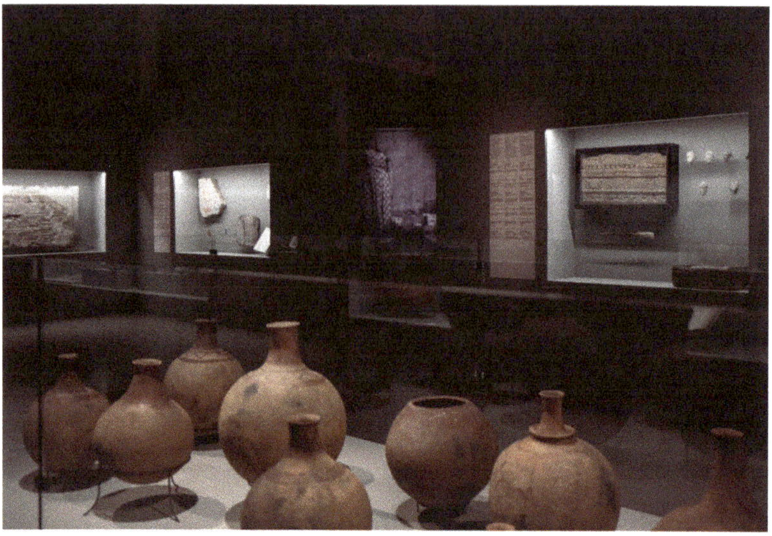

Figure 2.3 Sara Sallam's installation *The Fourth Pyramid Belongs to Her* at the Musées royaux d'art et d'histoire exhibition *Expéditions d'Égypte* in 2023. Courtesy and © of the artist.

1906. In the artwork the blocks gradually erase their decorated surfaces with a thin layer of salt in protest at their extraction from the Egyptian ground. The efficacy of this work was slightly muted as the removed pieces of mastaba were on display in the permanent galleries, some distance from the temporary exhibition area.

The final new commission, *If I Can Be Heard in the Place Where You Are*, featured a six-and-a-half-minute video installation showing clips from popular Egyptian soap operas in which people dramatically express grief. A calm, warm male voice meanwhile can be heard reading a love letter (originally written on an ostracon now held in the Louvre) from the eleventh-century BC scribe Butehamun to his departed wife. As Sallam wrote on the accompanying label, 'by likening his bereft words to those uttered nowadays in funerals, I wish to remind you that mournful tears of sorrow were once shed inside pyramids, temples, excavation pits, and tourist sites'. However, the decision was made not to use 'open' sound. In contrast then to *Come to Your House*, which projected sound into the space of the Sainsbury Centre through three small loudspeakers, in Brussels visitors would need to opt to put on the headphones to fully experience the artwork. In conception Sallam had initially felt that the headphones would bring an intimate experience with the work. What Sallam had not been prepared for, however, was the installation alongside her work of a full-sized image of mummified remains prior to their dissection and ultimate destruction by a surgeon's investigations in 1939. It was a body that had originally but incorrectly been thought to belong to Butehamun and had been purchased from Giovanni Belzoni's widow, Sarah. Today, only the head and some bandages remain in the collection (Delvaux and Van Caelenberge 2023, 24–5). The photographic portrait of the wrapped body was rendered at full size by the Egyptological curator for 'impact', a strategy that horrified Sallam when she encountered it just a few days before the opening. To mitigate, she requested that the physical distance between her work and the stark image of the deceased be increased. In this context, the use of open sound to break the traditional contemplative silence of the gallery might have provided a more direct critique of the display, in contrast to the intimate one-to-one engagement via the headphones.

The museum kept track of all print and online media advertisements, overviews and reviews of the exhibition in Belgium, which by June 2023 numbered some 124 individual sources.[14] With only a few exceptions (e.g. *La Libre* of 3 April 2023 and 12 April 2023), most of the press descriptions of the exhibition, 83 per cent of the total, focused exclusively on the Egyptological history presented in the exhibition or Queen Mathilde of Belgium's visit to see it, with none of the accompanying images giving any hint of Sallam's artistic interventions. Only a single feature led with Sallam's work, 'Antique next to contemporary' (Heylen 2023), but this comprised just a short descriptive preview of the show. Even in the expanded reviews (as opposed to advertisements), curiously no comment on the interventions was made whatsoever (e.g. Charles 2023; Ess 2023; Van de Weyer 2023), and in one case the feature even captioned a single image of *The Fourth Pyramid Belongs to Her* incorrectly as being a photograph of Egyptologist Jean Capart (Charles 2023). When her works were mentioned, this was typically tacked on to the end of the overview; 'a few interventions by the Egyptian artist Sara Sallam round it off', noted one reviewer without further qualification (Schelstraete 2023, 3). Named individual works of art were not referred to, unlike the ancient Egyptian artefacts, which were described in detail. In a six-page full-colour, richly illustrated magazine overview in the Belgian magazine *Archaeology* (Lichtenberg 2023), almost all sections of the exhibition were covered and pictured, but no comment upon the contemporary artworks was made. How the wider public responded is not fully clear as visitor evaluation was not available. A free-text comments book at the end of the exhibition mainly included generic praise, a mode of 'audience-contributed gesture of closure' rather than one that provided feedback (Katriel, cited in Macdonald 2005, 121). Such material can elicit some useful comments, but audience research through more specific, targeted questions was never undertaken even though the exhibition was an experimental one for the museum.

Collectively the omissions in the media suggest that despite the efforts of the curators to ensure Sallam's pieces were integral, the profile of the museum and regular visitors' unfamiliarity with contemporary art may have maintained traditional modes of reception. Preconceptions of what an Egyptology exhibition should be may have further led people to approach the museum with well-founded expectations that were not challenged by the overall narrative of the history of Belgian Egyptology presented. This centred on familiar reference points of royal patronage, colonial adventure and celebrated Belgian collectors and curators such as Jean Capart. But it might also be because the tone of the exhibition itself bifurcated, with two very different registers of voice on interpretive labels and panels. On the one hand, there was the museum's detached, authoritative but anonymous account of the history of the collection accompanying the ancient artefacts, while on the other, there was the artist's first-person counter-narrative. Such anonymity has long fed the myth of museum neutrality, but one that the public often has great trust in as a result (Crooke 2021, 114–15), as is further explored in Chapter 6. This separation was even starker in the full-colour, detailed exhibition catalogue published in two versions, French and Dutch, with the opening 235 sumptuous pages devoted to the collection's history and individual object descriptions before reaching the final 14 pages that introduced Sallam's work (Delvaux and Van Caelenberge 2023). The catalogue itself is more broadly reflective of the late stage at which Sallam's work was brought into dialogue with the research project team, who had already spent years developing their more traditional account of the museum's history.

While perhaps not part of the longer academic research that underpinned *Expéditions d'Égypte*'s narrative, the exhibition itself was a form of experiment. For instance, even once it opened, Van Caelenberge and Sallam felt that their intervention 'didn't go far enough' and they sought a way to comment upon it while it was still in progress. Time constraints precluded a new artwork, but in a public reflection panel Sallam pondered whether the installations had been too subtle or whether the narrative strategy of first-person labels had been effective, musing that a stronger narrative through the exhibition itself was something that would have been worth trying.[15] This sort of reflexive practice may go some way towards ameliorating a common issue with artist commissions, namely that they may be under great pressure to produce timely work to a brief, rather than explore their creative practice more organically (Bertola and Rich 2020).

*

In the range of installations described above, there are examples of research and interpretive processes of relevance to Egyptological research and presentation, be that in Bonn or Brussels, where conversations between artist and Egyptological curator are recognised to be of mutual benefit. Such an approach contrasts with that of inserting pre-existing works merely for aesthetic enhancement. In the case of Brussels the artist's invitation to intercede in the communication of pre-established results of research does raise the question: what might have been the result if artists had intervened earlier as part of the underpinning research itself? Looking more strategically at where artists might intervene could challenge perceptions of interdisciplinarity as just knowledge exchange (Bertola and Rich 2020, 159), especially with the iterative practices of artists such as Sallam, whose careful historical enquiry is driven by a commitment to subjecting orthodox historiography and narrative to critical scrutiny. These examples raise further points of discussion: what is the nature of any legacy in their host institutions or within scholarly discourse? To address these questions, I turn now, in Chapters 3 to 5, to three institutions that have relatively long histories of engagement with contemporary artists, starting from the 1990s: the British Museum in London (Chapter 3), the Museo Egizio in Turin (Chapter 4) and the Staatliches Museum Ägyptischer Kunst in Munich (Chapter 5).

Notes

1 19 November 2021 to 30 January 2022. See https://www.micfaenza.org/en/2021/12/faience-faenza-from-ancient-egypt-to-contemporary-art/ [Accessed 18 September 2023].
2 https://anja-schindler.com/en/work/der-tod-ist-himmelblau/ [Accessed 18 August 2023]. Author's translation from the original German.
3 https://anja-schindler.com/en/work/der-tod-ist-himmelblau/ [Accessed 18 August 2023]. Author's translation from the original German.
4 http://marilynarsem.net/projects/with-the-others/ [Accessed 30 May 2023].
5 Later acquired by the Tate Modern art gallery in London. A second iteration, *Grey Area (Brown Version)*, was acquired by the Brooklyn Museum of Fine Arts in New York.
6 https://dafbeirut.org/en/events/ETERNAL-LIGHT-SOMETHING-OLD,-SOMETHING-NEW [Accessed 30 May 2023].
7 https://dafbeirut.org/en/events/ETERNAL-LIGHT-SOMETHING-OLD,-SOMETHING-NEW [Accessed 30 May 2023].

8 The first 10 participating artists were Russian artist Alexander Ponomarev; American artist Gisela Colón; Brazilian artist João Trevisan; French artist JR; Italian artist Lorenzo Quinn; Egyptian artist Moataz Nasr; Egyptian-born, Los Angeles-based artist Sherin Guirguis; British artists Shuster and Moseley; British artist Stephen Cox RA; and Saudi Arabian artist HRH Prince Sultan Bin Fahad. https://www.unesco.org/en/articles/forever-now [Accessed 28 July 2023]. A second iteration that opened in November 2022 involved 12 large-scale sculptures by artists such as Pascale Marthine Tayou, Jwan Yosef, Therese Antoine, Ahmed Karaly, Zeinab Alhashemi and Natalie Clark.

9 https://nefertitihack.alloversky.com/ [Accessed 23 July 2024].

10 One new photomontage from her series *Home Outside of Home*, in which Sallam depicted a sarcophagus from the collection in Egypt, was included as part of a small 2023 Rijksmuseum van Oudheden exhibition of four artists, *Time and Again Kemet*, presenting personal visions and contemporary reflections on the past.

11 At the time of writing, a gallery refresh was in the initial stages of being implemented, including a new selection of objects, the removal of the fabrics in the showcases and the introduction of uniform, updated labels and wall texts.

12 The museum's full mission statement: https://www.artandhistory.museum/en/about-rmah#:~:text=Vision&text=Located%20in%20Brussels%2C%20at%20the,dialogue%20about%20pasts%20and%20futures [Accessed 16 August 2023].

13 https://www.artandhistory.museum/en/beforetimebegan [Accessed 25 June 2024].

14 All of these sources have been translated by the author from the original Dutch or French.

15 Forever is Now: Ancient Egypt in Contemporary Art. A conversation *(in English)* between artist Sara Sallam and curator Elisabeth Van Caelenberge on the role contemporary art can play in the Egyptological discipline, moderated by Alice Stevenson. Musées royaux d'art et d'histoire, Brussels, Sunday 3 September 2023. https://www.artandhistory.museum/en/activity/ah-sunday-expedition-egypt-56 [Accessed 25 June 2024].

3
Contemporary art and the British Museum

Since 1759 the British Museum in London has been a stage for experiments in the display of Egyptian antiquities. Moser's (2006) in-depth research has traced this history up until 1880, demonstrating some of the exhibitionary strategies that have influenced Western perceptions of ancient Egyptian culture, first through their opposition to classical antiquity and then as public spectacle. Displaying contemporary art alongside the British Museum's collection in the late twentieth century continued to challenge the place of Egyptian antiquities in art historical canons, shaping and challenging public viewing expectations instilled more than a century before. This chapter examines museum experiments in the Egyptian sculpture gallery of the British Museum, from the exhibition *Time Machine: Ancient Egypt and Contemporary Art* (1994) through to smaller-scale interventions and artist residencies in the decades following, variously highlighting the roles of architecture, staffing and cultural trends in shaping the experience and impact of such projects. By situating these exhibitions within their historical context, their overlooked radical propositions become more apparent, with artworks that I argue can still generate provocative challenges to how ancient Egypt has been viewed and understood.

Henry Moore, the British Museum and gallery design

Time Machine was not the first intervention of twentieth-century art in a British Museum gallery devoted to ancient societies. That accolade goes to artist Henry Moore. He was immersed in the modernist drive to break away from Greek-style modelling in clay towards direct carving of stone, for which the British Museum offered a wealth of examples. Moore's notebooks of his visits to the British Museum in the 1920s and 1930s abound with sketches of Egyptian, Sumerian and Cycladic art, alongside copies of Peruvian, Oceanic and Northwest Coast artefacts (Moore 1982). In 1969 Moore was invited to exhibit one of his sculptures beside Greek examples in the British Museum, to which he responded:

> I am delighted by your idea of a comparison between sculpture made nowadays and something made in 3000 BC. Such a comparison might help to show that common fundamental sculptural ideas persist – and it would support the optimistic belief that there is a continuity in ideas and their expression. Also it could suggest that the British Museum should not be looked on as a collection of dead art disconnected from our own times (Moore, cited in James 1992, 165–6).

Moore admired 'the monumentality of vision' and the 'timelessness' of Egyptian monuments (Moore 1982, 8), insights that were valued by the Department of Egyptian Antiquities Keeper, T. G. H. James, who deferred to the artist's assessment of sculptures on more than one occasion. Writing for the blockbuster exhibition *Eternal Egypt: Masterworks of Ancient Art from the British Museum* held at The Metropolitan Museum of Art in 2001, James quoted the artist at length in his account of the Old Kingdom striding figure of Meryrahashtef (James in Russmann 2001, 77) and cited Moore's own writings on Egyptian statuary for several other catalogue entries. Russmann (2001, 28) also took the opportunity in the same volume to use the public's familiarity with the modern art of Picasso, Matisse and de Kooning as reference points for illuminating Egyptian two-dimensional representation. James recognised this wider aesthetic milieu that modern artists had created, noting that

> the very wide range of styles which exist and are appreciated by connoisseurs and critics of modern art, should enable today's student of ancient art to approach the products of Egyptian artists with greater sympathy than at any time since the early nineteenth century when these products first become known in modern times (James 1985, 6).

James's comments acknowledge the long shadow that the British Museum's classical collection cast over Egyptian material (Moser 2006). His remarks also, however, assume that visitors and students would be able to deal intuitively with art, that it would be directly accessible to them, with their perceptions shaped by their experience of European art. But do these modernist ways of perceiving ancient Egyptian material serve to pull Egyptian creations further into our world rather than providing insight into previous ones?

According to curators interviewed, Moore's legacy left a 'massive impression' not only on British Museum staff, but also on the gallery space itself. When the gallery was redesigned in 1981, Moore was one of the principal benefactors and was consulted in the design process on the placement of monuments, the connections between them in terms of form and the overall vista of the gallery. It was into this space that the first interventions of contemporary art were placed 13 years later. The artists' installations were not, therefore, just in dialogue with the antiquities. They were also in concert with the gallery's architecture.

The Robert Smirke-designed hall had housed major works of Egyptian sculpture in high-ceilinged galleries since the 1830s. This gave the collection prime viewing space within the building, in an environment that was sympathetic to the scale of the monuments it contained (Moser 2006, 148). The space consisted of two wings over an area of 1,189.3 m^2: north and south wings, in which artefacts were arranged chronologically, except for the Rosetta Stone. The 1981 redesign altered the colour scheme, simplifying it by replacing the polished red Aberdeen granite plinths with warm grey sand-blasted concrete for the sculpture bases: 'the neutral colours of these new bases act as an unobtrusive connection between the existing Yorkstone floor and the many stone colours of the sculptures' (Robert Wade Design Associates 1981, 8). This explicit aim to withdraw the display apparatus into the background arguably reinforced a twentieth-century design modernism rooted in avant-garde constructivist aesthetics and placed it in subtle alignment with the ancient sculptures, potentially enhancing modernist sensibilities that some visitors might bring with them into the space.

The 1981 redisplay also introduced new side galleries, 'designed primarily to give a more intimate setting allowing smaller objects to be incorporated in the exhibition', and constructed to 'have a tomb-like character' (Robert Wade Design Associates 1981, 6).[1] The theatrical atmosphere of these more enclosed spaces was further enhanced by the deliberate use of rich and dark colours in comparison to the muted colour scheme of the main gallery (Robert Wade Design Associates 1981, 8). As a space, therefore, the British Museum's Egyptian galleries in the 1990s afforded both expansive vistas in the central wings and more intimate encounters in the adjacent rooms. In content, the size, mass and fame of the material exhibited would pose a challenge to artists seeking to compete for visibility and impact in the space. Yet it was also an enormous opportunity, given that in 1994, prior to the construction of Norman Foster's Great Court, the Egyptian galleries were the primary access route into the museum itself through which all visitors would have to pass.

Time Machine: an unusual proposal

Between 1 December 1994 and 26 February 1995, the Egyptian sculpture gallery hosted the creations of 12 international contemporary artists whose range of work represented a cross-section of late twentieth-century artforms (Table 3.1). It was conceived by James Putnam, who was then based in what he describes as a 'junior position' at the Department of Egyptian Antiquities. Funding was largely provided by Arts Council England with sponsorship in kind from Momart for shipping and the newly founded Institute of International Visual Arts (Iniva) for the catalogue's production. The exhibition was originally envisioned as a loan of several antiquities from the British Museum to a contemporary art gallery, but when transportation costs and venue difficulties arose, an easier alternative was found in the British Museum itself (Putnam 1995a). What emerges from the archives and interviews is the opportunistic nature of the project, which appears to have been driven by Putnam's personal vision, efforts and personableness, rather than being a direct response to museum policy or incentive. As curator for the exhibition, Putnam was the 'catalyst between the artist and the ancient artefacts and to develop an unrestricted "sketch pad of ideas and concepts"' (Putnam 1993).

Also integral to *Time Machine*'s delivery was the Keeper of the Department of Egypt and Sudan, Vivian Davies, who was not averse to working with contemporary artists and indeed was sympathetic to their practices, recognising them as key audience members of the museum who regularly visited the galleries to sketch. Davies steered the project through some of the controversies at the higher levels of museum management, a necessary role given the unconventional character of the project. The British Museum's then director, Robert Anderson, had stressed on several occasions that it was 'a historical museum rather than an art museum' (Gardner and Kleinitz 2000, 11). Nevertheless, he had also highlighted to the trustees that although it was a 'museum

Table 3.1 List of artists and installations in *Time Machine* at the British Museum, 1994.

Artist	Name of work	Related museum artefacts
David Hiscock	Transmutations: Rosetta Stone bar code, etched zinc plate, powder-coated and sand-blasted, 43.5 × 56 cm Water Clock, 5 × 4 transparency Kiki Smith's hand wearing ancient rings, 5 × 4 transparency	Rosetta Stone (EA 24) Water-clock (EA 938)
Rita Keegan	Girdle of Isis (The Goddess, Interactive Mummy and Daddy, Real Time)	Kaitep and Hetepheres painted limestone (EA 1181) Sekhmet statue
Kate Whiteford	False door of Ptahshepses, paintings	False door of Ptahshepses (EA 682)
Igor Mitoraj	Eclisse ('Eclipse') – white marble head, 35 × 29 cm, in libation bowl EA1292 Iron Shadows, 2.1 m Tsuki-No-Hikari ('Moonlight'), 3.14 × 3.49 × 2.45 m	Libation bowl of Mentuemhat (EA 1292)
Marc Quinn	Rubber Soul	Frog sculpture (EA 66837)
Jiři Kolář	Untitled replica of Gayer-Anderson Cat (38 cm H) Untitled, four views of pair-statues, one-cut collages (25 × 32.5 cm) Untitled (1993) torn postcard of Rosetta Stone	Gayer-Anderson Cat (EA 64391) Limestone pair-statue of Khaemweset and Nebettawy (EA 51101)
Stephen Cox	Stone bowls (1993) Flask (1991)	Grano-diorite statue of a king and the god Amun-Ra (EA 21) Porphyry bowl (EA 22823)
Martin Riches	RA (71 cm H), in EA 1134, sound installation	Ra in a granite monolithic naos shrine (EA 1134)
Peter Randall-Page	Ouroboros (76.5 × 191 × 187 cm)	
Andy Goldsworthy	Stonework, in EA 32 Sandwork, in EA 10 (L 3.13 m) Leafwork (2.75 m L), in EA 23 Leafwork (78 cm diam.), in EA 1386	Sarcophagus of the God's Adorer Ankhenesneferibre (EA 32) Sarcophagus of King Nectanebo II (EA 10) Sarcophagus of Hapmen (EA 23) Black basalt libation bowl (EA 1386)
Alexander Mihaylovich	Colossus of Menes, mixed media, 4.88 × 7.62 m	
Liliane Karnouk	Untitled installation	Wooden funerary box (EA 41549) Sarcophagus of Nesisut (EA 30)

of history, not of art … the Museum was expected to be innovative and develop new fields'.[2] His comments suggest that the wider social and cultural milieu in which the British Museum found itself in the 1990s, as outlined in Chapter 1, had a part to play in facilitating the realisation of the exhibition. Local economic and political contexts further draw his comment into relief.

The year 1989 had been billed as 'Museums Year' by the UK's Museums Association in celebration of its centenary. The sector, however, was struggling. National museums were facing a 'cash crisis' as Prime Minister Margaret Thatcher's 'rolling back of the state' devolved financial responsibility from government, cutting costs across all areas of public spending. National museum finances were squeezed, with the British Museum declaring its first deficit in 236 years, to the order of a million pounds.[3] The pressure was on to justify the use of taxpayers' money and to find new funding avenues, as Macdonald (2002, 31–40) has demonstrated for London's Science Museum during the same period. In this climate the government considered 'the public' the most important judge of museum performance, leading to a new emphasis on attracting visitors, and further catalysing the spread of 'experience economy' agendas throughout the museum world (see Chapter 1). Thus, although this was a period characterised by crisis, it was equally a dynamic time for museums in which the status quo was being challenged (Macdonald 2002, 37). In London new futures were being envisioned as the millennium approached, with fresh ambitions for the city's cultural sector. Amongst them was the Tate's announcement in 1992 that it intended to split off the modern foreign and British collections to establish a new, iconic museum of contemporary art beside the Thames River in central London. In these circumstances the turn to contemporary art, one of the major markets to have escalated in the 1980s (Feist and Hutchinson 1989), has a particular significance for the British Museum:

> The BM has for a long time had a reputation for being stuffy and aloof, run along the lines of an exclusive gentleman's club … yet under its new director, Robert Anderson, some attitudes appear to be changing … the most daring new development of all has just opened in the Egyptian Sculpture Galleries (Hall 1994).

The first mention of the exhibition in the British Museum's Trustee Minutes was on 26 February 1994, in which there is no indication that there was any resistance to its premise. It was tacked on without comment as the last item of Davies's Egyptian Antiquities Departmental Report:

> ... among the exhibitions planned was one of contemporary art inspired by the Department's collections. Ideas had been discussed with Allen Jones. A number of well-known artists had agreed to produce works of art for the exhibition, including Stephen Cox, Andrew Goldsworthy and Marc Quinn. The Department of Prints and Drawings had expressed interest in obtaining some of the preparatory drawings for these paintings.[4]

The use of the word 'paintings' here suggests that at this stage the exhibition was envisioned by senior staff in conventional terms, with no suggestion of the diversity or scale of materials that would finally be produced. Rather, what was proffered was a benefit to an existing department – that of Prints and Drawings – which already curated modern art collections. Moreover, at least one trustee, Allen Jones, was supportive of the project from the outset, as was further confirmed in curator interviews. Jones, a British pop artist, has been celebrated for his satirical and bold embrace of popular culture, and later confessed that he would have loved to see his own sculptures installed in the Egyptian galleries (Buck 2016). This highlights the role of creative artists in shaping policy and practice at the British Museum through their positions as trustees, with many coming to the table through the appointment criteria of the 1963 British Museum Act, which stipulates that of the 25 trustees, at least one should be nominated by the Royal Academy of Arts. Other trustees of the time were likely to have been equally sympathetic to the proposal, including Colin Renfrew and Henry Moore's daughter, Mary.

The initial list of contributors comprised up-and-coming artists, as well as more established ones whose careers were on the ascent. This included an approach to the *enfant terrible* of contemporary art, Damien Hirst, a member of the notorious, spectacle-driven Young British Artists (YBAs) who emerged from Goldsmiths College in the late 1980s. Hirst, like many of the other YBAs, was at that time funded by the highly successful advertising agency head Charles Saatchi, and the UK's contemporary art market had begun to boom under their combined influence. However, when Hirst was offered a vacant vitrine in the galleries upstairs, where the mummified remains were displayed, he declined. Three other artists who were approached enquired as to whether space could be made for their artworks by moving existing displays and artefacts out of the way so that their own artworks could be fully appreciated in isolation. These requests demonstrate the novelty of Putnam's project; such interventions were, at the time, relatively rare and so, in this case, misunderstood.

Time Machine: the exhibition realised

The final artwork line-up included 22 creations, comprising original paintings, photographs, sound installations and sculptures in a range of organic and inorganic materials, interspersed amongst, and sometimes within, the antiquities of the Egyptian sculpture gallery. The expectation was that this might create 'a harmony and conversation with the antiquities rather than merely a contrast' (Putnam 1994, 8). The chosen artists were generally ones who had never previously engaged with Egyptology, in the hope that they might express 'particular qualities of Egyptian art without drawing directly on Egyptian images and exploring the concept in a more thematic way' (Putnam 1994, 8). Many, nevertheless, expressed in my interviews with them their lifelong admiration for the British Museum's collection. Randall-Page extolled the 'power and strength' of its Egyptian sculpture collection, which he credited with having had a significant influence on his decision to become an artist. For Keegan, growing up in New York meant she 'always had museums and galleries at my fingertips ... at the end of my travel card and so it was really easy for me to spend time at the Metropolitan', where she had 'familiarity with the Egyptian collection'. Similarly, Mihaylovich's professional career as an artist grew out of a publications job at Getty Villa in Los Angeles: 'that is where it found me, you know, at the museum'. It is a reminder that while artist interventions are frequently perceived as a means of injecting a fresh perspective that is external to the institution (Deliss 2021, 27), it remains the case that museums may already have predetermined artistic imagination. The wider histories of mutual implication charted in Chapter 1 mean that there is a shared social field of discourse as well. As artist and critic Andrea Fraser (2005, 281) astutely observed, when artists shift 'from a substantive understanding of *the institution* as specific places, organisations, and individuals, to a conception of it as a social field, the question of what is inside and what is outside becomes more complex'.

Putnam's (1993) exhibition brief made it clear that it was 'not essential to make a direct juxtaposition with particular ancient works of art'; rather, the aspiration was that general themes of relevance to the show would emerge from the 'inner intensity of Egyptian art'. Thus, while many pieces were created in response to conversations with Putnam or to specific encounters with the space and the artefacts (including those by Keegan, Quinn, Mihaylovich, Hiscock and Karnouk), others were pre-existing works that resonated more generally with the artefacts on display. The latter included Stephen Cox's *Flask* and Randall-Page's ouroboros snake biting its own tail, both acting more as insertions than as interventions. Interpretation in the gallery was minimal, with objects accompanied simply by a label giving the name of the artist. This approach, Putnam stated, was to allow visitors to formulate their own impressions (Lancaster 1995). It also meant that the exhibition was relatively inexpensive, as bespoke display cases, graphic panels and special lighting were not required.[5]

One of the central pieces that was used to market the free exhibition was only physically present in the gallery for a few days. Andy Goldsworthy's 30-tonne *Sandwork*, made of compacted golden-yellow sand, was installed six weeks in advance of the show as an ephemeral offering, snaking around sculptures for just a few days (22–25 October 1994), since there had been a concern that otherwise it would have blocked one of the main gallery thoroughfares. It was constructed after-hours by Goldsworthy fans and a mixture of art, archaeology and architecture students from neighbouring London universities (Figure 3.1). A photograph of the completed installation was taken and mounted as a poster below the colossal statue of Pharaoh Ramesses II for the remainder of the exhibition's run, alongside a TV monitor showing a 42-minute silent film of the construction process.

Mitoraj's *Tsuki-No-Hikari* (*Moonlight*), a colossal fragment of a serene bronze face, served as a second primary icon for the exhibition, set on the lawn outside the museum. Without a plinth, sitting at an angle and in its fragmentary state, it sought to evoke a sense of encountering antiquity before its museumification. Inside the Egyptian sculpture gallery, the exhibition's opening panels were situated beyond the Rosetta Stone, where David Hiscock's etched zinc plates depicting a photograph of a script on the Rosetta Stone, distorted and blurring into the likeness of a barcode, were mounted. Flanking the exhibition's entrance, they acted as metaphorical doorways, drawing from the Rosetta Stone's history in unlocking the translation of hieroglyphs as a new means to access the ancient Egyptian past. For photographic art critic David Mellor (1995), Hiscock's piece in the context of the exhibition's reflections on time served to unsettle the Rosetta Stone through its ancient to modern transmutation, evoking its Orientalist and colonialist histories. Such a subtle reading, however, requires considerable historical contextualisation not then available to the majority of visitors to the gallery.

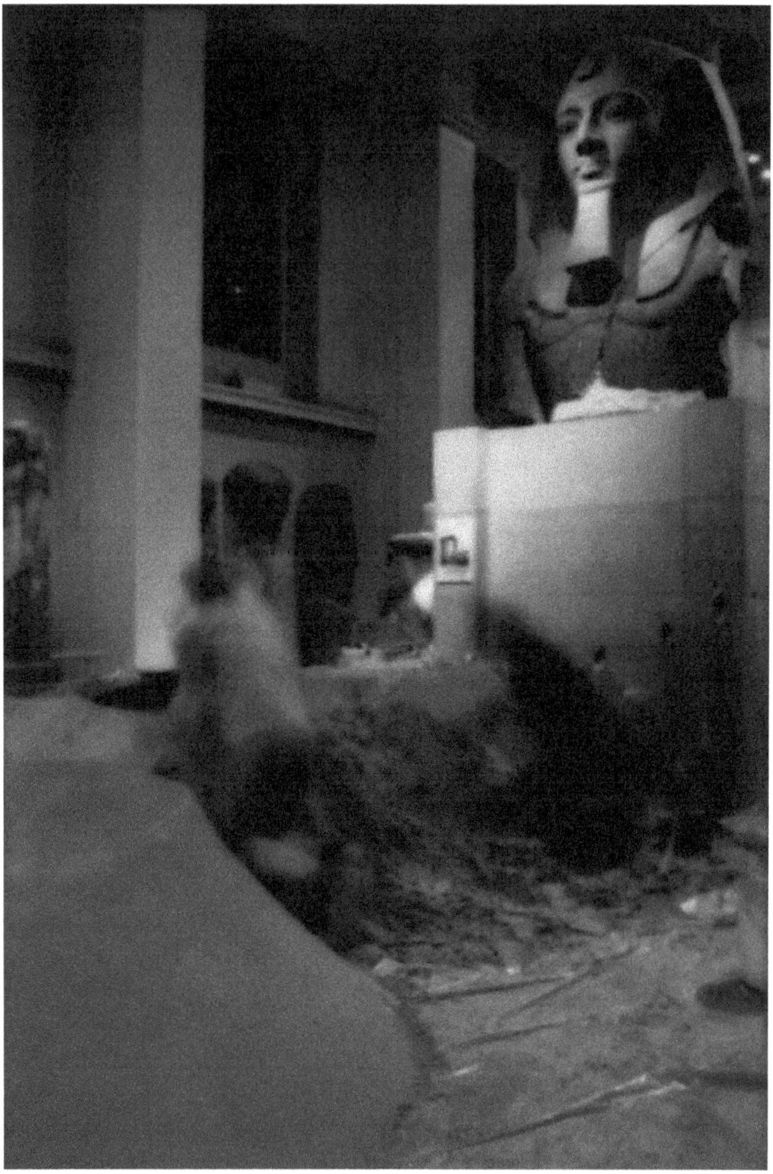

Figure 3.1 Photograph of the construction of Andy Goldsworthy's *Sandwork* at the British Museum, 22 October 1994. Photograph by and courtesy of James Putnam.

In the gallery space itself, in the absence of *Sandwork*, the panorama was dominated by a giant 20-foot-high oil painting, *The Colossus of Menes*, by Alexander Mihaylovich, which peered down at visitors from between two giant pillars at the far end of the gallery (Figure 3.2). Mihaylovich responded immediately to this location when first given a tour by Putnam, and it is clear from our interview that he views museum architecture as a display element itself worthy of interpretation, allowing for a 'grand new repackaging of antiquity'.[6] When he first proposed the piece, Davies took some convincing of the feasibility of the work and so Mihaylovich produced a scale model to help with the planning and visualisation, at which point Davies 'went pale when he realised how large this thing was'. The question of why it was that size was one that several visitors and reviewers would ask, a misunderstanding Mihaylovich believes was related to his identity as a Los Angeles-based artist and the assumptions of 'Disneyfication' and American largesse that accompanied that. The piece had, however, sought to reify the awe inherent in Egypt's monumentality and its time depth, harking back to the first mythical ruler of Egypt, Menes.

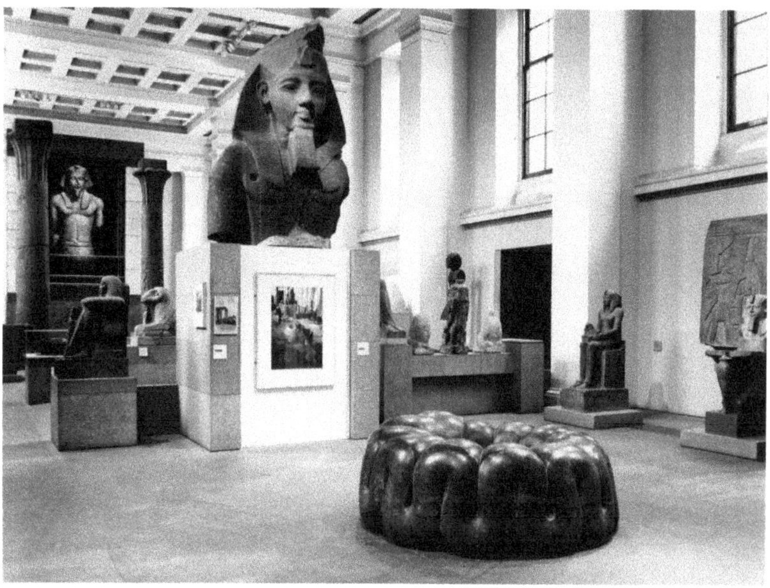

Figure 3.2 The installations of *The Colossus of Menes*, by Alexander Mihaylovich (background), and *Ouroboros*, by Peter Randall-Page (foreground), as part of the exhibition *Time Machine* (1994) at the British Museum.

In the area in front of Mihaylovich's *Colossus* were three separate, smaller interventions by Goldsworthy – *Leafwork*, *Pebblework* and *Sandwork* – 'responding to the underlying energies of Egyptian sculpture and a celebration of growth, death and rebirth', and nestled within a libation bowl and sarcophagi respectively (Putnam and Davies 1994). The other large contemporary sculptures for the gallery were ones by English artists Peter Randall-Page and Stephen Cox, together with a second work from Mitoraj – *Iron Shadows*, a seven-foot-high fragmented face in rusted cast iron. These sculptures largely echoed the muted tones of the ancient monuments surrounding them (indeed, Cox's was carved in Egyptian breccia from the Wadi Hammamat), with many visitors mistaking them for ancient pieces (Ovenden 2003, 46, note 9).[7] In contrast, for the audience the most eye-catching pieces are likely to have been Kate Whiteford's large, brightly coloured paintings. These were based on the False Door of Ptahshepses displayed in the gallery, realised using large blocks of red colour on which demotic-like script was painted in a bright blue, 'at maximum hues, as they burn themselves into the retina, creating an after-image in the mind' (Whiteford, quoted in Putnam and Davies 1994, 18). By these means, Whiteford confronted questions about the materiality and agency of colour, as opposed to simply colour perception and symbolism, ideas that archaeologists only really began to attend to in the following decade (e.g. Jones and MacGregor 2002).

The most controversial piece in the exhibition was by Marc Quinn, another artist affiliated with the YBA group of the 1990s. *Frog: Rubber Soul* responded to the association in ancient Egypt of the frog with a 'powerful protective deity closely associated with birth' (Putnam and Davies 1994, 26). In a vertical silver refrigeration display unit, Quinn mounted a living but frozen North American wood frog (*Rana sylvatica* in a natural state of hibernation) into a perspex sculpture of his own head, with the frog located to coincide with the dormant part of the brain. When word of the installation reached the director, he promptly issued a memo to the Head of Public Services highlighting that it was 'obviously a possible focus for criticism' from an animal welfare perspective, as well as a legal one.[8] Davies wrote back reassuring the director that appropriate experts had been consulted to ensure that the installation would not cause the frog any distress and that relevant specialists from London Zoo could be on hand to supervise the installation.[9] The sculpture was orientated relative to a large frog statue of andesite porphyry dating to 3100 BC.

Two installations appealed to senses other than sight. The first, a single sound sculpture, *RA*, was created by Martin Riches and placed inside a second-century BC granite naos shrine of Ptolemy VIII and Cleopatra II from Philae. When activated by visitors, bellows would emit the sound 'Ra'. The second was Rita Keegan's multimedia installation *The Girdle of Isis*, which was made up of three complementary components and included an olfactory element, bringing to the show an early example of the power of a more narrative-driven installation. The first component, *The Goddess*, was a linear video piece using photographs of wall paintings, tomb paintings and statues. Much of Keegan's work has involved a focus on female empowerment,[10] and her intervention in the British Museum was no different: 'Even though Egyptology and archaeology has had amazing women,' she remarked animatedly in our interview, 'we just see Indiana Jones.' Her second piece, *Interactive Mummy and Daddy*, drew on more personal reflections. As a Bronx-born woman of Caribbean and Black-Canadian descent, she perceived in an Old Kingdom (*c.*2300 BC) statue of Kaitep and Hetepheres the likeness of her parents. This prompted her to explore different qualities of time – spirituality, personal family, history and real time – by placing family heirlooms and photographs inside the vitrine beside the ancient objects. On seeing the installation, she was struck by how dehumanising the process was:

> When the cabinet was closed ... you have that separation if only through glass but the whole way museum artefacts are shown they become artefacts they are no longer art: they become facts not human ... it was quite painful (Keegan, cited in Ovenden 2003, 356).

Finally, *Real Time* comprised surveillance cameras around the gallery, linking to a split-screen monitor 'showing people interacting with the Egyptian collection to bring the outside of the gallery to the inside of the installation'.[11]

The annexe to the sculpture gallery, into which these elements were placed, was an appropriate setting for such a personal response to the collection, potentially providing visitors with 'a more private way of engaging' with the exhibit (Moser 2010, 25). It also offered Keegan a 'sanctuary sort of feeling' (Ovenden 2003, 357) in which she could intercede to dissolve the museumification of the space using smell:

> ... what happens in a museum is that you don't smell it, and life stinks and life smells, like, you know, life smells good, life smells bad and a culture that was so involved in perfumes, to

> walk through the British Museum and the Egyptian collection and you smell nothing you don't even smell humanity. I felt that it was really important to include that element of smell because it is a really important part of every culture (Keegan interview, Ovenden 2003, 357).

To redress this, she introduced a bespoke scent created on the basis of recipes from the *Book of the Dead*. This was infused as potpourri scattered on the gallery floor amongst sand, filling the space with the smell of frankincense, myrrh and other spices, elements that can profoundly shape museum experiences (Stevenson 2014).

Like Keegan's, Egyptian artist Liliane Karnouk's contribution was placed in one of the side rooms off the main gallery. Karnouk's installation surrounded the ancient Egyptian granite sarcophagus of Nesisut with Gothic, black-iron cemetery railings. A test tube containing a miniature palm tree was suspended between each railing, evoking the ancient Egyptian practice of placing germinated grains of corn in tombs to symbolise rebirth. In so doing, she hoped to bring Egypt to the British Museum as she felt that the artefacts needed to be contextualised 'in their original burial grounds' (Wattie 2019; see Chapter 6).

Time Machine: reception and reappraisal

As there had been little precedent for this sort of exhibition, unlike by the early 2000s when interventions had become much more commonplace, press reviews and the show's wider reception are especially informative. That said, it is also the case that some artists involved felt that there was quite limited media engagement, maybe because the British Museum staff were uncertain how to market it, or perhaps, one artist opined, because they did not want to. Nevertheless, the reviews of *Time Machine* that were published in the general press were mostly positive. *The Guardian* considered it 'a triumph' (Hall 1994), *The Art Newspaper* described it as a 'compelling juxtaposition of contemporary with ancient Egyptian statuary' (Bevan 1994) and *The Times* hailed it as 'brilliantly innovative' (Taylor 1994). *The Independent on Sunday*'s art critic was more scornful, framing it as 'this year's most bizarre exhibition' (Hilton 1994), *The Observer* nominated it as the most 'misplaced art of the year' (Feaver 1994) and *Time Out*'s reviewer felt the interventions merely compounded the 'appalling clutter of its [the British Museum's] displays' (Kent 1995). The *Telegraph*'s David Cohen (1994) wrote of the show as an 'exhibition of contemporary art', presenting the museum as if it was merely a venue rather than an integral part of the experience, which highlights a danger that more recent works can overshadow the ancient ones.[12]

Visitor responses were equally divided. Although 'great care was taken to ensure that the contemporary art would neither be too invasive on the permanent collection nor create too harsh a contrast' (Putnam 1995a, 6), there were members of the public who felt compelled to complain in strong terms to the museum about their 'shock' and 'dismay', or the 'offensiveness' of their encounter with contemporary pieces. Others felt the exhibition represented a 'lowering of standards' by the museum, demonstrating a lack of respect (visitor comments 245/94 and 15/95). The positive responses, on the other hand, were effusive, one describing it as 'inventive, exciting, thought provoking, fun' (visitor comment 83/95) and another commenting that it 'made us look anew at the Egyptian artefacts and sculptures which we have known or thought we knew, for a great number of years' (visitor comment 255/94). This feeling that the new inspired a fresh perspective on the old was also conveyed in a letter to Putnam saying that 'many pieces of sculpture hit me with an entirely new force, or from a previously unconsidered angle, juxtaposed with the modern pieces' (letter to Putnam, 7 January 1995). Visitor survey and interview data suggested that the exhibition brought in a new, younger audience from the 18–30-year-old range (Putnam 1995a, 7). Visitor comments support this, with one young individual additionally commenting that 'I had never particularly liked ancient Egyptian art, but was attracted to the new – I found that, for the first time, the ancient art had impact' (letter to Putnam, 5 February 1995). Notably, the Egyptian ambassador to the UK at the time, Mohamed Shaker, was said in one of the curatorial interviews to have considered the exhibition to be a 'tremendous idea'.

The exhibition sat between the contemporary art and Egyptology worlds, and consequently, Putnam felt, it was rather ignored by both. He recalled, for instance, a rather 'snooty' response from contemporary art critics and gallerists who, while noting the presence of bigger names like Marc Quinn, were more circumspect about the overall lack of famous artists. Egyptologists equally seemed to have taken minimal interest, with no reviews evident in any of the specialist academic journals,[13] although at that time many of the glossier Egyptology magazines that aimed beyond just a small scholarly community, such as *Egyptian Archaeology*, had yet to be launched. However, there are hints of a warm reception, including from Jaromír Málek, then head of the Griffith Institute at the University of Oxford, who wrote to congratulate Putnam on what he felt was 'the most imaginative thing the Egyptian Department has done for years' (letter to Putnam, 12 December 1994), and there was a letter of regret from Dietrich Wildung at not being able to see it in person. More directly, the invitation to reimagine the exhibition at the Museo Egizio in Turin at the end of 1995 speaks of its broader appeal (see Chapter 4).

As a form of museum intervention, *Time Machine* has been characterised as more 'benign' and 'poetic' than the more radical or critical intentions of institutional critique (Robins 2013), an observation Putnam largely agrees with, remarking in our interview that 'when I did *Time Machine*, there was no element of institutional critique'. From the perspective of the twenty-first century, that may indeed seem to be the case, especially considering the more recent uptake of decolonisation rhetoric in the sector, with the attendant imperative to challenge Western appropriations of ancient Egypt and offer meaningful opportunities for Egyptian interpretations of collections and their histories, which in the case of *Time Machine* was limited to a single Egyptian artist. Nevertheless, within the historical context of London in the early 1990s, this portrayal does not quite do justice to some of the intentions and effects of elements of the installations. As a deliberate 'experiment' (Putnam 1995a, 7), it did challenge and disrupt museum regimes of representation.

Take Goldsworthy's *Sandwork*, for instance. For some viewers it succeeded in evoking an imagined landscape in which the sculptures were originally set along the winding Nile River and in desert environs (Roberts 2013, 3; MacRitchie 1994). Others tellingly noted its resonance with 'its setting' in the museum (Málek 1999, 420). Some were more critical, commenting that under the artificial lights in the museum, the 'piece looked curiously dead and feeble among some of the greatest granite sculpture ever produced' and 'appeared sterile and perfunctory … it added nothing at all to one's understanding of the Egyptian sculpture' (Lee 1995). Whichever of these reviews is taken, positive or negative, the traditional view of Egypt itself seems not to have been disturbed by this intervention – a benign intervention that 'stabilises rather than problematises' (Robins 2013, 5).

Yet, overlooked by these reviews are other possible readings of the primary themes of Goldsworthy's work – growth and decay, construction and deconstruction. These are themes that archaeologists have found significant in their engagement with Goldsworthy's oeuvre (e.g. Renfrew 2003; Pollard 2004), helping them 'create for themselves the "intellectual space" required to think about the use of natural materials, and to sense the intimacy with the natural world that was part of prehistoric life' (Mithen 2004, 163). For Egyptologists, Goldsworthy's *Time Machine* installations potentially provide similar counterpoints to an image of Egypt defined in the British Museum's main statue galleries by the endurance of monuments. Like Schindler's installations at the University of Bonn's Egyptian Museum (Chapter 2), Goldsworthy's work calls attention to the more overlooked uses of natural materials in the ancient world – arrangements of plants and flowers, or the deliberate curation of unusually shaped or coloured stones. The archaeological record for Egypt is just as subject to the vagaries of site formation processes as elsewhere, thereby rendering vast swathes of material evidence of past life elusive, particularly organic materials when not in ideal conditions for preservation. Similarly, the need for perpetuity did not necessarily characterise all Egyptian monumental construction, and similarly to *Sandwork*, immense amounts of labour could be invested in building projects that were then actively decommissioned, as the First Dynasty (*c.*2900 BC) enclosures at Abydos attest (Bestock 2008, 47). Finally, the finished installation was itself a product of the efforts of many anonymous individuals, much like the monuments of the Pharaohs and those who removed them millennia later.

For the British Museum itself, the exhibition marked a significant break with past practices, ushering in a new approach to audience engagement. One of the curators interviewed referred to 'the old guard' and the 'public school boys' who had largely been in positions of power at the museum until the 1990s, gatekeeping traditional practices and resisting change. With *Time Machine*, however, there was a new sense of purpose to be more open to communicating with a broader public in novel ways. One curator reminisced about how the exhibition private view was 'completely different from anything previous'. Rather than the usual champagne reception for the well-heeled, a more casual approach aimed at a younger, more fashionable audience was taken. As they recalled with a chuckle, beer bottles had been provided through a Beck's Bier sponsorship,[14] which several guests nonchalantly drank from, much to the horror of a few who walked out of the event. For them, this was not a 'benign' intervention, but 'aggressive', with a strength of feeling that prevailing attitudes towards their work and public engagement were changing for the better.

The exhibition also must be situated within the context of the museum scene in the 1990s. As noted above, London's cultural sector was at that time shifting dramatically under pressure from the political climate, but it was also responding to new enterprises. One of those initiatives was brought about through Keegan, who engaged an organisation that would become the main collaborator on the exhibition: the newly founded (1994) Institute of International Visual Arts (Iniva). The organisation had been initially financed by Arts Council England, in response to calls for Black and Asian artists to be given greater opportunities to attain a platform in the mainstream visual arts sector. It was a long-standing concern. Naseem Khan's (1976) *The Arts Britain Ignores*, for example, charted the disregarded arts practices amongst the UK's ethnic minority communities that were unsupported by national institutions. Iniva's strategy to address this embraced a 'new internationalism' (see Chapter 1), seeking to identify and promote artists from around the globe whose creations might challenge Britain's predominantly Western-centric view of the visual arts. *Time Machine* was amongst its first collaborations and Iniva's director, Gilane Tawadros, provided a preface for the exhibition's catalogue in which she welcomed the opportunity to bring together the 'seemingly disparate worlds of Europe and Africa, the past and present, the museum and art gallery' as well as the opportunity to showcase the 'importance of ancient Egypt for artists today from a range of different cultures and backgrounds' (Tawadros, in Putnam and Davies 1994, 4).

One of the most overlooked, but arguably the most radical, works in the exhibition was Keegan's site-specific contribution, one she notably had to self-finance. It provides an example of how artworks might challenge museum presentations *and* offer an understanding of ancient Egyptian material itself. Not only did it bring a refreshing feminist angle, but the olfactory element of Keegan's installation, much like Marilyn Arsem's later 2011 performance in the Boston Museum of Fine Arts (Chapter 2), also had the capacity to induce strong affective responses and subtly question the depersonalisation of exhibitionary strategies (Figure 3.3). From a visitor's perspective, there are benefits to these multisensory interventions, as they encourage a more immersive experience and thereby create stronger emotive memories of the museum visit. There is also, however, a valuable disciplinary critique here for Egyptian art studies. In a review of the 2014 volume *A Companion to Ancient Egyptian Art*, Riggs (2017) notes the problematic methodological emphasis throughout upon *viewing* works of art via stylistic or semiotic analysis, rather than considering the social dimensions of aesthetic experience – who, where and under what circumstances viewing 'art' occurs. Keegan's work is a vital rupture in the museum context for the ocular-centric encounter with Egyptian material, drawing attention to the experience of visual culture, many examples of which would have

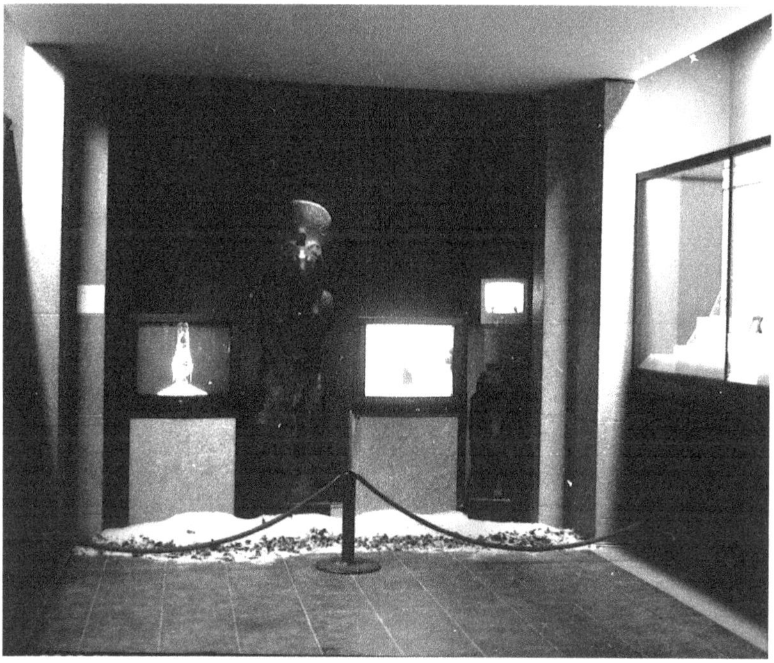

Figure 3.3 Rita Keegan's *Girdle of Isis* installation for *Time Machine* at the British Museum. Photograph by James Putnam and courtesy of Rita Keegan.

been animated in enclosed, sacred spaces infused with the aromas of unguents and offerings (Strong 2015; La Nasa et al. 2022).

Similarly, Riches' introduction of a sound-making device into a shrine shifts perceptual modes away from the visual. This is particularly appropriate for an elaborately decorated piece under the glare of a museum spotlight, since in ancient times it would have occupied the sacred recesses of the temple sanctuary in almost total darkness. It can therefore present an ontological shift, since Riches' mechanism occupies the space in which a cult statue would have sat, one that itself would have been expected to speak. Consequently, the artwork has potential to provide an affective cue to dislodge the experience of that artefact, redirecting attention to its audience and function, and also to the sonic environments of monuments. The role of sound in the use and perception of monuments has a strong methodological and theoretical foundation in archaeology (e.g. Watson and Keating 1999), notably through phenomenology, but this has been far less well attended to for the ancient Egyptian past, with some exceptions (Stevenson 2022a, 68).

There is therefore an argument to be made for the role of artists in broadening our perceptual reference points, dislodging the visual bias of much Egyptological interpretation and providing a counterpoint to dominant tropes. Nevertheless, the artworks arguably could not escape the totalising architecture of the museum itself, and they, like the ancient artefacts on display, are inextricably implicated with its project. Thus, although *Time Machine* foregrounded relationships with time through works that reflected upon questions of life, death, duration and survival, its place within the British Museum's 'universality of art' and lack of contextualisation nevertheless imposed a flattening of time by implying that chronological and historical arrangements might be abandoned. This can have the consequence of homogenising human experience, obscuring differences across cultures and histories.

On the surface, then, there seems to be an intractable tension between the need to provide didactic historical grounding, on the one hand, and allowing an unmediated aesthetic impact, on the other. As Peter Randall-Page observed during our interview, although a historical context for objects 'enriches museum collections in important and vital ways … it has been at the expense of the immediacy of the object'. Contemporary art, he argues, has a role in providing emotional cues and permission to partake in the 'revelry of the incredible achievements of cultures of the past'. To an extent, this is a question of museum display strategies, involving decisions on where, how and to what extent historical information and interpretation are provided, and also acknowledgement of the diversity of visitor backgrounds with variable reference points for the encounter with such material. Yet there need not be an 'either/or' between historicism and presentism. Perhaps the value of contemporary art alongside the remnants of past human lives is to cleave open the possibilities for 'multi-chronicity' (Kosmadaki 2021), in which the contemporary is not solely in the immediate moment and antiquity not just in the past. It might be possible, then, to make a distinction between those works in *Time Machine* that express the experience of the past, such as Mitoraj's sculptures, and those that might provide some prompt to fresh approaches to interpreting it, as in elements of Keegan's installation.

Time Machine was only displayed for three months, but it was well attended, being visited by more than a million people, selling in excess of 20,000 copies of its four-page guide and shifting 20,000 exhibition catalogues (Putnam 1995a). Once deinstalled, however, memory of it at the British Museum quickly faded. One curator stated in their interview,

'I have never heard it referred to by colleagues or the public and I suspect it has been forgotten.' Certainly, institutional memory of the exhibition is limited, with no mention of it on individual artefact records on the online database. The British Museum's own archive of the exhibition is restricted to a floor plan, marketing materials (posters and an education pack), a couple of memos and a few photographs. A film made by the education team at the time (previously recorded onto VHS and later copied to DVD), which includes artist and visitor interviews, was in a format that could not be played at the museum, rendering the data inaccessible, which highlights the fragility of certain technologies for institutional memory.

Nevertheless, there were some physical traces in the form of new acquisitions into the collection. Most were two-dimensional works on paper taken in by the Department of Prints and Drawings.[15] Only Mitoraj's 3-metre-by-3-metre bronze sculpture *Tsuki-No-Hikari* (*Moonlight*) was formally accessioned into the collection. Given its size, there was apprehension about its long-term display and storage, with discussion amongst the curators as to its fit to the collection since it was not ancient. But, curators recalled, it had been 'enormously popular' with the public, who 'loved it'. When the gift was listed for the Board of Trustees, the director confessed that it 'would be difficult to keep at the Museum for a long time, but that the Yorkshire Sculpture Park was interested in taking it on loan'.[16] The trustee Allen Jones put forward the suggestion that since the sculpture was a 'frontal piece', it 'could probably be installed at the north entrance of the Museum, and that it would add interest to the rather bleak aspect of the building'.[17] Allen's proposal was implemented[18] and the sculpture welcomed visitors to the British Museum for several years until the new director, Neil MacGregor, intervened almost immediately on his appointment in 2002 to have it removed.

While only one of the art pieces produced for *Time Machine* ended up being acquired by the British Museum, others led different lives. Goldsworthy's *Stonework*, for example, was sold by premier auction house Christies in February 2005[19] and Cox's *Flask* entered a private collection in Hong Kong,[20] raising questions about the role of museums in improving the commercial value of exhibited works, a point of discussion that Chapter 6 will take forward. Significantly, beyond the British Museum, the show had some impact on the museum sector. The Louvre's contemporary art programme director, for example, got in touch with Putnam a few years later and said that they had been 'totally inspired by seeing *Time Machine*'.

Their contemporary art programmes were launched in the subsequent decade (Chapter 1).

Collected (1997): Fred Wilson at the British Museum

Following *Time Machine*, Putnam was keen to undertake more projects, as were several of the artists. But the museum, he recalls, 'were not at all receptive', as the Great Court project began to consume staff attention. Frustrated with being unable to progress this new line of curatorial work, Putnam took a year's break from the British Museum. On his return he was contracted not to the British Museum's Egyptian Department but to its Education Department to head up a Contemporary Art and Culture Programme. Its aim was to enable experimental practitioners to engage more critically with the museum, not just around exhibitions, but through alternative smaller-scale interactions with the collections. The post was not funded by the museum itself, but rather had arisen fortuitously from external contacts leading to a series of small grants and sponsorships, including from the art philanthropist Tom Bendhem. The programme lasted until 2003 and staged conversations with contemporary artists such as Tracey Emin, as well as hosting international symposia.

Putnam felt that the British Museum's Education Department was 'the only department that had any amount of freedom' at that time, but also one which 'in curatorial terms is not taken too seriously'. Putnam's recollections of the British Museum in the 1990s resonate with observations made by multimedia artist Ernesto Pujol (2001) on artist residencies in the USA throughout the 1980s and 1990s. These, he noted scathingly, were largely supported by museum education departments, who began the hard work of challenging white upper-class institutional spaces long before curatorial departments: 'an unacceptable cultural landscape of parallel programming of "humble B-list" contemporary art programming alongside "curatorially generated A-list"' (Pujol 2001, 5). Similarly, while Wilson's *Mining the Museum* is most readily associated with the artist himself and the curator, often overlooked is the central importance of the education department at Maryland. As Wilson himself noted, 'there was a woman who worked in the museum in the education department. She was quite helpful. All of them were helpful actually, but she was the most helpful from the beginning' (Appiah and Wilson 2006, 6).

Most of Putnam's projects post-*Time Machine* were evidently conducted under the radar of the institution, never getting a mention in trustee meetings.[21] The one exception was a tribute to Henry Moore (on his centenary in 1998) for which Putnam staged the exhibition *A Sense of Form – Henry Moore at the British Museum*. This included Moore's large bronze *King & Queen* loaned from the Tate, juxtaposed with the ancient Egyptian pair statue that originally inspired it. In a separate vitrine were placed Moore's plaster maquettes, original sketchbooks from his British Museum visits in the 1920s (lent by the Henry Moore Foundation) and some related objects from the museum's collections. Other endeavours, as Putnam recalls, were 'relatively kind of clandestine things'. This included organising his own private views rather than them being delegated to one of the museum's own public relations teams. These private views, like the one for *Time Machine*, were more relaxed affairs, described by Putnam as involving 'a lot of young people there all drinking beer, a bit studenty kind of feeling'. Such informality has resulted in an almost complete silence in the museum's archives and contemporary media around the interventions. This is perhaps surprising since one of the most celebrated figures of institutional critique, Fred Wilson (Globus 2011; Chapters 1 and 2), was amongst the artists invited by Putnam into the British Museum, where he produced one of his lesser-known interventions in the Egyptian gallery as part of a multi-sited exhibition, *Collected* (April to June 1997), curated by artist Neil Cummings in association with the Photographers' Gallery.

For *Collected*, Wilson utilised one of the side alcoves off the British Museum's main Egyptian sculpture gallery (the one used previously by Keegan). Like his *Mining the Museum* project, this installation was fully site-specific (unlike most of the installations in *Time Machine*), relying only upon the artefacts and galleries of the British Museum itself. On this basis, his installation, *In the Course of Arrangement*, drew on the materiality of exhibitionary practice: old labels and display apparatus from the Department of Egyptian Antiquities. For instance, he exhibited the original vitrine that the Rosetta Stone had been housed in, accompanied by the rhetorical use of direct address in the captions, as in his *Re-Claiming Egypt* show, 'What are you looking at?', with the aim of prompting the museum audience to think beyond traditional museum interpretations (Putnam 2009, 134). Many of Wilson's installations have employed such prompts (González 2001), where they transform otherwise mute witnesses to the past into objects that speak. A similar strategy of repossessing the past is found in the second element of his British Museum composition, which comprised a displayed stone head, a photograph of a mummified human head mounted like a taxidermy specimen and a bronze bust of Giovanni Belzoni, with the labels 'remember when', 'remember this' and 'remember me' respectively positioned under each.

A second intervention in the Egyptian statue gallery, as part of the same show *Collected*, was Richard Wentworth's *Questions of Taste* (1997), in which the artist created a 'display' using a selection of ancient Egyptian drinking vessels intermixed with various modern drinks containers discarded in the museum vicinity. As part of the artistic process these modern tins, cartons and plastic bottles were individually photographed alongside a scale bar as if scientific specimens. They were then described on official-looking museum labels, including details of their manufacturing process and their individual find-spots, to initiate a dialogue between what was valuable and what was worthless, and the unique handmade object versus the mass-produced product, while also drawing into relief the documentation practices through which artefacts are disciplined (Putnam 2009, 133). Like *In the Course of Arrangement*, *Questions of Taste* seems to have left no archival trace in the British Museum.

Contemporary art interventions in the twenty-first century

Putnam's tenure at the British Museum was limited by short-term contracts, but his curatorial innovations did set a precedent for later projects that interspersed contemporary works through the permanent galleries. *Statuephilia: Contemporary Sculptors at the British Museum* (4 October 2008–25 January 2009), curated by external art critic Waldemar Januszczak and his researcher, the art historian James Fox, included six contemporary artists: Ron Mueck, Marc Quinn, Damien Hirst, Antony Gormley, and Noble and Webster. The latter pair's work saw contemporary art return to the Egyptian statue gallery in the form of *Dark Matter*, composed of carefully orientated taxidermised animals, including rats, mounted on a metal stand with light behind them to project two silhouette portraits of the artists onto the gallery wall. For the artists, this was an aesthetic challenge to viewers to be in awe of contemporary works as much as they are in the presence of ancient ones. The work tried to echo the ancient Egyptian belief that deities could take the form of animals such as cats, dogs and birds, as well as the practice of breeding these animals to later be mummified and offered back to the gods. As with previous shows, *Statuephilia* served to bring in a younger audience of visitors, under the age of 35 (Morris Hargreaves McIntyre 2009).

Visitor surveys also found, however, that most visitors did not expect to see contemporary art alongside the collection even though this was a display strategy that had been intermittently used for more than a decade prior to the exhibition. Nevertheless, the visitor feedback was largely positive, with the public enjoying the opportunity to see the collection in a more dynamic way.

Scholars have been more critical, noting that the pairings of material in *Statuephilia* were predicated upon rather superficial formal qualities and merely added to the traditional museological system, rarely responding to deeper themes or ideas (La 2017, 233). The insertion of Noble and Webster's shadow sculpture, although created specifically for the Egyptian sculpture gallery, is a case in point. It responded to rather generic themes not present in that gallery specifically, an observation made by several other visitors surveyed who, while admiring the craft and skill evidenced in the piece, felt that in such a large gallery of stone monuments it seemed out of place. Ten years on from *Time Machine*, technologies of audience outreach had shifted, with content now being produced by the museum for the internet as an integral part of exhibition marketing. This brought subject specialist curators to the forefront to comment on the significance of the work. In this case, the Keeper Neal Spencer used it as a departure point to reaffirm known facts about animal mummification rather than question them.[22]

Outside of the Prints and Drawings department, contemporary art has subsequently been a rare focus for British Museum exhibitions (Grayson Perry's 2011 *Tomb of the Unknown Craftsman* being an exception), nor have there been many interventions in permanent galleries (although collecting from contemporary artists has been an important acquisition strategy for the Africa, Oceania and Americas Department with regard to the representation of contemporary communities from those continents). The museum has, however, continued to include contemporary art in special temporary exhibitions with some regularity. As observed by the museum's Head of Interpretation, Stuart Frost (2019, 496), the 'use of a few examples of well-chosen, and well-interpreted, contemporary art in special exhibitions has often proven to be an effective way of engaging visitors intellectually and emotionally with subjects that otherwise might be seen as remote from their own personal experience'. So successful has this strategy been that in December 2020 the British Museum's popular radio show and best-selling publication, *A History of the World in 100 Objects* (MacGregor 2010), added a 101st object: *Precarious Passage*, a contemporary artwork by Issam Kourbaj which had been acquired for the permanent collection (museum number 2018,6003.5). This small, fragile creation – a miniature boat formed from bicycle mudguards, spent matches and clear resin – was one of dozens from the installation *Dark Water, Burning Worlds* that called attention to the European refugee crisis. It had been inspired by fifth-century BC model boats from the ancient port of Tartus in Syria, and was originally displayed alongside these at the Fitzwilliam Museum. In the British Museum iteration, one of these matchstick boats is seen wedged through a hole drilled into a hardback copy of *A History of the World in 100 Objects*, bringing the museum itself into a conversation about its past, present and future.

The other more recent engagement with the Egyptian collection has been through artist residencies. These have inspired fresh works that have the potential to provide valuable interventions and institutional critique, but which have had a more muted effect as they are physically removed from the works they were inspired by. Gala Porras-Kim's art residency is one example. In 2020 Porras-Kim undertook a residency at the Delfina Foundation in London where she focused on the funerary art of Egypt and Nubia in the British Museum, spending time in the galleries and speaking to staff and curators about alternative ways of conceptualising the afterlives of human remains and ceremonial objects held by the institution. Her artistic response, *Out of an Instance of Expiration Comes a Perennial Showing*, was installed in a small contemporary art space, Gasworks, three miles away from the British Museum in southeast London, for two months from 27 January 2022. The work explored the 'institutional frameworks that define, legitimise, and preserve cultural heritage, questioning the ethics of museum conservation and inviting the viewer to assign new meaning to artefacts extracted from their original sites and stored in archaeological collections across the world' (Porras-Kim 2022, 1). In doing so, Porras-Kim aimed to provide concrete proposals to improve the material and spiritual conditions of artefacts confined to museums.

On entering the small, white-cube exhibition space, visitors were confronted with a replica Fifth Dynasty sarcophagus, a reproduction of one displayed in the British Museum (Figure 3.4). In the museum the original faces southwest but in Porras-Kim's installation it is aligned with the cardinal points as would have been the case in the original tomb so that the deceased could face the sun rising in the east. Presented alongside this copy was a large, pitch-black graphite drawing, *Mastaba Scene*, portraying the interior of an Egyptian tomb. Part of her artistic practice is to engage directly with curators to challenge their practices.

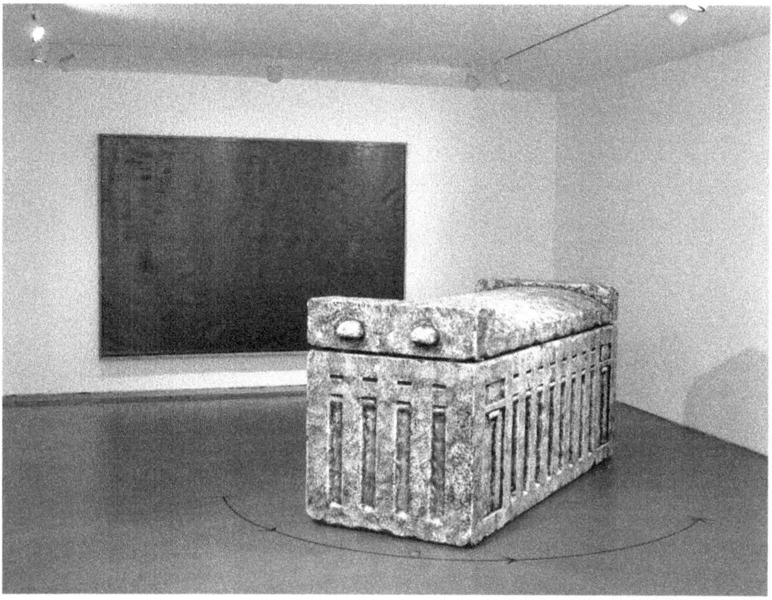

Figure 3.4 Gala Porras-Kim's *Sunrise for 5th-Dynasty Sarcophagus from Giza at the British Museum*, 2023, replica of sarcophagus EA71620, with *Mastaba Scene*, 2022, graphite on paper, at the London Gasworks' *Out of an Instance of Expiration Comes a Perennial Showing* exhibition. Commissioned by Gasworks, London. Photograph by Andy Keate.

In a letter to the then acting Keeper of the department, Daniel Antoine, which was exhibited in the exhibition, she proposed that 'since we cannot yet be certain of the mechanics of the afterlife, we could consider the perpetual plans of the persons under your charge as a guide for their care, and as such, their display'.[23] Her suggested interventions include a repositioning of the sarcophagus to align with the rising sun in the east and with the head pointing north, and to provide for 'views for sights beyond the grave', in this case the pitch-black graphite drawing to portray 'the interior of an impenetrable Egyptian tomb, not meant for the living' (Porras-Kim 2022, 2).

In these ways, Porras-Kim's work provides not just institutional critique and suggestions for stronger, more culturally specific museum interpretation that acknowledges an ancient individual's rights and agency, but also a disciplinary challenge that is of relevance to how we approach ancient societies. For example, Egyptologist Rune Nyord (2018, 73) has asked, 'How could we, and why would we, take Egyptian mortuary religion seriously?' For Nyord, frameworks for interpreting ancient Egypt emerge less from the sources than from earlier deductive

Victorian categories that have imposed a view of the 'afterlife' and a 'quest for eternal life' upon Egyptian material. In these discussions, Nyord draws from anthropology, where the 'ontological turn' has prompted scholars to transcend representationalist frameworks that treat cultures simply as systems of beliefs rather than a lived experience. Proponents see this as a methodological intervention to challenge presuppositions and to caution against the danger of predetermining interpretations by taking seriously questions about what sorts of things might exist and how (Holbraad and Pedersen 2017). This is what Porras-Kim's work potentially provides. It is a method of disciplinary disruption that Egyptologist Stephen Quirke has also reflected upon with reference to Goldsworthy's *Sandwork*:

> You have to get out of the aesthetics of modernity when you look at ancient material from the Nile valley. We have a very long way to go, not least because the material itself needs a colossal shock to our system to wake up.[24]

Porras-Kim's letter to the curators that was displayed in the exhibition seems not to have ever been sent directly to the department to form part of its correspondence archive, and it existed only as a performative gesture for the Gasworks' audience. The gallery did, however, reach out to the British Museum to set up a public panel discussion in which Porras-Kim presented her ideas. In conversation with the British Museum curator and Egyptologist John Taylor, Porras-Kim enquired whether the museum might be able to take up her suggestions. That, Taylor confessed, was a difficult proposition, not least because the physical museum space itself acted as a constraint on the sorts of presentations that would be possible.[25]

*

'It's one of my favourite museums in the entire world, I love everything Egyptian,' enthused artist Tracey Emin on her appointment in November 2023 to the British Museum's Board of Trustees as the first female representative of the Royal Academy (Ho 2023). Contemporary artists have had a subtle, but significant role to play in shaping the British Museum's Egyptian sculpture gallery, from Henry Moore's influence upon exhibition design through to Allen Jones's support for *Time Machine*. Since that exhibition, the types of direct artist engagements in the Egyptian collection of the museum have varied enormously.

Mostly these have sought to have an affective presence in the space rather than act as a deliberately disruptive intervention or institutional critique. Despite being one of the earliest examples of inviting artists to be interlocutors in an Egyptian gallery, *Time Machine* still highlights an ongoing issue – that to place an artwork identified as 'contemporary' in a space that is dedicated to the display of antiquity ostensibly sets up a dialogue between the idea of 'pastness' and that of 'nowness', but the result is irrevocably still a 'contemporaneous unfolding of an artwork, heritage, and viewer relationship' (Cass et al. 2020, 3), especially given the ways in which the modern space mediates the experience physically and intellectually.

Nevertheless, some of the installations were significantly disruptive, and very strict definitions of what is or is not institutional critique miss many of the nuanced ways in which they operated. For the museum as institution, *Time Machine* sat at a transformative time for the relationship between culture, audiences and professional power in the museum sector. For Egyptology specifically, the critique of the dehumanising nature of museum display through Rita Keegan's and Fred Wilson's work is an important reminder of the profound ways in which the museum has skewed, narrowed or mischaracterised how these ancient objects were once used and made to have meaning. More recent works like those of Gala Porras-Kim tap into ontological questions that are often hard to grapple with but do seek a closer alignment with past cosmologies. Collectively, therefore, this material provides a hopeful basis for interdisciplinarity in which Egyptologists, curators and artists might find common ground to intellectually engage in productive dialogue.

Notes

1 These side galleries were subsumed by the Great Court at the end of the twentieth century.
2 Minutes of the British Museum Board of Trustees, 3 April 1993, p. 5506.
3 Anon. 1989. British Museum faces £1m deficit. *The Times*, 18 October 1989.
4 Minutes of the British Museum Board of Trustees, 26 February 1994, p. 5675.
5 The projected costs for the project were £25,700, primarily covering expenses for the artists and the catalogue rather than the exhibition design and mounting itself. Funding was provided through the Arts Council and London Art Board, with Iniva providing support for the production of the catalogue (James Putnam, *Time Machine*, personal archive).
6 Notably in this vein, less than one month after the closure of *Time Machine*, artist Terry Smith took the opportunity to carve an enormous Ionic capital, inspired by the British Museum's main architectural motif, in the wall plaster of an upper gallery being refurbished (Putnam 2009, 182).
7 The three stone bowls he also lent to the exhibition were clearly based on and imitated ancient examples.

8 Memo from R. G. W. Anderson to Geoffrey House, 28 October 1994, British Museum Exhibition Archive, *Time Machine*.

9 Memo from Davies to R. G. W. Anderson, 4 November 1994, British Museum Exhibition Archive, *Time Machine*.

10 For example, the 2021 retrospective *Somewhere Between There and Here* at the South London Gallery. For more information, see https://ritakeeganarchiveproject.com [Accessed 27 June 2024].

11 Keegan, R. 1994. Girdle of Isis. Installation proposal. Document in possession of Rita Keegan.

12 All quotes taken from press cuttings of reviews of *Time Machine* held by Iniva (Institute of International Visual Arts), archive reference CA1-D2.

13 Although it was given a cursory, but positive review in *Antiquity* 69(262) 1995: 95.

14 In the 1990s Beck's Bier had a reputation for sponsoring the most 'fashionable' art private views, often with limited edition artists' bottles (artist-designed labels). They continued to provide beer for the special events staged by Putnam's Contemporary Arts & Culture Programme.

15 A charcoal drawing by Peter Randall-Page of his stone sculpture *Ouroboros* (1995.0225.13), a drawn study by Marc Quinn of his sculptural exhibition *Rubber Soul* (1995.0225.12) and the photographic print of Andy Goldsworthy's *Sandwork* (1995.0618.37–38).

16 Board of Trustee Minutes, 28 September 1996, p. 6130.

17 Board of Trustee Minutes, 28 September 1996, p. 6130.

18 Although it was first installed on the front lawn when that was relandscaped and subsequently reinstalled in a different position on the right of the front steps of the main entrance, it was never installed at the north entrance as Allen first envisioned.

19 https,//www.christies.com/en/lot/lot-4437537 [Accessed 27 June 2024].

20 https://www.stephencoxra.com/new-blog/flask-1989-91 [Accessed 27 June 2024].

21 Which at that time were preoccupied with complex logistical plans and financing of the Great Court project.

22 The British Museum. 2008. Statuephilia: Tim Noble and Sue Webster, Dark Stuff, at the British Museum. https://www.youtube.com/watch?v=Qc4xQ-iiPKk [Accessed 27 June 2024].

23 Letter from Gala Porras-Kim addressed to Daniel Antoine, 26 January 2022, displayed as part of the exhibition *Out of an Instance of Expiration Comes a Perennial Showing*, Gasworks, 27 January to 27 March 2022.

24 Quirke, S. 2021. Middle Kingdom birth tusks, and an enigmatic coffin in Turin. *YouTube Museo Egizio*, 9 July 2021. Available at: https://www.youtube.com/watch?v=Skx2rNiXHtg&t=448s [Accessed 10 February 2023].

25 Gasworks 2022. In conversation: John H. Taylor and Gala Porras-Kim. *YouTube Gasworks*, 24 March 2022. Available at: https://www.youtube.com/watch?v=C-cBz75MHd4 [Accessed 1 August 2023].

4
Contemporary art and the Museo Egizio

Founded in 1824, the Museo Egizio sits in the centre of the northern European city of Turin, housed in a seventeenth-century baroque building called the Collegio dei Nobili. It is one of the world's oldest museums dedicated to ancient Egypt but since the late twentieth century it has additionally hosted the works of numerous contemporary artists. *Les Egyptes Bleues*, for example, was hosted at the museum for a month between May and June 1987, showcasing the works of painter, photographer and engraver Henri Maccheroni (1932–2016), whose creative outputs span post-surrealism to the genre of 'socio-critical' art. These precedents facilitated a second showing of James Putnam's *Time Machine* at the museum in 1995. Subsequently, throughout the 2010s, the Museo Egizio gave space to a handful of contemporary artist exhibitions as the institution underwent radical redevelopment. What becomes clear in examining the motivations for mounting these exhibitions is the role of urban regeneration in the cityscape of Turin and the place of the Museo Egizio within a wider museum ecology – that is, a network of museums that implicitly or explicitly work in tandem – in shaping the museum's approach to contemporary art. At first this was opportunistic, but as the museum continues to reinvent itself physically and conceptually, a more critical consideration of the potential for collaboration with artists is evidently emerging.

Time Machine: antico Egitto e arte contemporanea

The second iteration of *Time Machine*, first held at the British Museum in 1994 (Chapter 3), arose fortuitously. The Polish artist Igor Mitoraj – who at that time had a studio in northern Italy – introduced Putnam to Alessio Luca, a senior executive of the Italian commercial vehicle company IVECO (Industrial Vehicles Corporation), which had headquarters in Turin (Fiat Veicoli Industriali). Luca had attended the British Museum show and was enthusiastic about bringing it to the Museo Egizio. IVECO eventually not only physically facilitated the exhibition through transporting artworks to Turin, but also funded its installation and controlled much of the public relations around it. The partnership materialised one of the most pressing challenges facing Turin in the 1990s: the renegotiation of a profound relationship between the car manufacturing company and the city.

Turin in the twentieth century had been a key node in northern Italy's 'industrial triangle', alongside Genoa and Milan. Its primary income had derived from the automobile industry, principally Fiat, so much so that the city itself was labelled as a 'Fordist' or 'one-company town' (Salice 2016). But from the 1980s, the city experienced a pronounced period of decline, redundancies and deindustrialisation. Consequently, from 1993 onwards, a local strategy for recovery placed fresh emphasis upon tourism as a means of regeneration (Gilli 2015), a common policy pursued by city authorities across Europe and North America during this decade (Griffiths 1993). Key to this new agenda was the development of a narrative of a city devoted to culture and to establishing a reputation as an international contemporary arts capital (Guerra 2021). Notably, just one year before *Time Machine* came to Turin, the city founded *Artissima*, a contemporary art fair, which since 1994 has evolved to become Italy's most important, combining the presence of an international market with a focus on experimentation and research.[1] IVECO's sponsorship can be understood, therefore, as part of Turin's shift from a manufacturing centre to a cultural and artistic one, but one that sought to maintain a dialogue between the old and the new, a key theme of *Time Machine*. This shift is further, perhaps, a reason why the IVECO chief executive officer, Giancarlo Boschetti, chose to open his foreword to the exhibition catalogue with a reference to Egyptian myths of rebirth, focusing attention upon change and progress (Putnam 1995b), and why IVECO took charge of invitations to the opening launch, bringing in local businesses and government officials. This sense of encouraging a new relevance and dynamism in the museum was similarly expressed by its director, Anna Maria Roveri Donadoni, who, in a video made by the British Museum's Education Department for *Time Machine*, explained that 'we are interested to show that Egyptian art is not dead art in the museum, museological things only ... this is an art which is living in our culture'.[2]

Time Machine at the Museo Egizio involved a modified line-up of 14 artists. Eight of the original artist roster from the British Museum re-exhibited their work,[3] alongside inclusions from Francesco Clemente, Brian Eno, Mimmo Paladino, Kiki Smith and Kan Yasuda. Henry Moore once again provided a point of departure; as the museum director recalled, Moore had admired prehistoric figurines in the collection (Putnam 1995, 4). Unlike in the British Museum, artworks were interspersed throughout the whole museum, rather than confined to a single gallery. Many found their way into the smaller, more intimate rooms, housing at that time old-fashioned wooden or metal-framed vitrines (Figure 4.1). Andy Goldsworthy's *Sandwork* was reinstated as a seven-day ephemeral installation, but this time constructed using black sand and paired with a snaking shadow formed from bracken fronds and thorns pinned to the museum's ceiling (Figure 4.2). For the length of the exhibition run, it was Mitoraj's *Hadrian* sculpture that welcomed visitors entering the museum (Figure 4.3). As the public then turned towards the galleries, they encountered Japanese artist Kan Yasuda's *Tensei/Tenmoku* ('Door without Door'). In this context, the meaning of his monumental two-part arch sculpture was retrofitted to echo the false door of ancient Egypt, the threshold between the world of the living and that of deities and spirits.

Few pieces were produced by working with the Turin collection in advance. Those by Cox, Hiscock, Mitoraj and Riches were directly transferred from the British Museum to the Museo Egizio. For example, Riches' *Ra* sound machine was accommodated in a similar type of shrine to the one used at the British Museum. Randall-Page's sculpture, like his offering for the British Museum, was not one specially made for the exhibition, but rather was a commission already in progress. Marc Quinn's 'bread hands', meanwhile, had been a feature of his artistic production for six years prior to the Turin installation, but by chance it could speak to examples of ancient bread that had survived in the New Kingdom tomb of Kha (*c.*1425–1353 BC) at Deir el-Medina and which were now on display in Turin. Kiki Smith's pieces, although produced for the show, were based on a generalised and long-standing interest in ancient Egypt and her love of going to museums where she felt 'confirmation' (Close 1994). She had latterly been involved with *Time Machine* at the British Museum in so far as she was a happenstance feature of one of David Hiscock's photographic interventions.[4] Putnam, on meeting her later in New York, offered her the chance to be part of the Turin version, for which she produced two works that he then flew back over to Turin to place within museum spaces where he felt that they would have

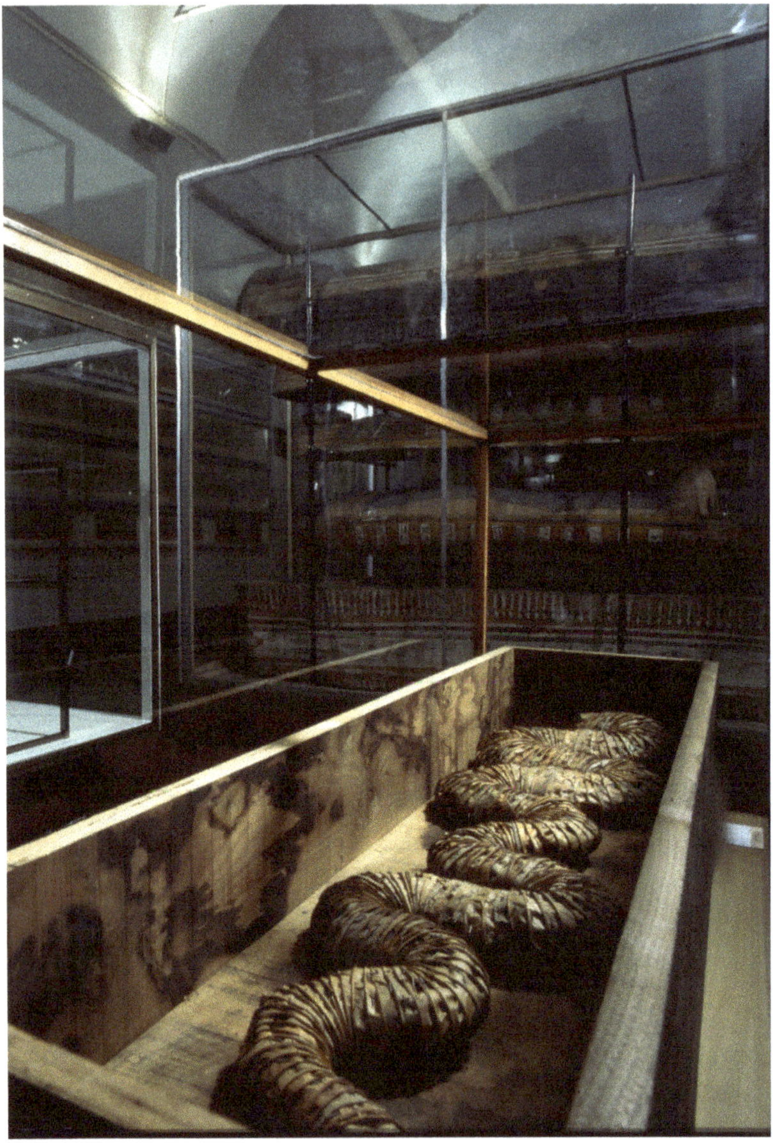

Figure 4.1 Andy Goldsworthy's *Leafwork* in the Museo Egizio's 'mummy room' as part of the 1995 *Time Machine* exhibition. Courtesy of the Museo Egizio, photo by Andrea Di Dio.

the most resonance. In the case of *Southern Hemisphere*, for instance, it was set in the Predynastic galleries where the naturally desiccated bodies of individuals who had died in the fourth millennium BC were displayed (Figure 4.4), providing for at least one visitor a scene that they

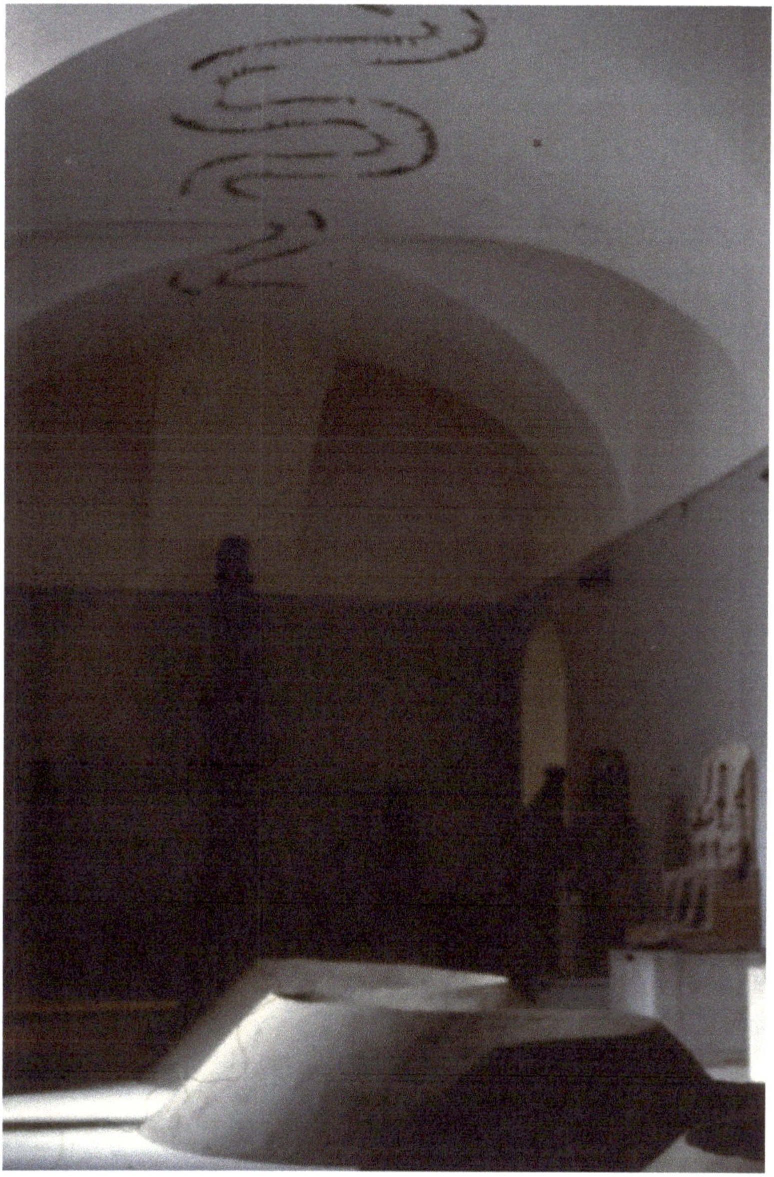

Figure 4.2 Andy Goldsworthy's *Sandwork with Leafwork* in the Museo Egizio as part of the *Time Machine* exhibition. Courtesy of the Museo Egizio, photo by Andrea Di Dio.

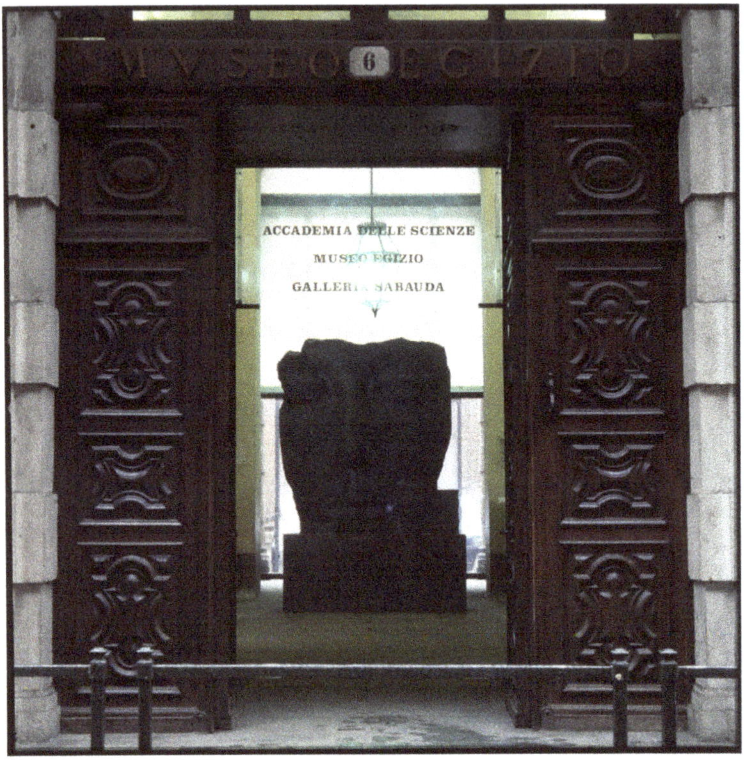

Figure 4.3 Igor Mitoraj's bronze *Hadrian* sculpture in the entrance of the Museo Egizio for the *Time Machine* exhibition. Courtesy of the Museo Egizio, photo by Andrea Di Dio.

considered to be 'very dramatic'.[5] Brian Eno's coloured light installation in the interior of the rock temple of Ellesyia was an exception, with the artist visiting the museum to produce the work, coincidentally in a year where he travelled to Egypt as a tourist for the first time.

Other installations were equally insertions of previous work inspired by ancient Egypt generally (or indeed just had parallel themes) rather than emerging from engagements with the collection specifically. This was the case for all three Italian artists who were invited to exhibit in order to bring in local artistic relevance: Francesco Clemente, Mimmo Paladino and Giuseppe Penone. The former two are noted as principal figures in the Italian Transavanguardia ('beyond the avant-garde') movement of the 1980s, which rejected formalism and conceptual art in favour of symbolism and figurative art, while the latter, Penone, is considered a leading representative of Arte Povera, an Italian critical theory that rejected traditional artistic languages. Clemente's inspiration

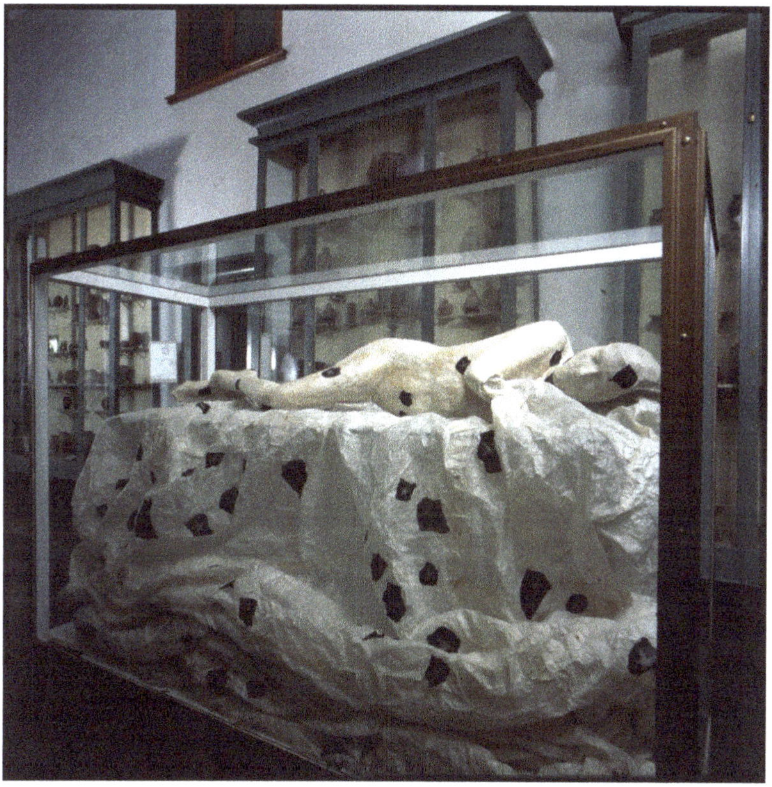

Figure 4.4 Kiki Smith's *Southern Hemisphere* amongst the Predynastic display of the Museo Egizio as part of the *Time Machine* exhibition. Courtesy of the Museo Egizio, photo by Andrea Di Dio.

came after vising Egypt and the Valley of the Kings in 1986, resulting in a series of 'funerary paintings'. One of these appeared in the Turin exhibition alongside another work from 1988, *Nec Spe Nec Metu* ('Neither Hope nor Fear'), featuring the figure of the jackal-headed god Anubis. For Paladino, Egyptian imagery had been one source of inspiration amongst many for the religious imagery he evoked in paintings and sculpture (Figure 4.5).

The artists' works were placed near artefacts that generally resonated with their creations, such as a kneeling statue of Amenhotep II and a statuette of a crocodile. Local Turin-based artist Giuseppe Penone is known for large-scale sculptures of trees, an example of which appeared in Turin's *Time Machine*. Putnam visited him at his studio where he was shown a few works in progress and they selected one that was completed for the show, *Albero Porta – Cedro/Door Tree Cedar*.

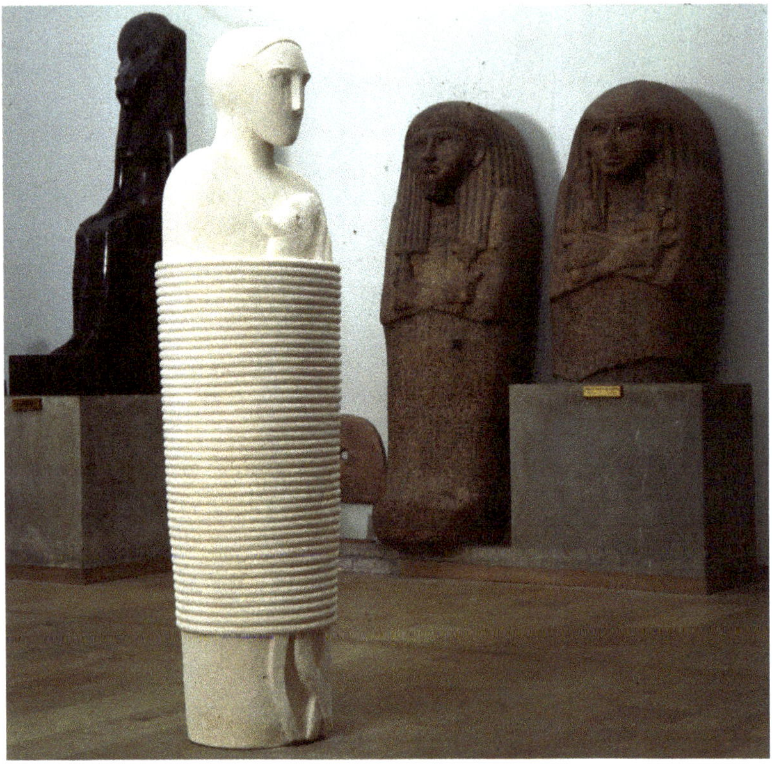

Figure 4.5 A Mimmo Paladino sculpture (untitled) in the Museo Egizio as part of the *Time Machine* exhibition. Courtesy of the Museo Egizio, photo by Andrea Di Dio.

For this, Penone had carved a large rectangular opening in a 10-foot-high tree trunk to reveal within it a slender, sculpted pine. This artwork proved to be a logistical challenge to install in the galleries (Figure 4.6). The material of the artwork, cedar, was seen to reference the material of the coffin of Khepeshet and, in the catalogue, the work was illustrated next to the wall painting of a tree goddess depicted in the burial chamber of Pharaoh Thutmoses III (Putnam 1995b, 48).

Overall, this was a very different type of artistic production from its London-based predecessor, with insertions rather than interventions more strongly defining the curatorial approach. Since few works were designed specifically for the show, there was less dialogue with curators or the collections in preparation. Pieces were chosen primarily for local relevance, or because of stylistic or thematic resonances that complemented rather than challenged the interpretation of the collection. Consequently, the contemporary art acted to reinforce the museum's

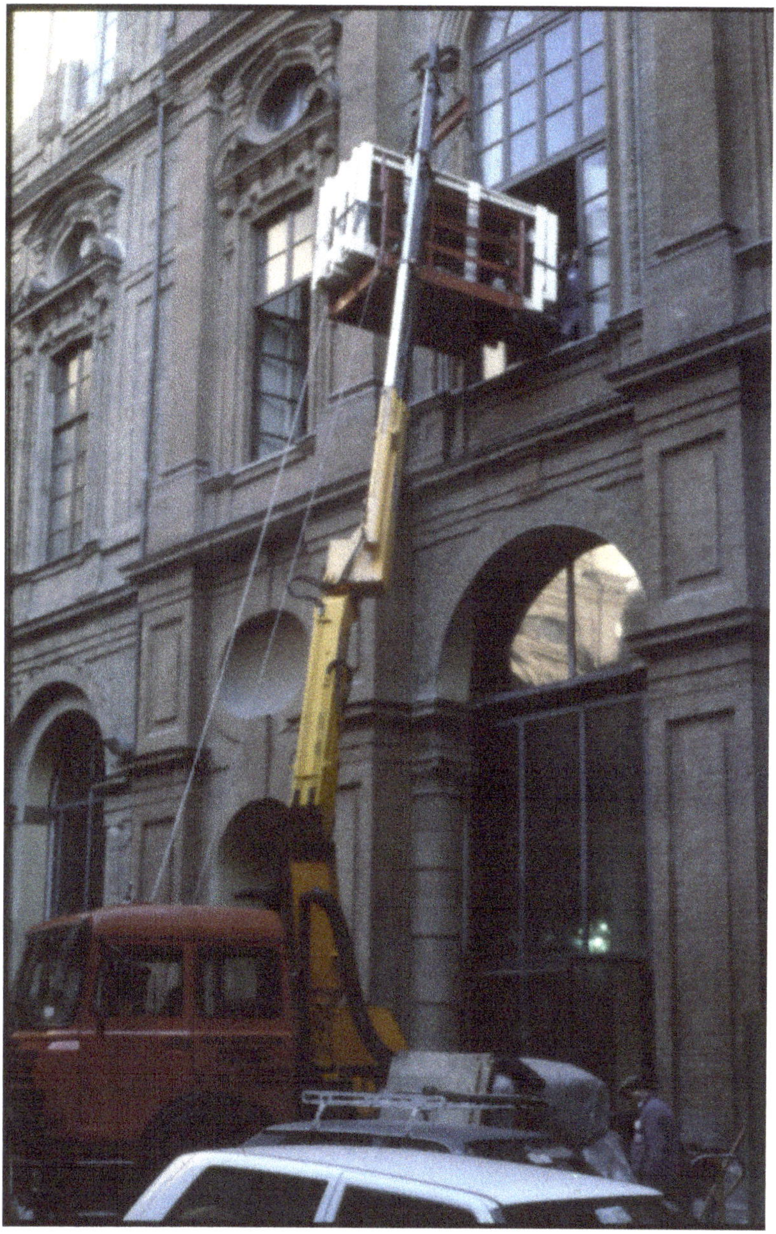

Figure 4.6 Giuseppe Penone's *Albero Porta – Cedro* had to be lifted into the galleries through an open window due to its size and weight, as shown in this photograph. Courtesy of the Museo Egizio, photo by Andrea Di Dio.

pre-existing interpretations, with themes such as bread, trees, life and rebirth being used to explain ancient Egyptian concepts rather than to develop, question or act as a counterpoint to them. The line-up too was far less diverse – only a single female artist was included, and no individuals of colour nor Egyptians were involved. Nevertheless, for the director at the time the exhibition had a radicality in being part of a concerted effort to 'remove the Museum from that "mummy complex" of which those who visited it in other times or as children often fall victim' and to bring about a meeting of the ancient past with the present day (Donadoni 2006).

The Turin-based *La Stampa* newspaper published several articles describing the show,[6] warmly appraising it as an invigoration of a 'dusty' but revered institution (e.g. *La Stampa* 13 December 1995; 21 November 1995; 19 January 1996). One reviewer, however, was more scathing about the ability of contemporary artists to 'compete' with ancient sculpture; the contemporary works were assessed as 'messing up' the museum, Eno's installation was regarded as an 'invasion' of the tomb it was set in, and Riches' sound sculpture was dismissed as 'slightly kitsch' (Vallora 1995). Only Mitoraj's offerings were complimented, suggesting that the reviewer held very particular Orientalised and romanticised ideas about what 'Egypt' and the museum should be. But the director was not discouraged by the few negative reviews, and she once again welcomed four contemporary artists into the museum in 2003 in a push against public perceptions of 'the mummy museum'. *Ostrakon: The Memory of Times* again involved contemporary artworks being interspersed amongst the antiquity displays throughout the museum (Barbero 2003). Nearly a hundred pieces – terracottas, brasses, paintings and a tapestry – were installed, with each of the artists dealing with one of four themes: beauty (Enrico Colombotto Rosso), costume (Camillo Fancia), culture (Riccardo Licata) and fashion (Giovanni Bonardi).

Ostrakon was the only contemporary artistic intervention in the 20 years after *Time Machine*. In part this could be attributed to what has been described as 'a distinctively conservative museological tradition' in Italy, with a divide in Europe between Anglo-Saxon and southern European models (Vecco and Piazzi 2015, 222; Mossetto and Vecco 2001). The former is generally characterised as more visitor-focused, the latter as more concerned with the care and conservation of artefacts. The influx of contemporary art into historic spaces is thus often identified as a phenomenon that diffused into Italy from elsewhere in Europe, with the long-standing Venice biennial acting as a conduit for avant-garde movements (Giannini 2022). But more significant in the Museo Egizio's case were the extensive changes within the museum itself – in its management, staffing and building – together with ongoing shifts in the social and cultural circumstances in the city of Turin itself.

A fresh space: Museo Egizio, 2005–17

The industrial crisis from the 1980s did not abate, and in April 2002 the 69th edition of the Salone dell'Automobile (Turin Auto Show) was cancelled. The historic Mirafiori plants were emptied and a more urgent investment in art and culture was pursued. Arts-led regeneration projects included the establishment of the Turin Contemporary Art Triennial in 2005, but it was really the award of the 2006 Winter Olympics, and the accompanying cultural Olympiad required by the Olympic Charter, that catalysed infrastructural investment and cultural enhancement. At the Museo Egizio these wider developments translated into radical changes in its management and funding. In 2004 it established a unique model of Italian public cultural heritage management – a private–public partnership deriving its income from geographically rooted public bodies (the city and regional authority), private sponsorship and marketing. In the galleries, preparations for 2006 manifested in the appointment of the Oscar-winning Hollywood costume and set designer Dante Ferretti, who staged a spectacular and dramatic view of the Egyptian statuary through the creative use of lighting rigs and mirrors, rendering the museum's statue gallery a movie set by boxing in the walls and lowering the ceiling. As he did so, Goldsworthy's ceiling artwork from *Time Machine* was concealed from view. Although initially designed as a temporary installation, Ferretti's gallery has remained in place for more than 20 years. And behind its façade, an artwork that was also conceived of as transitory was unwittingly preserved, perhaps one day to be rediscovered.

After the Olympics, and as part of a wide-ranging redevelopment plan aimed at improving Turin's cultural offerings, the museum launched a competition for a renovation project. It was won by a group led by Turin-based architectural practice Isolarchitetti and once again it involved Ferretti. The culmination of these efforts was the dramatic renovation of the Collegio dei Nobili, involving the removal of four floors, the creation of underground galleries and the redisplay of more than 35,000 objects. All the while the old and new were balanced with building works sensitive to original structures while providing modern sections. The completely redesigned museum opened on 1 April 2015, with a fresh curatorial team, a new director and different management structure. Although this meant that there was limited institutional memory of past activities, the future vision was firmly established by the director, Christian Greco, as that of a modern archaeological museum, focused upon context, research, dialogue and care, rather than an antiquarian one.[7] The newly created displays were considered 'far from being the only and final outcome of this process of renovation', and the museum hoped to keep 'experimenting with new approaches to communication and outreach' (Del Vesco 2016, 18).

The balance of old and new did not include contemporary art until 2017, when the museum participated in *Like a Moth to a Flame*, which formed part of the inaugural Visual Arts Program, another regeneration scheme. This time, redevelopment was focused upon Turin's Officine Grandi Riparazioni (OGR), a site built between 1885 and 1895 for the maintenance of railway vehicles that was transformed into a 20,000-square-metre arts and innovation centre for the promotion of culture and technological innovation in the fields of the visual and performing arts. The event also served as a celebration of the 25th anniversary of the Fondazione Sandretto Re Rebaudengo's collection of contemporary art, bringing together more than 70 works from the foundation together with hundreds of objects from Turin's historic holdings and 'offering a portrait of Turin and its engagement with the world through the collecting habits of the city and its citizens' (Anon. 2017). The Museo Egizio contributed several items from its collection to be displayed in the cavernous postindustrial spaces of the OGR. One was an Osirian head of a king, while in its place in the Museo Egizio *Unfired Clay Torso* (2005) was mounted, a fragmentary figure evocative of an archaeological find sculpted by Dutch artist Mark Manders and held in the collection of the Fondazione Sandretto Re Rebaudengo. For Bard College professor Tom Eccles, one of the show's curators, Manders' figure reminded him of a Pharaonic head in the 'quality of the sculpture, the very soft facial features, the slightly mournful quality' (Spence 2017). The exhibition's curators also borrowed a monumental second-millennium BC black marble statue of the Egyptian lioness goddess Sekhmet, pairing it with kinetic art movement artist Gianni Colombo's *Bariesthesias* (1974–5), which took the form of black asymmetrical steps.

Although the exhibition materialised the shift to the contemporary to revive, regenerate and make more relevant historic collections, during the press promotion for the exhibition Eccles proffered an alternative dynamic between past and present, flipping the direction of influence:

> *Like a Moth to a Flame* is just the latest in a series of exhibitions in recent years that have brought together objects from past and present. Why are they so popular? 'The last two decades have seen such an explosion in the contemporary art world, people are feeling almost overwhelmed by it, as well as the pace of the world,' says Eccles. 'The slowness of historic art [provides a] solace that people find compelling.' (Spence 2017)

This was an initiative external to the Museo Egizio, who reacted to an opportunity presented to it by the wider museum ecosystem. But also acting on this dynamic was the contemporary art market. The exhibition was included as part of *Artissima*, with the Museo Egizio installation deemed one of the highlights as part of the Notte delle Arti Contemporanee (Contemporary Art Night) circuit for art fair participants (Artnet News 2017).

In January and February of the following year, 2018, creative photographer Sharon Ritossa exhibited in the entrance hall of the museum, an opportunity created by the regional tourism board.[8] Her *#EnjoyEternity* project played on the theme of technology and images, employing images of New Kingdom sphinxes reconstituted with hundreds of smartphone photographs; bold, brightly coloured graphics of small artefacts from the collection arranged in grid-like patterns on the surrounding walls; and a female body wrapped in a light-emitting thread in the exhibition area. That same year, another multi-sited exhibition was held across Turin as part of the 'European Year of Cultural Heritage', involving 12 months of events and celebration brought together under the banner 'Our heritage: where the past meets the future'. Turin's offering, *Anche le Statue Muoiono* (*Statues Also Die*), with a title drawn from the short documentary film *Les Statues meurent aussi* (1953) by Chris Marker and Alain Resnais, was initially conceived as a means to bring together the reflections of contemporary artists on the theme of the targeted destruction of heritage in areas recently affected by conflict in places such as Iraq, Iran, Lebanon, Syria and Egypt (Calderoni 2018, 64). Similar types of exhibitions were prevalent in European and American museums around the same time, many using contemporary artists to articulate the violence, loss and human impact of conflict in these diverse regions. The Ashmolean Museum's 2021 *Owning the Past* exhibition, for instance, was inspired by attempts by ISIS (also called Daesh) to erase identities and histories in Iraq, and featured a commissioned installation by British artist Piers Secunda. The University of Pennsylvania's Museum of Archaeology and Anthropology, meanwhile, mounted the exhibition *Cultures in the*

Crossfire: Stories from Syria and Iraq between April 2017 and November 2018. This represented a collaboration between the museum and the Syrian contemporary artist Issam Kourbaj, who had displayed works like *Dark Water, Burning World* alongside archaeology collections in institutions such as the Fitzwilliam Museum in Cambridge, the British Museum and the Museum für Islamische Kunst in Berlin (see Chapter 3).

Such projects frequently defer to one of the most pervasive and compelling narratives of 'heritage' present in the public and academic domains, that of 'destruction' – a narrative that has dominated conversations about the heritage of the Middle East in particular, eternally casting it as being 'at risk' (Rico 2017). The danger of such an approach is that the concept of 'European' becomes defined in opposition to the Middle East, taking the Orientalist view of Europe as a place of safety, salvation and authority, in contrast to the East. Overall, such installations, Rico (2017) reminds us, can be focused on object and perpetrator, overlooking the deeper implications of looting destruction and colonial legacies for contemporary local communities, and sidelining alternative narratives of heritage outside the academy and the museum. While *Cultures in the Crossfire* at the University of Pennsylvania's Museum of Archaeology and Anthropology garnered widespread acclaim, this was insightfully tempered by Raha Rafii's (2019) review, which cautioned that 'rather than acting as a timely response to the then-ongoing threat of ISIS, such framing enlisted ISIS' destructive spectacle in the service of the claims of museums and other institutes to their collections'. These issues were mitigated to a considerable extent, although not entirely transcended, in *Statues Also Die* through a curatorial triangulation of themes. Although the first theme did feature destruction and looting in the Middle East, the latter two firmly cast a critical eye over Western institutions themselves, first by looking at the power of images as bearers of numerous meanings and instruments of dominance, and secondly by questioning the role of Western museums in the preservation of cultural heritage, including implications of the 'museum container' and colonial legacies.

Statues Also Die, like *A Moth to a Flame*, represented a collaboration of four institutions across the city – the Museo Egizio, the Musei Reali (a museum complex in Turin established in 2014), the Centro Ricerche Archeologiche e Scavi di Torino and the Fondazione Sandretto Re Rebaudengo. To support the exhibition's narratives, the decision was taken to provide relatively extensive interpretive labels, captions and wider context to highlight the processes underlying the display of objects within museums, rather than leave the art open-ended as is often the case (Ciccopiedi and Del Vesco 2021). As the introductory text panel at each site asserted, the 'physical proximity of ancient artefacts and contemporary artworks spurs reflection on how the forerunners of the current practices of destruction and pillage lie in other historical, geographical and ideological contexts'.

At the non-profit, private contemporary art foundation Sandretto Re Rebaudengo, works of artists Mark Manders, Simon Wachsmuth, Lamia Joreige and Kader Attia were exhibited. The foundation occupies a modern city-centre building (Centro per l'Arte Contemporanea), opened in the former industrial area in 2002 and designed by architect Claudio Silvestrin, known for his use of contemporary minimalism. Consequently, ancient and modern artworks were set into a familiar aesthetic setting emphasising the nature of the encounter in the present, not wholly inappropriate for the exhibition's themes. Algerian artist Kader Attia's *Arab Spring*, which was previously shown at Basel's Art Fair in 2015, sat at the core of the foundation's portion of the exhibition. It comprised 16 museum showcases modelled like those in Cairo's Egyptian Museum, then smashed by the artist to recall the popular revolt in Egypt in 2011 when a group of demonstrators broke into the museum on Tahrir Square, devastating numerous vitrines and stealing many objects that were representative of pre-Islamic culture in Egypt. Sharing the expansive space with Attia's installation were two artefacts borrowed from the Museo Egizio as examples of acts of *damnatio memoriae* (condemnation of memory) towards political and religious representatives: a mid-second-millennium statue of Hapu (inventory number C. 3061) and a similarly aged stele of Amenhotep (C. 1523). In the case of the statue of Hapu, the act was the erasure of the god's name 'Amun' during the Amarna period, while on Amenhotep's stele his name and image were gouged out. Both artefacts were rather apologetically set against the wall, out of the sightline of the gallery's main entrance, a vista dominated by Attia's installation. The liaison between past and present here was therefore somewhat tokenistic, not just in context but in physical placement. This strategy is equally apparent from the accompanying catalogue, in which the publishing house preferred a traditional presentation, with ancient material and the contemporary artworks discussed separately rather than placed into discourse with each other (Ciccopiedi et al. 2021).

At the Museo Egizio, *Statues Also Die* was housed on the third floor of the Collegio dei Nobili, in a dedicated, enclosed, muted white space for temporary exhibitions, set apart from the collections. A small selection of artefacts from the collection were brought into the space and paired with a few, although not all, of the contemporary artworks. For instance, the exhibition commenced with Mimmo Jodice's *Anamnesi* (2014), a series of nine black and white photographs of statue faces with their mouths wide open, placed opposite the fragmented faces of the ancient Egyptian governors of Qau el-Kebir (1900–1850 BC) from excavations in their rock-cut tombs led by the museum's curator, Schiaparelli, in 1905–6 (Figure 4.7). Both offered reflections on what the passage of time does to sculptures. The exhibition closed with a Middle Kingdom wooden statue (1900 BC) from the Assiut tomb of Upuautemahat (S. 8786). The statue's eyes had been hollowed out by looters to extract the hard stone and bronze inlays and it was this feature that was deliberately spotlighted to resonate with Kader Attia's *Untitled (Sacred) and Untitled (Violence)* installation of glass fragments arranged on a light box to bring appreciation to their broken and jagged edges. The artworks by Jananne Al-Ani, Morehshin Allahyari, Liz Glynn, Walid Raad and Simon Wachsmuth were selected for their ability to problematise and respond to themes of heritage destruction and Western museum appropriation, rather than to address Egyptian antiquity specifically. This was echoed in a subsequent roundtable following the exhibition, where the curators reflected on the project. Their discussion on the relationship between contemporary art and archaeology described a unidirectional influence of archaeology upon contemporary artists and the relevance of heritage in the contemporary world (Ciccopiedi and Del Vesco 2021, 31–5).

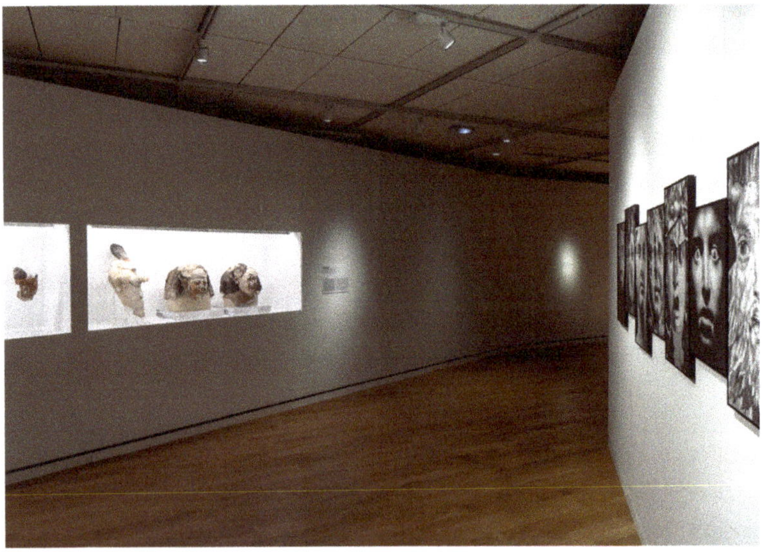

Figure 4.7 Juxtaposition of Mimmo Jodice's photographic prints *Anamnesi* with ancient Egyptian fragmentary statues, part of the *Statues Also Die* exhibition. Courtesy of the Museo Egizio, photo by Nicola Dell'Aquila.

Only two installations referenced Egypt directly, those of Ali Cherri and Iman Issa. In Cherri's *Fragments II* (2016), this was overt, with the inclusion of small, portable Egyptian artefacts procured from auctions in Europe alongside other antiquities from Peru, Greece and Indonesia, amongst other countries. These Cherri arranged on a backlit table to deprive the objects of their shadows and, without labels that might give them provenance, to decontextualise them. Amidst this assortment of commercially acquired heritage, a taxidermised bird of prey loomed large, symbolising the West's rapacity. The statue of Neshor, which had been modified on the antiquities market, was placed in sight of Cherri's installation, together with a Ptolemaic coffin piece of Djedthotiuefankh (C. 2241), an example of an artefact whose identity, function and meaning had been stripped away during its circulation on the market and its museum life (Figure 4.8). Egyptian artist Issa's *Heritage Studies* 1 (2015) was part of an ongoing series of sculptures paired with texts, brought together to explore the gap between history and artefact. Each minimalist geometric sculpture was installed as if it was a museological display, accompanied by a didactic label. In the case of *Heritage Studies* 1, this took the form of a large wooden pyramidal structure accompanied by a deliberately absurd label that misidentified the material, history and dimensions of the work displayed.

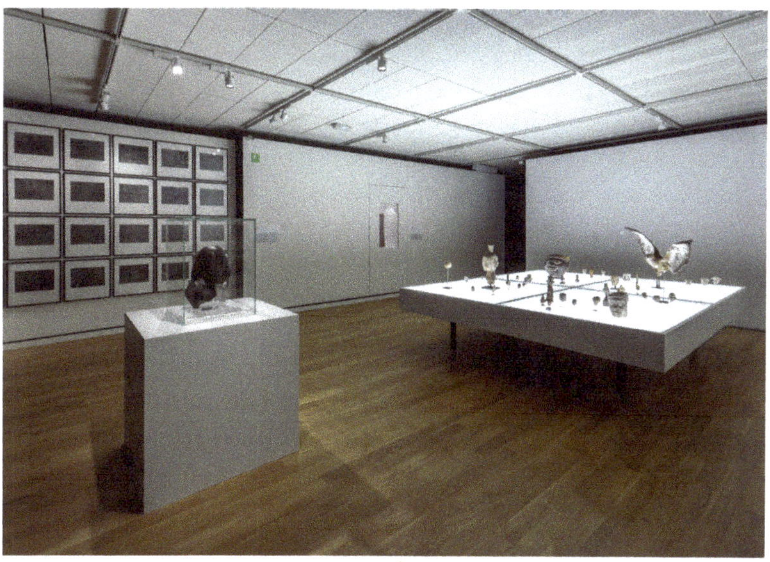

Figure 4.8 Installation of Ali Cherri's work in the *Statues Also Die* exhibition together with artefacts from the Museo Egizio's collection. Courtesy of the Museo Egizio, photo by Nicola Dell'Aquila.

The role of contemporary art at the museum was confidently identified as being 'key to interpret archaeological collections', helping 'curators in communicating more effectively with the public, since it seeks to bridge the past-present gap with contents that are neither sterile nor superficial' (Ciccopiedi and Del Vesco 2021, 33). Finding a way to do that, however, can be challenging. In her review of *Cultures in the Crossfire*, Rafii (2019) opined that the contemporary art 'seemed to sit on top of, rather than inform, the rest of the exhibit'. In Turin, however, it was the antiquities that were at risk of seeming ancillary, although informal feedback from visitors and tour guides was considered positive by the staff, and the exhibition attracted some 183,338 visitors (Museo Egizio Report Integrato 2020).[9] It seems that one of the most notable impacts was indeed on helping the curators, but not necessarily in communicating with the public. Instead, the contemporary artworks facilitated the development of the curators' own ideas on the value of such interventions. Several staff members conducted tours for groups during the exhibition's run and on each iteration their confidence grew in narrating the significance of the juxtapositions between contemporary artworks and the antiquities, allowing them to elaborate their insights for the visitors. For instance, one staff member recalled that the opening exhibit's pairing of the Qau statues with the creative photographs of Jodice began to impact their own awareness of museum practices and how they shift the meanings of collections. Curators observed, with great surprise, how Issa's false labels were often taken at face value by the audience and they were struck by the power of text panels to provide leading interpretive assumptions about an object. As the museum develops its future plan and interpretation strategy, these are lessons now at the forefront of their minds.

2022: Egyptology's anniversaries

Popular history has thrived on anniversaries. Egyptology is no different, establishing memory cultures around 'great' historical figures, 'iconic' events or famous objects as part of ongoing disciplinary self-fashioning. The year 2022 occasioned three such anniversaries for Egypt around which dozens of seminars and museum programmes were organised: 100 years since the opening of Tutankhamun's tomb, 200 years since the decipherment of hieroglyphs and 100 years since Egypt's independence from Britain. Most events focused on the first two, celebrating and promoting Egyptology, and feeding the media with conventional wisdom that rarely challenged standard narratives (Carruthers 2022). In Turin a temporary exhibition of contemporary artwork did, however, seek to bring a critical voice to authoritative accounts: the voice of Sara Sallam (see Chapter 2). By this time, the copresence of ancient and contemporary art had become a more common curatorial practice within Italy itself (Ferri 2021). 'An art place that does not have relations with the work of living artists is unthinkable,' declared Antonio Lampis, former director general of the state museums (2017–20), while the president of the Marino Marini Museum in Florence, Patrizia Asproni, acknowledged that it 'is right that contemporary art enters the places of ancient art', and the director of the National Archaeological Museum of Naples, Paolo Giulierini, stated that 'hosting contemporary art makes sense' (Ferri 2021).

The initiative to invite Sallam to Turin was taken by curator Paolo Del Vesco almost immediately following the first screening of her video *I Prayed for the Resin not to Melt* at the Birmingham conference *Performing Tutankhamun: One Hundred Years of Retellings* in July 2022. For her exhibition in Turin, *Through Tutankhamun's Eyes: Alternative Perspectives on Egyptology*,[10] Sallam and Del Vesco agreed on three pieces that would resonate most strikingly with the collection. The newest, *I Prayed for the Resin not to Melt* (2022),[11] an effecting and poignant video installation, features a photograph of the unwrapped, decapitated head of Tutankhamun appearing briefly on the monitor before fading to a blank black screen, a rejection of how the excavation has been portrayed visually and popularly consumed. Sallam then quietly gives voice, in English, to the dead Pharaoh's apprehension as archaeologists desecrate his tomb, providing a powerful counternarrative to the dominant one of the excavators. She whispers prayers that are etched into his golden death mask as the sounds of digging get closer. The image of the boy king's embalmed head returns intermittently, gradually becoming covered in gold leaf and fresh textiles, to convey a body being treated gently and receiving something of what was taken from him.[12] Although the work was not itself produced in dialogue with Turin's collection explicitly, it is one grounded in Egyptological research and archives (Sallam 2019), drawing inspiration from the writings of scholars such as Christina Riggs (2014b, 2019, 2021).

Sallam's second presentation in Turin, *A Tourist Handbook for Egypt Outside of Egypt* 1 (2020), offered a walking tour of the streets of Paris. The piece incorporated Egyptian site names from the places and battles of the Napoleonic expedition to Egypt into Parisian street names. In so doing, Sallam's work provided an alternative historical narrative to the dominant, Eurocentric one. Although first produced as a hand-sewn book, for Turin (as in Brussels; Chapter 2) the work was refabricated, and in its Turin iteration it was narrated by Sallam, who could be heard by visitors through the headsets provided (Figure 4.9). The third installation in the exhibition comprised the large-format prints of her *Home*

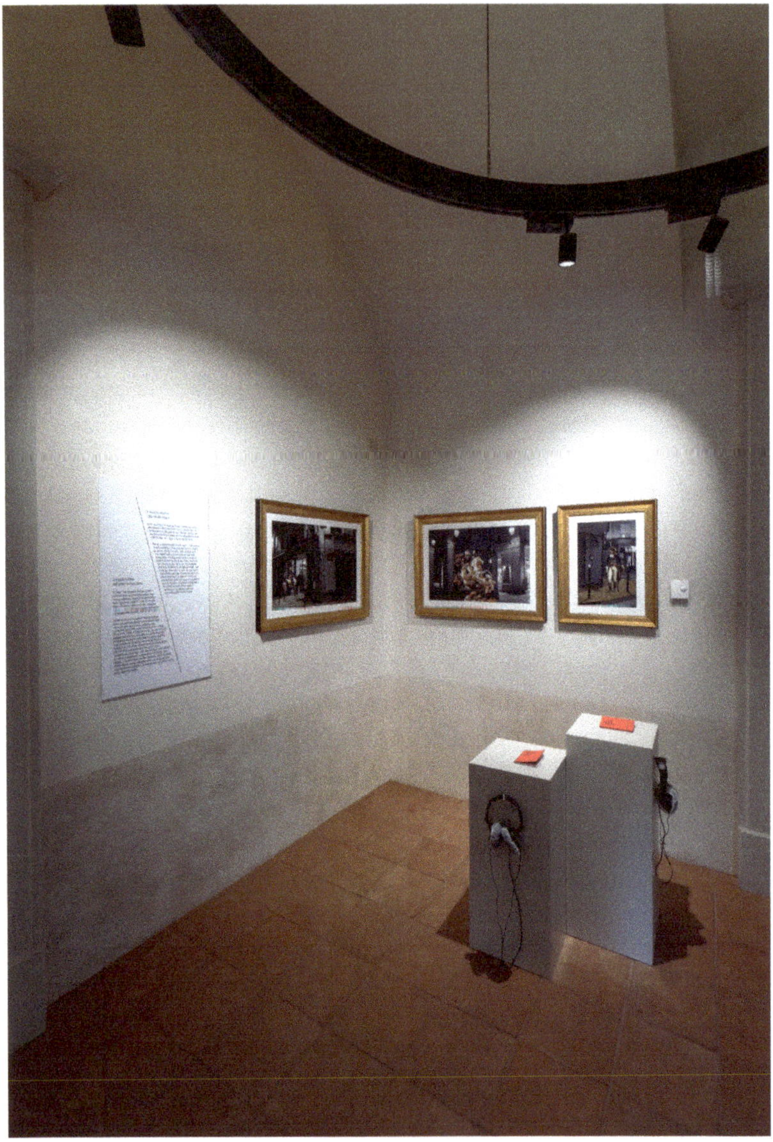

Figure 4.9 The Museo Egizio's installation of Sara Sallam's *A Tourist Handbook for Egypt Outside of Egypt* in 2022.[13] Courtesy of the Museo Egizio, photo by Nicola Dell'Aquila.

Outside of Home series, although on this occasion there had not been time to produce a bespoke version based on the Museo Egizio.

There had been extensive dialogue via email and online meetings with Del Vesco and the Turin design team to establish themes and interpretive text for the exhibition. However, it was not in conversation with the collection or the museum space, in part due to the extremely tight schedule between invitation and exhibition. In the end Sallam's artworks were installed in an area next to the conference hall as this provided direct access from the outside. The exhibition was integrated with the *Artissima* programme and its chosen location meant that it would be freely accessible during its 'Night of the Arts' even when the museum was closed. However, security guards reported to Sallam that general museum visitors found the exhibition hard to locate, making the critique she offered an optional and not integral reading of the museum's narrative. Riggs (2023) concluded that the 'alternative perspective' promised by the exhibition's title did not impinge on the authoritative voice of the institution. Other areas within the institution could have offered a more effective location for her work, such as beside the human remains displays, which would have benefited from *I Prayed for the Resin not to Melt*. However, at the time it was simply not possible to build a dark room for the projection in that gallery and, in any case, the museum staff countered that it is not always necessary to show one thing next to another for visitors to make a connection. Sallam's vivid portrayal of the sanctity of the tomb and the young Pharaoh's body engages both intellectually and emotionally with ancient and recent pasts. These are powerful combinations, and it has been demonstrated that affective presentations of knowledge provide substantive, long-term learning opportunities, heightening the experience of other parts of museum display even with distance (Robins 2013, 164).

Visitor surveys were not undertaken but anecdotes from security staff and the curatorial team suggest that many visitors were extremely moved by their encounter with Sallam's installation and returned to the galleries more contemplative. Some were said to have emerged crying from the projection room. A few members of staff were less enthusiastic about the place of contemporary art within the museum, preferring more traditional approaches. Egyptology scholars were reportedly more likely to express scepticism about the value of the intervention than non-Egyptological museum professionals in the building. Other curators found the installation provocative, galvanising an unease with the recently redesigned display of mummified remains opened in June 2021 and leading them to continue to question modes of interpretation and contexts of viewing. Here contemporary art interventions in the museum emerge less as a means of public communication or audience engagement than as a reflexive tool for the staff themselves – not research per se, but an ongoing course of contemplation on the disciplinary practices of archaeology and Egyptology. Moreover, they act as experimental adjustments in a rapidly shifting museum sector where external social and political pressures have demanded that institutions change.

While anniversaries may be primarily retrospective, they do offer moments of synthesis, benchmarks for future research and action. For the Museo Egizio, Sallam's 2022 installation was a turning point in its collections policy. Previously, the museum's policy prevented new acquisitions, due to the problems of the antiquities market and a recognition that legal restrictions in Egypt prohibit the export of ancient artefacts. In effect, the collection had been a closed one. However, the museum was keen to acquire all of Sallam's displayed installations and these could not be collected without a longer-term re-evaluation of the place of contemporary art within the institution. The group of curators who had worked on the *Statues Also Die* exhibition, and who also led on bringing Sallam's work to the Museo Egizio, came together once again with a proposal for the director: a new, long-term contemporary art programme. This included plans for artist residencies to coincide with the bicentenary in 2024, with opportunities for artists to respond to the collection and for their products to be subsequently acquired as an official part of the collection. Concurrent with this policy evolution was the further transformation of the physical structure of the Collegio dei Nobili itself. A second architectural effort was now undertaken to transform the museum, implemented by architects David Gianotten and Andreas Karavanas, creating a covered courtyard and a series of connected rooms within the museum, opening pathways and spaces. It is hoped that Sallam's work and that of other artists will be better accommodated in this reinvented building and that experiments in display can be conducted in the reconfigured floorplan.

*

Prior to 2022 the place of contemporary art within the Museo Egizio had never been well established. There was no focused programme or curatorial strategy of inclusion. Despite *Time Machine*'s artworks pervading the whole institution in the mid-1990s, subsequent enterprises were consistently billed as a 'first' for the museum. For instance, *Statues Also Die* was claimed to be 'the first time, contemporary art arrives at the Egyptian Museum' (Giraud 2018) or to represent 'an unusual and innovative partnership between the ancient and the contemporary' (Macaluso 2018). Nor were any of the interventions included in recent historical retrospectives on the institution (e.g. Moiso 2016), highlighting how these had not worked back on the museum. The freshly renovated institution in the 2000s at first only incorporated alternative presentations somewhat tokenistically. Most were included as reactions to external impetuses, whether these involved regeneration, civic cooperation or participation in initiatives of international bodies such as the European Commission.

It is only more recently with *Statues Also Die* and the invitation to Sallam that there has been greater involvement internally from curatorial staff as the practice of artistic intervention gained more traction within the Italian museum sector. Practice has generally followed a model of insertion of pre-existing works, but dialogue with the collection and the curators is emerging. As with the previous case study of the British Museum, what constitutes effective institutional critique is challenged by this case study, as staff have defended the use of contemporary art in spaces set apart from the collections. Is direct juxtaposition a necessary condition for effective reflection? Regardless, the introduction of recent artworks is beginning to transform policy by helping to redefine contemporary collecting within the institution. The museum collection in Turin may be more than 200 years old, but the staff see it as relatively young. It is still in a state of becoming both in terms of its infrastructure and its outlook, constantly shifting in its local and international contexts, negotiating between continuity and change, the old and the new.

Notes

1 https://www.artissima.art/en/about/ [Accessed 12 May 2023].

2 Film made by the British Museum's Education Service in 1995. I am grateful to James Putnam for sharing his VHS copy with me as it is not held in the British Museum's library or archives (in any department or centrally). A DVD copy in the British Museum could not be made to work.

3 Stephen Cox, Andy Goldsworthy, David Hiscock, Jiří Kolář, Igor Mitoraj, Marc Quinn, Peter Randall-Page and Martin Riches. Mihaylovich's work was simply too large to ship over, while the reason for Rita Keegan's exclusion is unclear – she does not recall being invited and it was perhaps on account of the technical, multimedia nature of the work that it was deemed to be unsuitable in the more traditional Turin Museum where almost all artworks that were included were static, sculptural pieces.

4 Produced using the British Museum's peripheral camera that she had a shared interest in, resulting in a picture of her hand wearing an ancient Egyptian ring being featuring in the final show.
5 As recorded in the British Museum Education Service's 1995 film of *Time Machine*. Copy held by James Putnam.
6 Quotations are translated by the author from the original Italian.
7 http://web.philo.ulg.ac.be/x-bound/portfolio-item/christian-greco/ [Accessed 23 September 2023].
8 Thanks to the support of Hangar Creativity, a project supporting young artistic talents promoted by the Department of Culture and Tourism of the Piedmont region and coordinated by the Piedmont Foundation Live.
9 Available at: https://museoegizio.it/esplora/notizie/pubblicato-il-primo-bilancio-integrato-del-museo-egizio/ [Accessed 3 September 2024]
10 On display at the Museo Egizio from 4 November 2022 to 31 January 2023.
11 A reference to Carter's decision to move the body of Tutankhamun outside the tomb into the sun in an attempt to melt the resin that had adhered the body and mask.
12 Sallam, S. 2022. Through Tutankhamun's eyes: Alternative perspectives on Egyptology. Lecture given at Museo Egizio, 9 November 2022. Available at: https://www.youtube.com/watch?v=DWbdJSjkJXM [Accessed 19 May 2023].
13 This image was taken prior to a final modification by Sallam. The white framing around the images was removed before the exhibition opening in order to have just the golden frames around them in direct contact with the images so that they looked more like older paintings.

5
Contemporary art and the Staatliches Museum Ägyptischer Kunst

The Staatliches Museum Ägyptischer Kunst (SMÄK) today occupies a glass and concrete building in Munich's Museum Quarter (Kunstareal München), which opened to the public in 2013 following an architectural competition. The winning design by Peter Böhm resulted in a new home for the state collection of Egyptian art, providing it with three times as much exhibition space as it had previously. This modernist museum space can be understood as a broader manifestation of the long tradition of German art-historical scholarship (charted in Chapter 1) that has led Egyptology to emphasise visual culture rather than original contexts. The museum's architecture, the interior design of its galleries and the pioneering temporary exhibitions of contemporary art it has hosted have been influenced by former director Dietrich Wildung (1975–88), but it owes a more considerable debt to the vision of his wife, Silvia Schoske, who succeeded him in the position (1989–2021). Their combined interests and the parallel developments they led in Munich and Berlin, where Wildung was director of the Egyptian museum for more than 20 years from 1989, are especially informative for the reciprocal influences of contemporary art and architecture, the commercial art market, Egyptology and museums. What stands out in this case study is the long-term institutional commitment to contemporary art as a communication and engagement strategy. Nevertheless, there remain opportunities to embrace institutional critique and develop further openings for collaborative research with, rather than just around, the collection.

Ägyptische und moderne Skulptur: designing museum spaces

Egyptologist Heinz Herzer, having first trained in art history, worked for the German Archaeological Institute in Cairo for several years. Throughout the 1960s and early 1970s, he facilitated the sale of Egyptian antiquities to some of the largest museums in the USA, such as the Brooklyn Museum of Fine Art,[1] The Metropolitan Museum of Art[2] and the Boston Museum of Fine Arts.[3] He went on to establish a commercial art gallery in Munich in 1976, Galerie Heinz Herzer, selling contemporary artworks alongside Greek and Egyptian antiquities, much like the dealers who founded galleries in London and Paris in the 1920s (Chapter 1). Whenever a substantial piece of ancient Egyptian material culture entered his possession, his first call would be to Dietrich Wildung, whose personal interest in art was informed by his father, an artist. Together with Schoske, Wildung would promptly visit the gallery, where they would be confronted by both Egyptian artefacts and contemporary works (Schoske and Wildung 2020). In 1982 the two visited Herzer's gallery and were struck by a pairing of a Kushite-period statue head and an abstract sculpture of three vertical iron plates by Ernst Hermanns, placed next to each other. The ensuing conversation between the dealer and the curators focused on the formal and stylistic aspects of the pieces, rather than dating and iconography, leading them to a fresh emphasis in their own work on detaching ancient Egyptian materials from 'their original function and historical context' and towards placing antiquities 'on an equal footing with works of art by other epochs and cultures' (Schoske and Wildung 2020, 58).

Their sentiments can be seen as broadly reflective of the museum sector in the German-speaking world in the 1980s, a decade that saw a renewed emphasis on objects, in a similar vein to the shifts witnessed 60 years before. Curators, such as ethnologist Gottfried Korff, were critical of German didactic displays of the 1970s that foregrounded texts and graphics as the primary bearers of meaning in the museum, obscuring its objects. In contrast, the culture-historical exhibitions that he and his colleagues mounted in the 1980s embraced audiovisual media, as well as more art and design features to create self-explanatory environments in which the object was the 'historical informant' and the 'core and quintessence of the museum' (Habsburg-Lothringen 2015, 331–5).

From the 'initial spark' in Herzer's gallery arose a proposition to organise an exhibition allowing for a direct encounter between ancient and modern art. With a specialist in contemporary art from Morsbroich

Museum in Leverkusen, the director Rolf Wedewer, *Ägyptische und moderne Skulptur* was conceived. Launched in January 1986, the exhibition compared 37 works by 23 modern artists (including Rodin, Picasso and Giacometti) with 48 ancient Egyptian sculptures, set into the then recently reopened baroque surroundings of the Morsbroich Museum palace, a museum whose physical contrasts between past and present underpin its interdisciplinary mission.[4] The exhibition was shown again in Munich, although space restrictions in the museum meant that it had to be hosted in the Hypo Kunsthalle in the centre of Munich, about five minutes' walking distance away. One result was that the exhibition was not terribly successful for the venue, attracting only 20,000 visitors. Nonetheless, it led Egyptologist Friedrich Junge (1990, 26) to ask, 'was denn ausmacht, was man gemeinhin "ägyptische Kunst" nennt?' ('what constitutes that which is generally called "Egyptian art"?'). His subsequent reflections were primarily art-historical, concerning how juxtapositions are a means to assess quality and visual appeal, but his comment also highlights modern and contemporary art's ability to provide a critical juncture, a productive disruption that serves to open discourse even if not a sustained engagement.

The show also set a precedent, opening up the Egyptian collection in Munich itself as a potential setting for the presentation of contemporary installations. These were highly unusual in Germany in the 1990s and early 2000s. In contrast to the wider cultural trends in the UK explored in Chapter 1, the inclusion of recent works outside of art galleries alongside other types of collections was not at all common. It has only been more recently, in the late 2010s and early 2020s, that this trend has become apparent as the German museum sector tries to address colonial and 'hidden' histories, most visibly in ethnographic institutions (Dittgen 2022; Küster 2022; Penzel 2022; Wonsich 2018). The installations in Munich, however, were an accident of circumstance rather than a product of design, since at that time the museum was poorly housed in the Munich Royal Residence where there was limited exhibition space. Thus, artworks had no alternative but to fit amongst the existing displays. In this way, the museum accommodated Burkard Backe's bronze sculptures in 1989 – *Sonnen und Skulpturen* – followed by further installations from student and professional artists, such as Traude Linhardt's *Zeitzeichen* (1997). Marlies Poss's work featured twice at the Residence: *Über Leben* (1995) and *Arte Animale* (2002), both of which were inspired by ancient Egyptian forms generally. The latter, for instance, gave an opportunity for the museum to discuss the role of animals in divine representation in ancient Egypt. There were also mixed shows of young artists, like *Out of Egypt* (1996), which did respond directly to the collection, under the guidance of the Professor of Sculpture James Reineking, at the Academy of Fine Arts, Munich.

By 1989 Wildung had taken up the post as director of the Ägyptisches Museum und Papyrussammlung der Staatlichen Museen zu Berlin and he oversaw its move to the Neues Museum. His development of the galleries in Berlin presaged similar approaches in Munich, including several installations of modern and contemporary art, such as work by Ugo Dossi in 2002 and Giacometti in 2008 (Klemm and Wildung 2008). In the early 2000s Wildung encountered a monumental neon installation by Maurizio Nannucci that 'captivated' him, displaying the words 'ALL ART HAS BEEN CONTEMPORARY' (Wildung 2004, 32). Allied with his conviction that our familiarity with ancient Egypt is 'self-explanatory' since ancient Egypt is so closely linked to Western culture in comparison to 'all cultures of the Orient and Africa' (Wildung 1988, 8), Nannucci's implication of original modernity catalysed Wildung's 'programmatic decontextualization' of the permanent galleries of the Berlin Museum, opened in 2009 (Wildung 2004; Widmaier 2017, 100). Here, Wildung's objective was to allow visitors to experience the museum's collections as being as fresh as they were in their original times, as most consistently applied to the museum's Amarna collections (Widmaier 2017, 98–121). With Italian architect and designer Michele De Lucchi, known for his industrial aesthetic, and the architect David Chipperfield, Wildung positioned individual artefacts within their own monolithic vitrines of a standardised size and shape, set on top of a concrete pedestal, and staged under spotlights so that they seemed to radiate of their own volition. Going further than T. J. H. James's (1985, 6) belief that modern art could create a milieu that might facilitate a more direct appreciation of Egyptian art than in the nineteenth century (Chapter 3), Wildung's approach actively modernised the collections in Berlin, abstracting them and challenging their historicity. This, however, was not a sudden break with Neues Museum display practices but rather a realignment with some of the principles introduced by Egyptian art historian Heinrich Schäfer 70 years previously as part of the wider reorientation of the aesthetic regimes of that time and their emphasis upon objects (Chapter 1).

This highly modernised aesthetic was adopted in an even more explicit way for the new SMÄK building where *l'art pour l'art* ('art for art's sake') informed Schoske's curatorial approach (Dercon et al. 2014, 27–8): 'to accept and understand Egyptian art as an historical source, to appreciate the art on the same level as for instance archaeological or textual sources'. To this end, as she emphasised in our interview, she worked closely with architects throughout the design process to create a bespoke space based upon the 'aesthetic needs of the objects'. The new museum was planned and developed during a period in which the city authorities were attempting to counter impressions of Munich as being 'posh' or 'boring'. For example, their 'Munich loves you' campaign, launched in 2005, aimed to reposition Munich's brand as 'an international, open metropolis with a special flair, a sports city, a young city as well as a traditional city, with a focus on being a modern dynamic economic place' (Vallaster et al. 2018, 55). By moving the collection to Munich's museum quarter and within this broader policy environment of cultural development, the more modernist and contemporary aspirations of the museum could be readily realised: 'Never before have our pieces looked so modern as they do in this neighbourhood where we are surrounded by art from all ages, literally, with the Alte Pinakothek and Pinakothek der Moderne and the Lenbachhaus all a stone's throw away' (Schoske in Dercon et al. 2014, 31).

From 2013 the now subterranean museum could be entered by descending a staircase towards a small opening in a monumental portal façade. Despite being underground, the atrium housing the first sculpture gallery challenges visitor preconceptions of darkened tombs as they instead enter a concrete, nave-like interior full of daylight provided by a series of integrated triangular supports (Figure 5.1). These pillars, while evoking the atmosphere of ancient temples in the language of modern architecture (ArchDaily 2016), do not imitate the monuments of antiquity, as they were explicitly constructed in such a way as to avoid a sense that this was merely Egyptianising architecture. While Böhm conceived of the structure, the interior space of the museum was designed by Munich-based Die Werft, an interdisciplinary planning practice composed of architects, designers and art graduates. The vitrines were fashioned to be 'extremely minimal ... to ensure the whole focus of attention is on the extraordinary objects of the collection' (Die Werft n.d). To achieve this, the materials used to showcase the exhibits were limited to the same materials as the building itself: blackened steel, exposed concrete and non-reflecting glass. For the designers, 'the combined effect of the ultra-modern, linear ambience and dramatic architecture will serve as a contemporary stage for these masterpieces from ancient Egypt' (Die Werft n.d). Here interior design and architecture worked in concert to reinforce a message of quality,

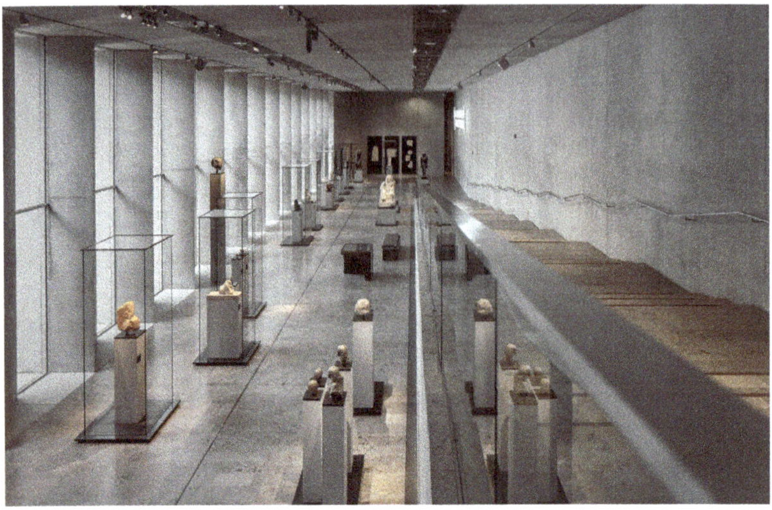

Figure 5.1 The Kunst und Form opening gallery of the Staatliches Museum Ägyptischer Kunst. © Staatliches Museum Ägyptischer Kunst, München. Photograph by Claus Rammel.

meaning and importance, a common strategy to transform artefacts into fine art (Clifford 1988, 224).

Reinforcing this sentiment was the commissioning and 'permanent loan' of a specially modified white neon-light iteration of Nannucci's *ALL ART HAS BEEN CONTEMPORARY* (Figure 5.2), still seen by staff today as integral to the museum's identity and presentation. Similarly, as part of the development and construction of the new museum, and in connection with the Pinakothek Sculpture Park, a competition for an installation outside the building was held.[5] This was finally awarded to Dutch sculptor Henk Visch for his *Present Continuous* sculpture (Figure 5.3), a four-metre-tall aluminium figure bent over staring at the ground, its ray of thought represented by a bright red plastic rod, emanating from its forehead and penetrating through the ground into the underground hall of the Egyptian museum where it continues, hanging from the ceiling in the 'Art and Time' room (Schoske 2018). To fully appreciate the sculpture, passers-by need to become museum visitors, which the QR code beside the figure above ground encourages by employing a link to a short film in which the earth tears open to reveal the galleries below. Both eye-catching works of art were placed strategically at key entranceways to the museum – Visch's near the building's entrance and Nannucci's at the first gallery's – distinguishing the institution from traditional Egyptological displays and standing apart from the exhibits

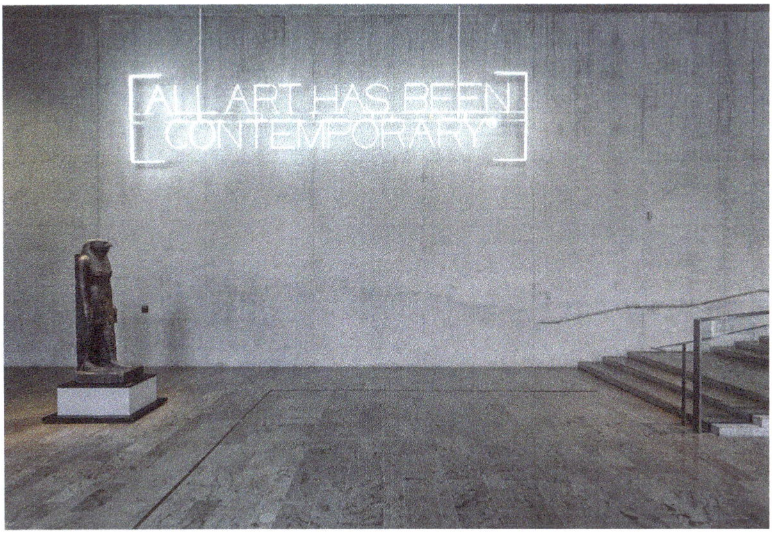

Figure 5.2 White neon-light art installation *ALL ART HAS BEEN CONTEMPORARY* by Nannucci on display in the opening Kunst und Form gallery of the Staatliches Museum Ägyptischer Kunst. © Staatliches Museum Ägyptischer Kunst, München. Photograph by Claus Rammel.

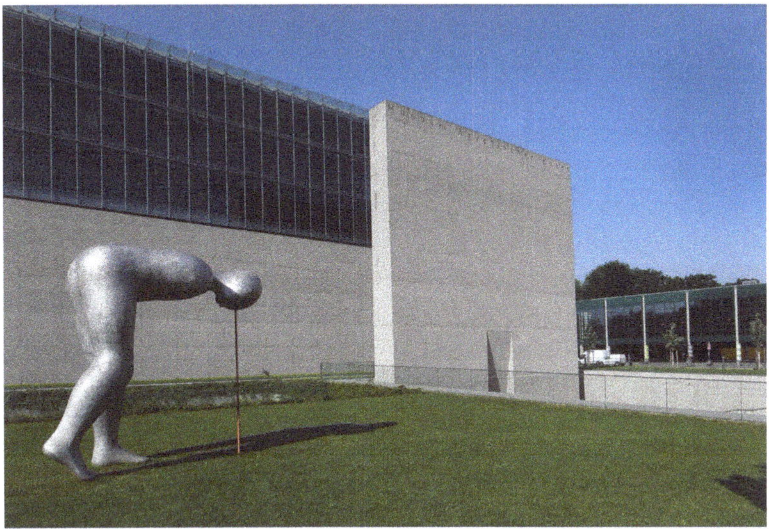

Figure 5.3 Dutch sculptor Henk Visch's work *Present Continuous* outside the Peter Böhm-designed entrance to the Staatliches Museum Ägyptischer Kunst. © Staatliches Museum Ägyptischer Kunst, München. Photograph by Marianne Franke.

to express wider institutional perspectives. These commissioned pieces take on a significant responsibility, therefore, in projecting the self-image of the museum and its contemporary, aesthetic approach to the ancient collections it houses.

The contemporary framing has been further creatively enhanced by a composition of electronic music by Mark Polscher, much of it recorded within the museum galleries themselves. Throughout the museum there are carefully placed speakers that, since the museum's opening, have established an auditory environment with sounds that are played on the first Tuesday of every month. The 64-channel soundscape fills the galleries with abstract, haunting electronic sounds mixed with montaged texts spoken (in German) from ancient Egyptian poems. Each room plays its own mix, with 63 minutes in total of sounds emanating, unexpectedly, from different directions, rising and falling. The result is an extension of the contemporary intervention not only into visual aesthetics, but additionally into the imaginative and subjective experience of the space and the objects that occupy it. This aspect is more invention than perhaps any of the other modalities of artistic installation previously explored, but one that is firmly about the past in the present and experience in the here and now.

In organisation, the museum rejected a chronological narrative in favour of a thematic one. Its opening 'Hall of Statues' gallery focuses on the topic 'art and form' and is organised like an art-historical description, with material grouped to convey ideas of form, iconography and style. This is followed by a second room of statues brought together under the theme 'art and time'. Both deliberately offer views to other rooms where the scenography of sculptural placement and architectural framing were designed to be in harmony and to orientate visitors in the space. Throughout, this aesthetic approach is maintained by keeping interpretive text panels and object labels to a bare minimum. For those who want more contextual and chronological detail, information is provided through audio guides and interactive media stations within each room. The minimalist didactic therefore preserves the conceptual and physical space for artistic interventions, of which there have been many, drawing visitors to the museum to see Egyptian art, on the one hand, or contemporary art, on the other. Such a strategy can attend to the multi-chronicity of artworks and may go some way towards transcending the tension identified by Randall-Page for the *Time Machine* exhibition between mediated and direct experience of art (Chapter 3). As the exhibition progresses, the design does give way to more contextualising approaches, such as the re-creation of the viewing conditions for an Old Kingdom statue-pair through a small slit-like window (*serdab*), the use of imitation sand for the denser display of funerary goods and the illustration on the accompanying wall of the city of the dead in Islamic Cairo.

Tea with Nefertiti

The first special exhibition in the new SMÄK was *Tea with Nefertiti: The Making of the Artwork by the Artist, the Museum and the Public* (May–September 2014), curated by Lebanese-German duo Sam Bardaouil and Till Fellrath. Together they had cofounded Art Reorientated, a multi-disciplinary curatorial platform based in Munich and New York. Its name derived from their philosophy that art exhibitions should be focused less on the art world and more on how an audience might interpret them and use that art to open dialogue. Bardaouil and Fellrath's interest in exploring how museums create ways of viewing and knowing other cultures and artworks led them to conceive the ambitious project *Tea with Nefertiti* in 2010. Egypt, they decided, was a rich case study given its long and varied history of colonial exploration, appropriation and display, while the ancient Egyptian queen provided an iconic artwork with an expansive biography ripe for unpacking how time, location and context can alter an artwork's agency. It is not my intention to exhaustively discuss each artwork in this rich and complex exhibition, nor to elucidate all the many intellectual themes or interpretations of the installations. This is aptly covered by the essays produced to accompany the exhibition (Bardaouil and Fellrath 2014). Instead, my focus is the history and legacy of the exhibition, as well as how it functioned within the space and the nature of any dialogue it had with the antiquities in the SMÄK's care.

Tea with Nefertiti debuted with an installation at Mathaf, the Arab Museum of Modern Art in Doha (17 November 2012–31 March 2013), before going on to tour three further institutions: the Institut du monde arabe in Paris (23 April–8 September 2013), the Institut Valencià d'Art Modern in Valencia (7 November 2013–26 January 2014) and finally the Staatliches Museum Ägyptischer Kunst in Munich (7 May–7 September 2014). It originally showcased works of some 55 artists to create a series of non-chronological juxtapositions of historic, modern and contemporary archives and artworks dating from the second millennium BC to the present day. As announced in the press release, the exhibition promised that:

> Through revisiting the contested histories of how Egyptian collections have been amassed by numerous museums from the 19th century onwards, *Tea with Nefertiti* explores the mechanisms by which artworks come to acquire a range of meanings and functions that can embody a number of diverse, and at times conflicting narratives.[6]

Mathaf, the Arab Museum of Modern Art in Doha, was founded by Sheikh Hassan bin Mohammed Al Thani, a prominent member of the Qatari royal family. Based on his private collection of art from the Arab world, the museum had opened in a converted former school in 2010 with the founding principle to act as a twenty-first-century 'post-museum' of Arab art, one that would be transparent and interaction-orientated (Al-Maria 2010, 43). Bardaouil and Fellrath contributed to the inaugural exhibition and returned three years later with *Tea for Nefertiti*, providing a platform to promote Egyptian artists, such as Mahmoud Moukhtar and the Art and Liberty Group, as well as those from the Middle East more widely, thereby aligning with Mathaf's mission. In content, the exhibition's message, that art becomes a tool in which the past is appropriated for present gain, was therefore also realised as part of a concerted effort to position Qatar as a prominent cultural hub, globally engaged with the contemporary art world.

It was in Paris that Schoske encountered the exhibition and she immediately began envisioning it in Munich amongst the SMÄK's newly erected displays. A slot in the touring schedule of the exhibition presented the chance to realise her ideas. It had always been the intention of the *Tea with Nefertiti* curators to utilise historic Egyptian collections, and numerous conversations had been started with German museums, resulting in the loan to Mathaf of some parts of the collection from the Roemer und Pelizaeus Museum Hildesheim.[7] Nonetheless, its installation at the SMÄK meant that this was the only venue on the *Tea with Nefertiti* tour with an ancient Egyptian collection, resulting in a very different and more expansive conception than the British Museum's *Time Machine*. From the outset it was explicitly intended to be critical and political. Its curators did not see this, however, as a blunt intervention, but as a dialogue, and in our interview they described the project as a 'true joint collaboration', facilitated by an alignment of views on the value of contemporary art, the shaping of museum environments and the possibilities for engaging audiences.

In its Munich incarnation, the exhibition was shown under a different title: *Nofretete – tête-à-tête,* a quotation from a poem by Austrian author Roda Roda.[8] Given the exhibition's initial establishment outside of the SMÄK, most of the selected works were not ones negotiated between the artists and the space but were preconceived and requested from 47 lenders comprised of national and commercial galleries, private collections and archives. A total of 46 artists'[9] work was placed into the SMÄK's permanent galleries under Schoske's guidance, as well as arranged in the temporary exhibition hall, bringing into the museum canvases from nineteenth-century painter David Roberts through to early modernist sculptures by the likes of Moukhtar and Chinese dissident contemporary artist Ai Weiwei, alongside archives and historic artefacts. The show was also founded on a much stronger narrative arc than the other exhibitions so far examined, being divided into three sections each presenting artworks from a different perspective: the artist, the museum and the public sphere. In each of these realms, the curators argued, artworks could be seen to accrue multiple meanings, shaping discourse and cultural production in time and space. For Schoske, meanwhile, the exhibition indirectly criticised the tendency for museums holding Egyptian collections to limit their focus to 'mummies and magic' (Dercon et al. 2014, 35).

It was hoped that by interspersing the artefacts throughout the SMÄK, visitor perceptions of the ancient Egyptian artefacts would be transformed. This intention was supported by the exhibition design team, provided again by Die Werft, the original designers of the museum's permanent galleries. They employed semi-transparent screens and plinths inspired by 'Oriental' ornamentation to make the modern artworks more prominent in their surroundings, but also to link them thematically to the permanent gallery displays (Figure 5.4).[10] Special seating was created, based on the design of Nefertiti's crown, as an invitation to visitors to stop and reflect on the exhibition's themes. In keeping with the minimal interpretation in the galleries, the company limited explanations to a few introductory panels outlining the ideas of each section – 'artist', 'museum' and 'general public' – with more detailed information made available in a trilingual (Arabic, English and German) leaflet. Where labels accompanied the artworks, these were carefully designed to stand out from the museum's own labels since, in that shared modernist interior, several pieces of modern sculpture, such as Giacometti's, looked as though they were from ancient Egypt.

As in the previous case studies, despite the well-articulated curatorial insistence on the effect of a 'series of juxtapositions and groupings of historic, modern and mainly contemporary artworks and documents' (e.g. Dercon et al. 2014, 25–31; see also press release),

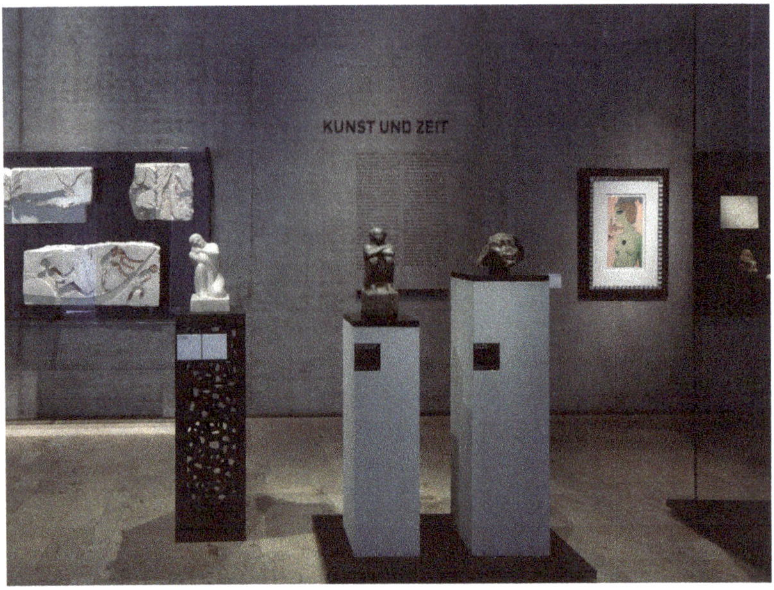

Figure 5.4 Photograph of the 2014 *Nofretete – tête-à-tête* exhibition in the Kunst und Form gallery of the SMÄK, featuring Mahmoud Moukhtar's 1928 sculpture *Al-Qayloulah (Siesta)*, on a plinth designed for the exhibition by Die Werft, and Kees van Dongen's painting *La Marchesa Luisa Casati* (1950). © Staatliches Museum Ägyptischer Kunst, München. Photograph by Marianne Franke.

the space of the museum itself acted powerfully to level interactions to one temporal plane. For instance, while the SMÄK's architecture is technically minimalist, intended not to detract from the artefacts, such imposing modernism has been argued to be particularly problematic for world cultures, crystallising Western cultural hegemony, erasing colonial pasts and nullifying cultural diversity (Wang 2021). In this setting *Tea with Nefertiti*'s efforts to form a critical perspective on modes of presentation that frame cultural otherness, and for the art to speak for itself, were rather undermined and were skirted over in the curators' critical discussion (Dercon et al. 2014). Artworks, both ancient and modern, are comfortably accommodated in this space – they 'fit almost like a glove', as one of the curators remarked in our interview – with the architecture drawing them together. But in so doing, it potentially muted the disruptive effect of the insertions. Similarly, Die Werft's homogenising 'Oriental' ornamentation did little to support the exhibition's intention of 'breaking away from more familiar museum classifications that have been conventionally based on geography, periods and/or styles'.[11]

In content, each section of the show opened with an image of the bust of Nefertiti, alternatively emphasising a different agency in its interpretation and providing a metaphorical thread through the exhibition. The first section of the exhibition, 'Artist', opened with Egyptian photographer Youssef Nabil's hand-coloured, gelatine silver print of the bust (Figure 5.5). No context was given, just a close-up of Nefertiti's face, which Nabil had coloured to resemble the texture of golden-age Egyptian films rather than the reality of the limestone and stucco bust, thereby emphasising its status as a work of art and signalling the theme of individual artistic exploration and negotiation. The second section, 'Museum', featured Candida Höfer's series of large-format colour photos of the bust in an unoccupied Neues Museum as it was on its reopening in 2009, both in its isolated tall glass vitrine and also giving a view of the space from the bust's sight line (*Neues Museum Berlin XII*). The third iteration of Nefertiti, introducing the 'Public' section, was a work by Little Warsaw (artists András Galik and Bálint Havas), comprising a headless bronze sculpture of a body proportional to the bust, together with a film of the brief moments when the original bust was placed upon the sculpture. In so doing, this artwork was intended to reference the public

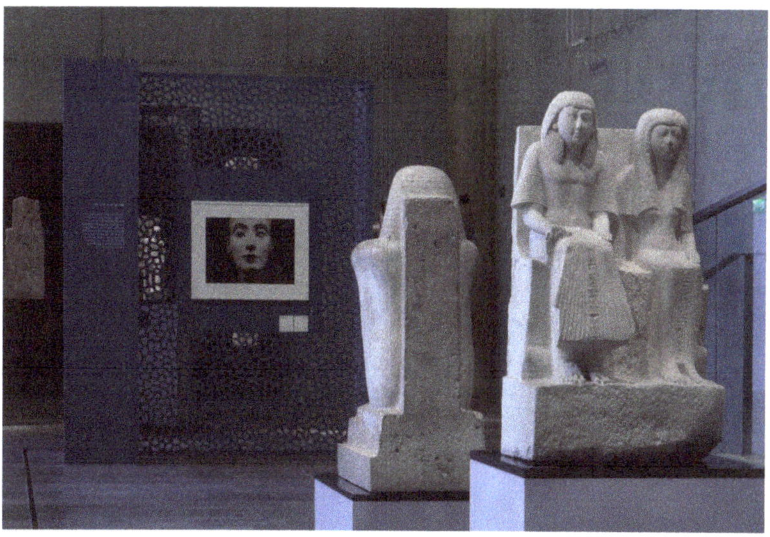

Figure 5.5 Photograph of Egyptian statues in the Kunst und Form gallery of the SMÄK with the introductory panel for the 'Artist' section of the *Nofretete – tête-à-tête* exhibition. A gelatine silver print of the face of the bust of Nefertiti by Egyptian photographer Youssef Nabil is hung on a mount created for the exhibition by Die Werft. © Staatliches Museum Ägyptischer Kunst, München. Photograph by Marianne Franke.

controversy generated by the intervention after it was first exhibited for the Hungarian Pavilion at the 2003 Venice Biennale.

The first section, 'Artist', with its emphasis on practitioners' productions in their own historical time and place, compared ancient forms with the types of artwork they inspired in a similar fashion to many previous exhibitions. This included Fayum portraits as an inspiration for Paula Modersohn-Becker's *Selbstporträt* (1906), Amarna statuary as the basis for Modigliani's *Portrait of Hanka Zbrowoska* (1917–18), Ptolemaic portrait heads as comparative pieces for Giacometti's *Lotar* II (1964–5) and Coptic symbols as reflected in Moukhtar's bronze *Ibn Il-Balad (The Native)* (1910). In addition, numerous responses to the pyramids as a geometric, rather than political, symbol were explored, with works by Lee Miller, Van Leo and Mamduh Muhamad Fathallah, all produced between 1937 and 1945. In keeping with the general theme of museum 'icons', Brazilian artist Vik Muniz's *Tupperware Sarcophagus* (2010) – a life-sized representation of a mummified body placed within a translucent plastic coffin with a blue rubber lid – was set upon a pedestal amongst the museum's own collection of coffins to highlight the appropriation and commercialisation of Egypt by such institutions. The curators' contention that the meaning of the artworks shifted significantly through the change in exhibition venue is particularly clear with the inclusion here of Nida Sinnokrot's (2009) imitation of raised blessing arms, *Ka (JCB, JCB)*, with two mechanical excavator shovels (Figure 5.6). In Qatar, it had a wider social resonance with the frenetic pace of construction activity in the Gulf States and the worship of globalised capital, a narrative not as powerful in Munich when shown in isolation as merely an example of 'artistic inspiration'. An alternative conjunction of works might have made reference to the Egyptian state's own modernisation construction projects or else appropriations by private construction contractors that have displaced communities and torn down historic buildings (Hanna 2013).

The more innovative 'Museum' section shifted the focus onto how museum space can alter the meaning of artworks. Further examples of Moukhtar's work were placed in this part of the exhibition but presented this time in front of wall-sized projections of their original staging in the 1920s and 1930s, drawing attention to how display strategies alter the evaluation and reception of an artwork. The role of museum classifications and distinctions – between high and low art, fine and decorative art, original and replica, authored and anonymous artworks – was drawn into relief through the unconventional grouping of three very different pieces: Grayson Perry's ceramic *Wise Alan* (2007), Ai Weiwei's

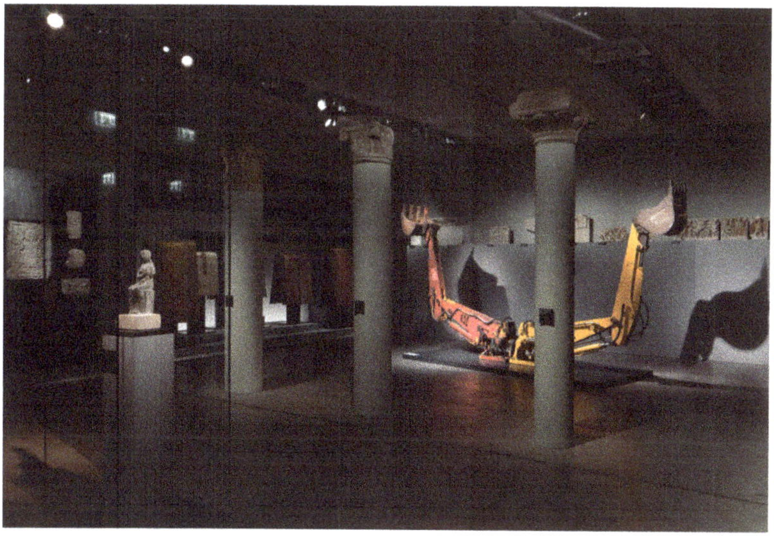

Figure 5.6 Photograph of Nida Sinnokrot's *Ka (JCB, JCB)* of 2009 installed in the 'after the Pharaohs' gallery of the SMÄK as part of the exhibition *Nofretete – tête-à-tête*. The seventh-century AD Coptic stela with the gesture imitated by the digger arms can be seen in the far left of the photograph. © Staatliches Museum Ägyptischer Kunst, München. Photograph by Marianne Franke.

Coca-Cola Vase (1997) and a twelfth-century Ayyubid glass base. Viewed individually, the latter is typically classified as Islamic decorative art, but the curators' grouping with the two other works sought to question how it might be transformed from a generic example of decorative Islamic art to an individual artwork through the signature of the artist. The inclusion of Ai Weiwei's creation, a Neolithic Chinese pot disregarded by Chinese authorities but rebranded by Weiwei with the Coca-Cola label, aimed to illustrate how value could be created in the commercial art market. Meanwhile Perry's *Wise Alan* – which featured in his 2011 British Museum show *The Tomb of the Unknown Craftsman*, and which depicts his teddy bear in an Orientalised pose with seemingly traditional motifs that on closer inspection are revealed to be representations of the modern world – tried to challenge the audience's categorisation of decorative arts. Together, the trio also helpfully highlighted the fragile distinction between 'artefacts' and 'artworks' (cf. Gell 1996).

The final section, 'Public', included examples of artworks that have had effects beyond the walls of the museum, in particular historical moments, such as in the recruitment of Pharaonic-inspired art for the promotion of specific ideologies such as nationalism. For instance, Kriemann's *Ramses Files* considers the removal of the Ramses II statue from Bab el-Hadid outside Cairo's main train station in 2007. This section also included the only work created specifically for the exhibition and its space: Bassem Yousri's *It's Not as Easy as it May Have Seemed to Be*, drawing out the theme of the public's relationship to the museum but also helping to 'create a voice of dissent from within' and further encourage viewers to criticise the exhibition's proposition (Dercon et al. 2014, 31). Hundreds of small, playful figurines in a variety of poses (Figure 5.7) engaged with the museum's display structures such as plinths and vitrines, sometimes in acts of looking, sometimes in more disobedient gestures like pushing them over. This installation can be a reminder of the wide range of human emotions and dispositions that art can draw out in museum spaces, inclusive of humour. Several works in this section acted as an excursus into the history of surrealism in Egypt, specifically in Cairo in the 1930s and 1940s. Here writers and artists drew from European surrealist experimentation as a form of cultural dissent, but modified it to speak to their local context. In the space of the SMÄK these inclusions held additional significance as a means of challenging the hermetically sealed image of Pharaonic Egypt divorced from the modern country, revealing what artist and academic Liliane Karnouk (2005, 3) has described as the double dilemma for Egyptian artists of the last century: 'the search for a balance between loyalty to an imposing past and the effort to liberate oneself from its burden'.

While admirably seeking to disrupt museum strategies, fostering a critical look at appropriations of Egypt, and providing a platform to promote Egyptian modern and contemporary art, there were instances throughout in which the curators fell into their own trap of ignoring the 'historical framework through which the contemporary moment of artistic production and perception is evaluated' (Bardaouil and Fellrath 2014, 19). One such instance was the highly problematic grouping of William Kentridge's *Carnets d'Égypte* (2010), produced for the Louvre (Chapter 1), alongside Xenia Nikolskaya's photograph *Wild Cats, Agricultural Museum* (2010) and Emily Jacir's video installation *A Sketch in the Egyptian Museum* (2003). In the exhibition catalogue, Bardaouil and Fellrath (2014, 83–5) leverage Kentridge's work of emulating curatorial research to reference one of his imaginary dialogues between two individuals who variously argue whether they want antiquities to be returned from the museum or to stay. The curators then turned their attention to the only two representations of Egyptian museums in the exhibition, both implicated uncritically in a long-standing colonial trope that heritage is not safe in Egypt: Nikolskaya's 'life-size photograph of a dilapidated interior from the Cairo Agricultural Museum' (Bardaouil and

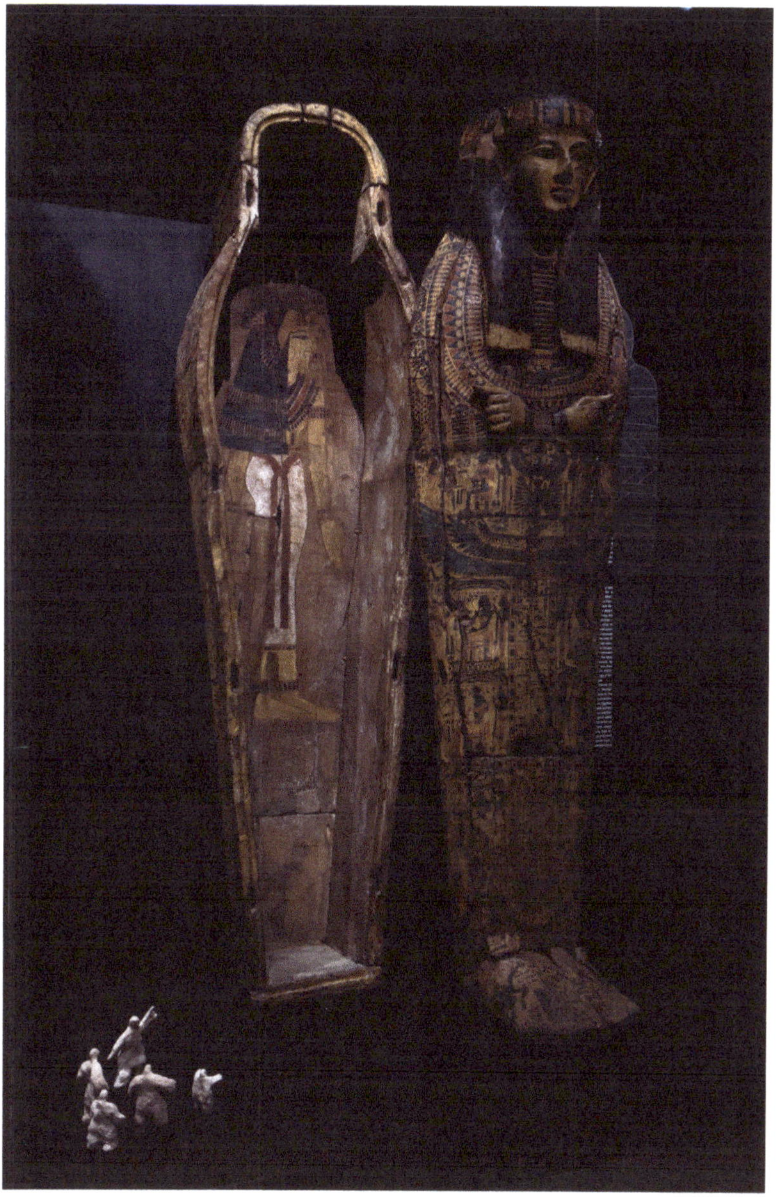

Figure 5.7 Photograph of five of Bassem Yousri's interventions, created for the exhibition *Nofretete – tête-à-tête*, in one of the vitrines containing ancient Egyptian coffins in the 'Realm of the Dead' gallery at the Staatliches Museum Ägyptischer Kunst. © Staatliches Museum Ägyptischer Kunst, München. Photograph by Marianne Franke.

Fellrath 2014, 83) and Jacir's video installation in which 'a cleaning man recklessly wipes an ancient stele beckoning the question of safety and care that such works require' (Bardaouil and Fellrath 2014, 85). This leads the curators to take on the role of devil's advocate and ask, 'wouldn't it be better perhaps for Nefertiti to remain where she is?' Despite the claims that Jacir's film somehow illustrates 'improper cleaning' (Vogel 2013) or a 'conservator's worst nightmare' (Bardaouil and Fellrath 2014, 85), such rhetoric is misplaced given that the artefact in question is a massive, hard-stone monument that even the most vigorous cleaning is highly unlikely to damage. A film of the British Museum's sculpture gallery made for *Time Machine* (Chapter 3) captured the boisterous engagement of schoolchildren with the artefacts displayed there, dangling over the sides of sarcophaguses, as well as tourists rubbing the feet of statues. Instead, encoded in the *Tea with Nefertiti* juxtaposition is an imperially derived rhetoric of preservation and entrenched assumptions about who has the right to care for heritage, under what conditions and where that should take place (see Carruthers 2015).

Using the curator's own logic of how alternative juxtapositions can tell a different story, a conjunction of other works in the exhibition might have better challenged this colonially biased narrative. Little Warsaw's installation is one. Their film of the brief setting of the original Nefertiti bust onto their bronze artwork was shown at a conference in Madrid in January 2014, in conjunction with *Tea with Nefertiti*'s opening in Valencia. Clips were introduced by the curators noting that the director of the Neues Museum, together with a specialised art handler, was supervising the bust's safety during the transfer to and from the artwork. As the film begins to play, the audience can be heard nervously laughing as the bust teeters precariously, as the handlers fumble with the plastazote supports and as the roughness of the plinth that this irreplaceable, priceless artwork rests on is revealed.[12] Again, the question could be provocatively posed back to the curators: is the Nefertiti bust really safe where it is?

Reception of *Nofretete – tête-à-tête*

The German press was largely positive about the 'remarkable, intellectually sophisticated show' (*Tagesspiegel*, 7 August 2013), finding many installations to be 'a real joy' (*Kunst + Film*, 7 June 2014), 'pleasurably colourful, stimulating, informative' (*Merkur*, 6 May 2014) and 'an exciting dialogue with Munich masterpieces' (*Ganz München*,

7 September 2014).[13] Any criticism tended to comment on the complexity of the show, 'an intellectual puzzle, but one that is unfortunately overloaded with ideas ... [so that] it is difficult to keep track of everything' (*Tagesspiegel*, 7 August 2013). The exhibition's curators, meanwhile, noted 'the positive reception that the exhibition has had by art professionals, fellow colleagues and museum visitors at large' (Bardaouil and Fellrath 2014, 9). Striking by their absence in this comment are Egyptologists and the possibilities for how the ancient past might be approached differently. Staff at the SMÄK recall that there was 'no interest whatsoever' from the Egyptological community in the exhibition. However, this was not a concern for the curators, who never considered specialists as one of the audiences for the show. When asked 'How do you want specialized and sceptical scholars to look at your interpretations, connections and inventions?', the duo responded that they 'are certainly no Egyptologists or Islamic art scholars ... we never claim to shed new scientific knowledge so to speak about the artworks themselves within the disciplines of study to which they are conventionally ascribed' (Bardaouil and Fellrath 2014, 43). This was a firmly contemporary art exhibition with a call 'for more research in areas that have been less explored by curators of contemporary art' (Bardaouil and Fellrath 2014, 19), achieved through the exhibition themes that transcend the specificity of Egyptian history and culture in order to speak to issues of global constructions of knowledge and art (Rabbat 2013).

Nonetheless, the exhibition could also be seen as a departure point for more research in areas less explored by curators of Egyptian collections and those who study them. Ala Younis's documentary-style installation *Nefertiti*, based on the sewing machine bearing the queen's image, is one possible example. Younis had first come across the pistachio-coloured sewing machine in a Cairo flea market in 2008, where she bought five examples. These prompted a meticulously detailed and wide-ranging research project examining the sewing machines' social, political and economic contexts and significances. Such everyday items, produced after Nasser's 1952 revolution as part of his grand modernisation project, were 'an attempt to empower households in a time of obsessive decolonisation: a functional symbol of anticolonial project' (Younis 2019). Her purchases informed the 2008 exhibition *Nefertiti*, hosted in downtown Cairo and organised by the Contemporary Image Collective at the Hungarian Cultural Centre. For the show she cleaned the machines and displayed each on a white pedestal, forming a production line, set against an 11-minute film projection of memories of the sewing machine shared by those who had used it.

Nefertiti was subsequently exhibited in London at the Delfina Foundation in 2010, before it became part of *Tea with Nefertiti*, and it was in London that curators from the British Museum attended a talk given by the artist on the history of the Nefertiti sewing machine. Afterwards they enquired if she might have any works on paper produced as part of the project that they might acquire, but she replied that no such work existed (Younis 2019). Six years later the British Museum's 'Contemporary Egypt project', coordinated by the Department of Egypt and Sudan, collected one such sewing machine and accessioned it into the collection (EA87550), as part of a concerted effort to represent the material culture of more recent, and not just ancient, Egypt (Spencer 2016). No reference to Younis's artwork was made, but the research and profile given to the artefact, through which it was transformed into a museum piece, are likely to have contributed to its serious consideration by British Museum staff. However, the British Museum's acquisition lacked the richly textured histories that Younis had documented and articulated in her installation. Here there is inspiration from art to Egyptologist, with a promise of interdisciplinary practice that recognises the multidirectionality of heritage interpretation and meaning-making (Stevenson 2022a). But as *Tea with Nefertiti* highlighted, context remains everything in the display of art and material culture.

While this was never an exhibition about ancient Egypt, nor indeed antiquity generally, in Munich it took on a different character because it was in concert with the Egyptian collection. Nevertheless, any opportunities for gaining insight into the ancient past itself were fairly limited because the organisational core of the exhibition – the bust of Nefertiti – meant that narratives gravitated more strongly towards the interpretation of recent centuries of representation. After the bust's public unveiling in Berlin in 1924 in the modernist-styled Amarna Courtyard of the museum (Chapter 1), it quickly transformed into a metonym of the German *Kulturnation* (Breger 2006), entangled in complex dialogue with the new aesthetics of cultural institutions, symbolic nationalism and international geopolitics. As noted in Chapter 1, the extrication of Egyptian forms from their archaeological contexts and their cohabitation within a wider ecology of modernist imagery throughout the 1920s meant that the antiquities rarely translated back into substantial engagement with archaeological themes. Such engagements were a symbol of being modern, not a sign of archaeological fascination (Stevenson 2019, 155).

Other interventions

Since *Nofretete – tête-à-tête*, the SMÄK has continued to pursue its mission to be not just a museum of Egyptian art, but a museum for art more broadly. A strong museum ecosystem has complemented these aspirations, with the SMÄK's central geographic position between the classically framed Glyptothek and the contemporary Pinakothek providing an audience primed to cross temporal and artistic boundaries, especially on Sundays when all museum entrance fees across the city are capped at one euro. Similarly, Schoske opened up the temporary exhibition space to wider use by these other institutions and their artistic projects. For instance, the museum has, like the Petrie Museum (Chapter 2), annually granted a space for art students, such as those from the Münchner Künstlergenossenschaft königlich privilegiert. It has even provided catwalks for fashion designers Susanne Wiebe and Hans M. Bachmayer. The museum staff value these events as they bring in new audiences while introducing those interested in Egyptian history to contemporary art.

The SMÄK's ongoing temporary exhibition programme has included *Rollenbibliothek* by Zygmunt Blazejewski (2018) and Mats Staub's *Erinnerungen ans Erwachsenwerden* (2019), neither of which were based on the collection nor inserted amidst it. Both were featured in many other institutions. Nonetheless, loose analogies were made to the collection, as with Blazejewski's installation in the temporary exhibition hall, which comprised 210 rolls of pictures, produced as part of a long-term painting process from 1992 to 1997, combined and arranged into a massive library wall. Its placement within the SMÄK was said to be a 'fitting place' as 'they become current evidence of a practice of recording, preserving and communicating cultural heritage that is deeply rooted in the past'.[14] However, in creating such opportunistic, generic links, such efforts do run the risk of devaluing the individual significance of both the contemporary art and the Egyptian material. As one of the curators, who was more sceptical of such insertions, remarked in our interview, 'they only work when it's really done with that merging of expertise. Otherwise, I think it's just a gimmick. Then one uses the other … you don't really get to something meaningful.'

Complementing the collection more closely are exhibitions that have been inspired by ancient Egypt, as with a series of oil paintings and drawings by Egyptian artist Alaa Awad that were hung in the special exhibition hall in 2022–3. This exhibition was developed under the direction of Schoske's successor, Arnulf Schlüter, who has continued to maintain the SMÄK's commitment to contemporary art. *An Egyptian Story* (29 November 2022–5 March 2023) grew out of a series of large-scale street murals that Awad painted from 2012, many of which were located on Mohammed Mahmoud Street just off Tahrir Square in Cairo, a site of bloody battles between protesters and security forces during the Egyptian revolution of 2011. Many Egyptians were killed on this street and the murals commemorated the clashes and the mourning of those who died. For the exhibition, Awad used brushes and acrylic paint rather than stencils and spray cans, bringing together ancient motifs with these modern events and concerns, although the latter are ignored in the exhibition's catalogue in favour of a sanitised, aesthetic account of his work (see Chapter 6).

Similarly, Ugo Dossi's 2021 exhibition at the SMÄK, *Zeichen und Wunder*, reinterpreted ancient Egyptian material using large-format colourful tableaus, sculptures, holographic projections and virtual realities to focus on hieroglyphs. The exhibition was subsequently reinstalled in 2023 at the Reiss-Engelhorn-Museen (REM) in Mannheim, where his work's 'reduced symbolic and pictorial language' was considered 'the perfect complement' to the *Egypt – Land of Immortality* exhibition.[15] In addition, a smaller selection of Dossi's creations were inserted alongside ancient Egyptian material in the REM's World Cultures gallery. As noted in Chapter 2, displays of ancient Egypt throughout Germany have only since the late 2010s embraced contemporary art in their galleries. Arguably, this has been spurred on by the agenda set by the SMÄK and the Neues Museum, which have, through their regular programming, normalised the practice.

Motivations to be broadly accessible to a wide range of art were made explicit in the promotional material for *Adam, wo bist du?*, on display at the SMÄK from June 2020 to January 2021, which saw Munich artist Ilana Lewitan explore the relationship between individual and ascribed identity.[16] Lewitan's exhibition also highlights the museum's desire to be of contemporary relevance, with her installations pointing to similarities and fractures between the familiar and the foreign, between locals and foreigners, between migrants and locals, and between the privileged and the disadvantaged. In particular, her exhibition responded to the anniversary year '1700 years of Jewish life in Germany', with Lewitan looking back on her own Jewish heritage in Germany (Figure 5.8). Using the example of predominantly Jewish biographies, the 10-station gallery path led to a large 4.6-metre-high cross with a 3.3-metre-tall body in the form of a concentration camp uniform. The SMÄK's own locational history is implicated in these narratives. In the year before *Adam, wo bist*

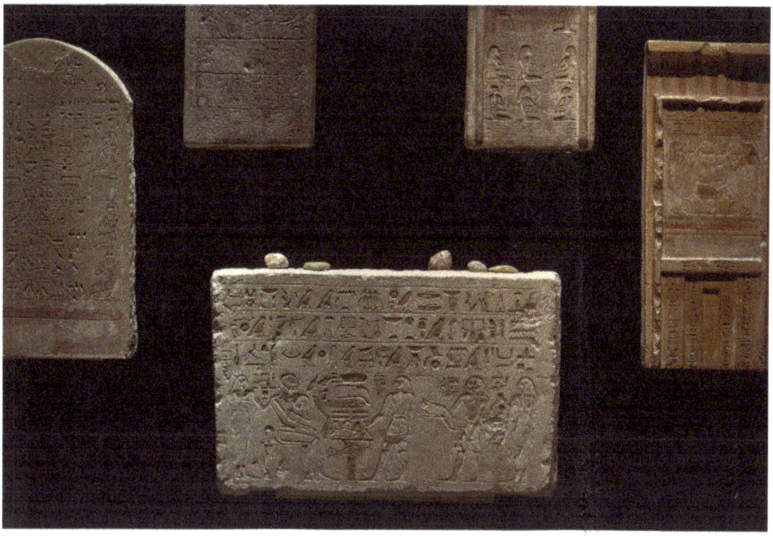

Figure 5.8 Visitation stones placed on an ancient Egyptian offering stela by artist Ilana Lewitan in 2020, evoking Jewish bereavement practices. Part of the exhibition *Adam, wo bist du?* at the SMÄK. © Staatliches Museum Ägyptischer Kunst, München. Photograph by Marianne Franke.

du?, the museum's relationship to Nazi history had been memorialised in the form of six brass plaques or 'stumbling stones' (Stolpersteine), a type of popular, albeit controversial, installation initiated by German artist Gunter Demnig (Cook and van Riemsdijk 2014), placed in the ground in front of and within the museum's foyer. By these means the SMÄK commemorates the former inhabitants of the area and their fate during the Nazi era when the site was selected for the erection of a chancellery building, which in the end was never completed (Wetzel 2020).[17]

In addition to the main exhibition in the temporary display hall, Lewitan's exhibition saw newly created artworks inserted alongside the permanent collection thematically. For instance, this included a hard drive placed beside an inscription bearing the hieroglyphic rendering of Ramses II's name to reflect a general theme of technologies of memory and information (Figure 5.9), and first-aid kits underneath a small figure of Imhotep, protector of scribes and doctors. For the Egyptian material, the inserted art thus acted as an interpretive device to draw out pre-existing knowledge rather than speak back to collection. These insertions were an afterthought rather than an integral part of the exhibition narrative, not being included in the accompanying catalogue as the exhibition was also to be shown in a church in Berlin at a later date.

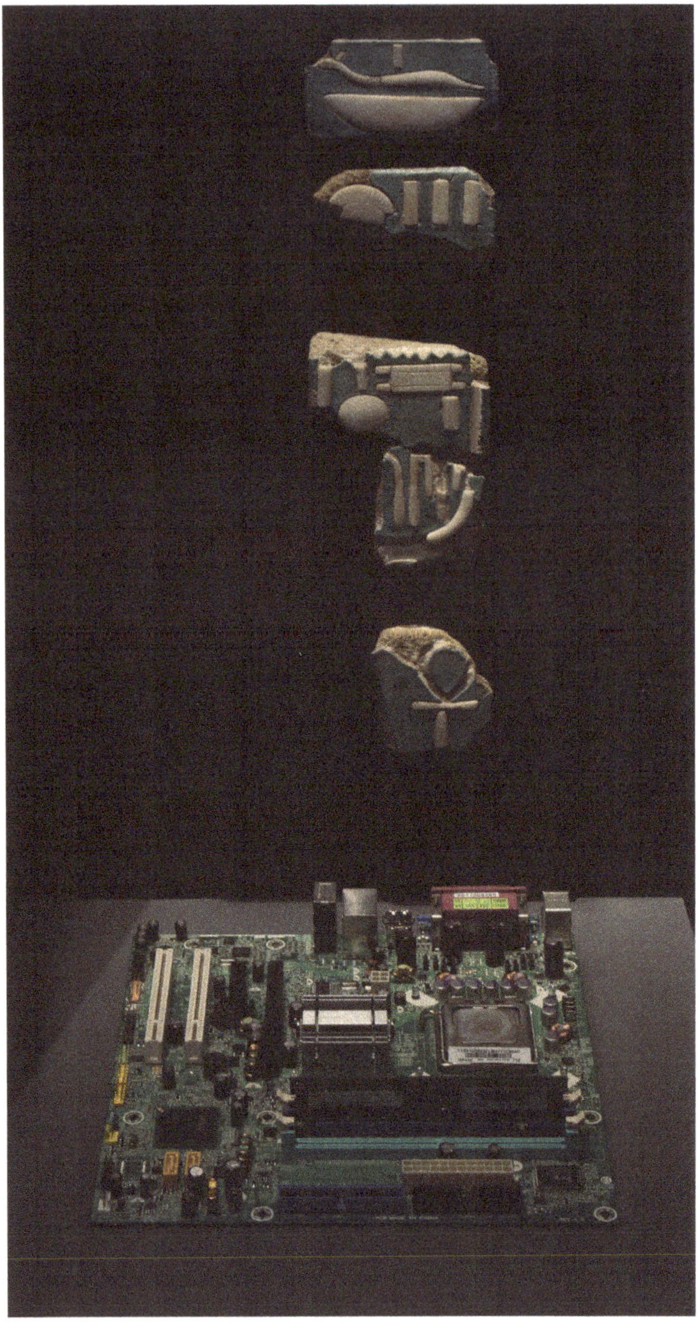

Figure 5.9 Photograph of an installation from *Adam, wo bist du?* at the SMÄK. © Staatliches Museum Ägyptischer Kunst, München. Photograph Marianne Franke.

The juxtapositions, Schoske confirmed, were opportunistic, having arisen in conversation with the artist, whom she encouraged to bring in additional pieces that would resonate with the permanent displays. Plans had been made for commentary in the form of a leaflet, but these were abandoned due to the COVID-19 pandemic.

Other contemporary artworks have used the museum more as a backdrop or venue than as a site-specific juxtaposition of ancient and modern, such as Frepoli's *Begegnungen*, hosted throughout the Egyptian galleries in 2017. Frepoli's art focuses upon portrait sculpture, creating expressionless busts and full-length figures of individuals from different social groups and backgrounds. Her sculptures were not made exclusively for the SMÄK and the exhibited works subsequently toured other historic venues, including the Weser Renaissance Museum. In the SMÄK they were comfortably set amidst the statue galleries of ancient heads of nobles and royal Egyptian figures, with one figure, *Purple*, subsequently being presented to the SMÄK on long-term loan, where it is displayed today in the outside terrace between the obelisk and entrance façade (Figure 5.10). In November 2023 the work was officially acquired for the SMÄK collection. Another long-term resident of the galleries is the abstract painting *Weiß* by Georg Baselitz, on loan from businessman Joe Kaeser. Its presence there is a recognition of the space's welcoming of artworks generally, but notably in opposition to the Pinakothek der Moderne where Kaeser's loan would not have stood out from the rest of the collection. In both these cases, the dialogue is not between past and

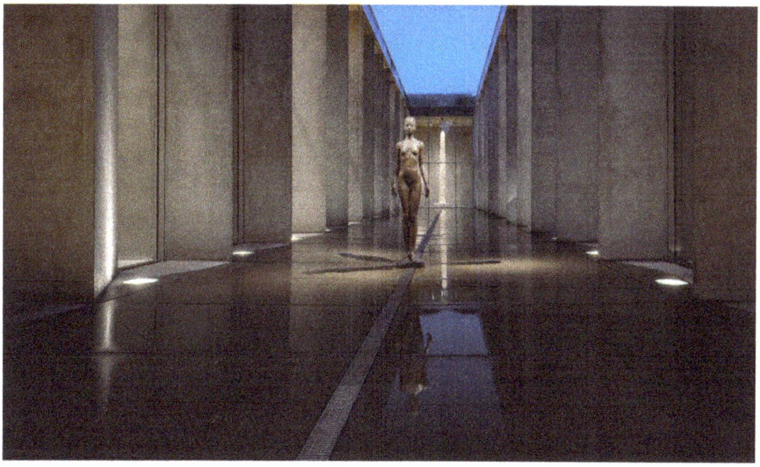

Figure 5.10 Photograph of Frepoli's *Purple* at the SMÄK. © Staatliches Museum Ägyptischer Kunst, München. Photograph by Claus Rammel.

present, but primarily between the artworks and the architectural frame, as well as the novelty provided by the SMÄK's collection.

*

Nannucci's *ALL ART HAS BEEN CONTEMPORARY* has acted as a significant leitmotif for the SMÄK. It not only serves as the foundational interpretive framing device for the collection on entry to the permanent galleries but is also invoked in almost every one of the catalogue prefaces to contemporary art installations held in the museum. Usually, it acts as an invitation to see the contemporary relevance and present-day potential of Egyptian art. It further underscores that the SMÄK's principal mission under Schoske was not necessarily to reflect on Egyptological discourses, but to influence art history more broadly as a discipline with the aspiration that it might accept Egyptian art as art. Indeed, she refers to herself as 'an interpreter of Egyptian art to contemporary people'.

The most expansive insertion of recent artworks into the displayed permanent collection, *Tea with Nefertiti*, was a highly intellectual exhibition, driven by scholarship and far less concerned with aesthetics, affect or sensorial immersion than an exhibition such as *Time Machine*. Although important critical contexts were established, this was not as disruptive an intervention as perhaps it might have been in a different architectural setting. The modernist physical structure of the venue provided a comfortable space for contemporary art, meaning that preconceived ideas that already resonated with the mission of the SMÄK, and its emphasis on letting art speak for itself, could be further developed. The central icon of Nefertiti also placed the intellectual centre of the exhibition in the recent rather than ancient past, provocatively questioning museology's platforms. While clearly sensitive to postcolonial scholarship and the power of institutional critique, the authorship of the exhibition was firmly Eurocentric, giving space but not voice to Egyptian artists or other 'communities of implication', that is, those other groups who ethically may be affected or implicated by the displays (Stevenson 2022a).

Tea with Nefertiti, as with the SMÄK's other ventures, has generally been a successful means of demonstrating the museum's relevance to present-day concerns and expressions, but it has offered fewer interventions into how the Egyptian past itself is interpreted. This is not a terribly surprising conclusion, given that the modes of presenting Egyptian art in the SMÄK are a very natural evolution of Egyptology's twentieth-century alignment with modernist trends in museum design and art market discourse – especially in Germany (Chapter 1), where concepts of form, iconography and style are foregrounded. In terms of process, while the museum has played host to almost two dozen contemporary art exhibitions or individual artist displays to date, most have comprised generic insertions or are linked by general themes inspired by Egyptian collections, rather than deep collaborations or in-depth collections research. Consequently, these can be seen as constituting what has been termed 'creative programming' for museums, where the focus is on developing novel, diverse and effective means of attracting and engaging with museum audiences (Chapter 6). In terms of strategy for opening the museum to people who may not have an interest in ancient Egypt and becoming more accessible to different groups, the SMÄK has had great success as the only state museum in Bavaria not to lose visitors after the COVID-19 lockdowns, with around 120,000 visitors in the year since it reopened fully.

Perhaps surprisingly, it has yet to accommodate artist residencies, so few artists other than students have critically engaged with or interrogated the collection or researched its histories as part of their artistic process. The historical aspect has only more recently been an emergent interest of the institution, with a set of panels on the history of the collection tacked on at the very end of the path through the exhibits in 2021. The museum is therefore well placed to take forward new modes of dialogue between curators and artists, a dialogue that takes the idea of *ALL ART HAS BEEN CONTEMPORARY* not only forwards, but also backwards to examine how the ancient materials might have been made meaningful as part of lived experience in past environments.

Notes

1 Mostly through correspondence with Bernard Bothmer; Brooklyn Museum Archives, General Correspondence series, Dealers, H. [Herzer 1966–1977].
2 See, for example, Metropolitan Museum of Art object records for 65.119 purchased by Herzer from the Egyptian Museum Cairo's Salle de Vente.
3 For example, 1971.294 purchased in 1971 from Herzer.
4 https://www.museum-morsbroich.de/museum/geschichte/ [Accessed 1 July 2024].
5 Federal guidance obliges public authorities in Germany to subsidise and include contemporary works of art within the framework of publicly funded building projects.
6 Press release available at: https://universes.art/en/nafas/articles/2012/tea-with-nefertiti [Accessed 17 April 2023].
7 Including a Dynasty 19 block statue of Ramses II (1250 BC) and a first century AD stela.
8 *Berliner Morgenpost*, 7 April 1930.
9 Ai Weiwei, Armand (b. Armenak Arzrouni), Mohamad-Said Baalbaki, Taha Belal, Adam Broomberg and Oliver Chanarin, Honoré Daumier, Fouad El Khoury, Mamduh Muhamad

Fathallah, Hans-Peter Feldmann, Francis Frith, Georg Frey, Alberto Giacometti, Gilbert & George, Georges Henein, Candida Höfer, Iman Issa, J&K (Janne Schäfer & Kristine Agergaard), Emily Jacir, Brandt Junceau, Ida Kar, William Kentridge, Susanne Kriemann, Little Warsaw (Bálint Havas and András Galik), Maha Maamoun, Luigi Mayer, Lee Miller, Paula Modersohn-Becker, Amedeo Modigliani, Mahmoud Moukhtar, Vik Muniz, Youssef Nabil, Xenia Nikolskaya, Amy Nimr, Lorraine O'Grady, Grayson Perry, David Roberts, Nida Sinnokrot, Thomas Struth, David G. Tretiakoff, Kees van Dongen, Franz Lenbach, Van Leo (b. Alexander Boyadjian), Ala Younis and Bassem Yousri.

10 http://www.diewerft.com/en/projects/nefertiti.html [Accessed 1 July 2024].

11 Press release available at: https://universes.art/en/nafas/articles/2012/tea-with-nefertiti [Accessed 17 April 2023].

12 A recording of the conference and the audience's reaction is available on YouTube: https://www.youtube.com/watch?v=bUb60kY-wUE [Accessed 17 April 2023].

13 All press quotes translated by the author with the help of Elaine Charwat.

14 https://SMÄK.de/ausstellungen/rollenbibliothek-anima-mundi/ [Accessed 16 July 2023].

15 *Zeichen und Wunder*, 29 July 2023 to 30 June 2024. https://www.rem-mannheim.de/ausstellungen/sonderausstellungen/ugo-dossi-zeichen-und-wunder/ [Accessed 28 July 2023].

16 https://www.youtube.com/watch?v=_lvcy9pqHfo&t=9s [Accessed 2 July 2024].

17 https://smaek.de/news/stolpersteine/ [Accessed 2 July 2024].

6
Inspiration, intervention or interdisciplinarity?

Performances, site-specific artworks, conceptual pieces, multimedia films, sounds, smells and sculptures placed next to, around and within ancient artefacts. What does such contemporary art do when it is an interlocutor in a permanent gallery of ancient material culture? The case studies brought together in this book highlight a range of agencies, motivations and outcomes. In this final chapter, I first review some of the shared themes of the previous case studies – relationships with the contemporary art market, motivations for working with artists and the nature of dialogues between past and present – before going on to advocate for more engagement with one modality: interdisciplinarity, an interactive meeting and transformation of ideas and attitudes. In other words, it is a way of working which does not just privilege the end product of artistic engagement, but can work back on academic perceptions of the source material. That being the case, I also turn to the question of what might form shared ground for productive dialogues between artists and Egyptologists. How could academics or curators become involved in the creative process, and how might artists form part of academic research so that artworks do not just sit adjacent to collections but inform them? It should not simply be assumed that artistic intervention by itself will be beneficial to an institution, strengthen interpretive strategy or indeed automatically provide an external criticality. Rather, I suggest, such projects should build in time for dialogue, reflection, evaluation and documentation.

Relationships with the contemporary art market

The late twentieth-century and early twenty-first-century penchant for pairing antiquity and contemporary art was forged much earlier in the twentieth century. Chapter 1 charted this relationship between contemporary artworks, the art market and Egyptological discourse, but of course contemporary art and antiquities continue to intersect today within a powerful global market, driven by commercial sales, auction houses and high-end dealers. For Dubrovsky and Graeber (2019), the art world, despite 'all the importance of its museums, institutes, foundations, university departments, and the like, is still organized primarily around the art market'. It is a condition, they argue, that leads it to effectively act as an extension of global finance. It is no coincidence that the Museo Egizio's hosting of *Time Machine* in 1995 followed the 1994 establishment in Turin of *Artissima*, Italy's largest contemporary art fair. Meanwhile, Henry Moore's relationship with the British Museum was a primary catalyst to the development of the Egyptian galleries and displays of contemporary art in the 1990s, examples of which went on to be sold commercially. The inspiration for Berlin and Munich's interactions with contemporary art came directly from encounters with modern and ancient art in a Munich dealer's commercial private gallery.

Studies have demonstrated a relationship between the museum display of antiquities and their commercial value on the market (Yates and Smith 2022; Austin forthcoming; Al-Azm and Paul 2019) and archaeologists have emphasised the role that market demand has played in intensifying illicit market activity and incentivising site looting (e.g. Parcak et al. 2016). To what extent, therefore, should museums be concerned about the commercial impact of temporary artists' interventions? Commodification was certainly one source of anxiety for some senior staff members at the Musées royaux d'art et d'histoire in Brussels in the run-up to the 2023 exhibition *Expéditions d'Égypte*, which featured contemporary art interventions from Sara Sallam throughout (Chapter 2). Arguably, the exhibitions under consideration might be seen as a catalyst for the return to cross-collecting from both the antiquities and contemporary art markets, which has seen something of a resurgence in the twenty-first century.

Take, for instance, *Artempo: Where Time Becomes Art*, hosted in the nineteenth-century Venetian-Gothic Palazzo Fortuny, Venice, in 2007, which ran concurrently with the Venice Biennale. It was co-curated and financed by Axel Vervoordt, head of a renowned art gallery, an interior design business and an arts and antiques trading organisation, in collaboration with Jean-Hubert Martin, curator of *Magiciens de la Terre* (1989). The show positioned ethnographic and archaeological material (including an eighth-century BC basalt statue of an Egyptian priest) together with classical and modern art, as well as contemporary installations. Many of the usual artists who have featured in the previous chapters were represented, including Bacon, Giacometti, Picasso, Moore, Kapoor, Kentridge and Warhol.

In the winter of 2015–16, meanwhile, Helly Nahmad Gallery, New York, organised an exhibition mixing Greek and Roman antiquities with the work of surrealist Giorgio de Chirico (Coolidge 2016). In the same year over in Europe, Galerie Cahn (Basel) collaborated with Jocelyn Wolff (Paris) on a joint show designed by the French contemporary artist Guillaume Leblon and involving 'a dialogue between Greek, Egyptian and Roman sculptures and contemporary works by Zbyněk Baladrán, Katinka Bock, Guillaume Leblon, Franz Erhard Walther, Prinz Gholam'.[1] The gallery has continued to stage pairings since then, opening Cahn Contemporary in 2019 as a dedicated space for dialogue between contemporary creations and archaeological material.

A few years later, The European Fine Art Foundation (TEFAF) New York hosted a collaboration of two art dealers, Sean Kelly Gallery and Charles Ede Gallery, to pair contemporary and ancient works of art in an effort to encourage a 'dialogue between past and present' (Rubinstein 2021). In this case, previous museum experiments, such as the Getty's 2011 *Modern Antiquity: Picasso, de Chirico, Léger, and Picabia in the Presence of the Antique*,[2] were explicitly noted as 'helping to drive the interest of collectors' (Coolidge 2016). In 2023 nine antiquities galleries presented their holdings at TEFAF, seeking to tap into the cross-collecting market because, it was suggested, sellers and buyers had become more concerned about provenance, making 'top quality antiquities ... scarce'. In response, dealers had a closer focus on creating 'aesthetically striking presentations highlighting the artistic qualities, not just the historical significance' of antiquities (Morris 2023).

A further indicator of the burgeoning market for cross-collecting comes from one of the world's premier contemporary art platforms, *Frieze*, which is responsible for producing art magazines and international fairs. In 2012 they inaugurated *Frieze Masters*, dedicated to art from ancient to modern times. Around 130 commercial galleries participated, showcasing six millennia of art and 'creating a destination where visitors can discover art history anew'.[3] At the 2017 fair, New York-based commercial galleries Salon 94 and Antiquarium Ltd joined forces to pair the work of contemporary artists and ancient Egyptian objects in their exhibition *Egyptomania*, as for instance in a coupling of a Predynastic decorated pottery vessel (3350–3225 BC) with a decorated ceramic (*Untitled*, 1987) by Keith Haring (Small 2017).

In contrast, less commercially focused but nonetheless indicative of this trend for wedding ancient and modern was the launch in 2022 of the practice-based *Mass Sculpture* magazine for artists exploring 'undervalued and neglected skills and processes that deliver the thrill of manipulating form in space, in both historical and contemporary contexts'.[4] Their first issue featured the *c.*25,000–30,000-year-old 'Venus of Willendorf' on the cover, while the second included a conversation between sculptor Marianne Walker and Egyptologist Elizabeth Frood (Walker and Frood 2023), itself a model of how Egyptology and contemporary art can productively question and think in parallel.

One collector buying from both markets is former investment manager Christian Levett. His personal collection of antiquities and contemporary art was opened for the public in 2011 as a private museum, the Musée d'art classique de Mougins, in a small village near Cannes in southern France. Amongst his collection of Egyptian and classical antiquities are the works of several artists who have featured in the British Museum – Damien Hirst, Marc Quinn and Antony Gormley. In 2018 the Mougins museum loaned several pieces to *The Classical Now*, a two-month-long exhibition mixing objects from contemporary art and antiquity displayed in London at Somerset House through a partnership with Kings College London (Squire et al. 2018). Subsequently, one of the artefacts, a 'Greek Bust of Cleopatra', was sold at TimeLine Auctions and featured as the cover image for their auction catalogue.[5] Despite the lack of provenance prior to 1972 (in contravention of the UNESCO 1970 Convention on the Means of Prohibiting and Preventing the Illicit Import, Export and Transfer of Ownership of Cultural Property), the *Classical Now* exhibition and its museum display provided it with a pedigree that bolstered its status and value. Two years later, in August 2023, the Mougins museum closed to make way for Levett's new collecting interest: female artists. To accommodate this new enterprise, almost the entire collection from the Musée d'art classique de Mougins was sold at a series of auctions in London and New York. Despite the lack of verifiable provenance for many of the antiquities, the 'museum quality' collection achieved exceptional prices.

Opened in the same year as Levett's museum, the acclaimed Museum of Old and New Art (MONA) was the brainchild of professional gambler and antiquities collector David Walsh. In this unconventional space, Walsh's intermixed collection of contemporary art and ancient material, including an Egyptian sarcophagus and mummified remains, is irreverently arranged around the concepts of sex and death, producing an aesthetic experience and cultural destination (Franklin 2019, 84–105). Despite claims that MONA's displays are exceptionally original, Walsh's inspiration appears to have been *Artempo* (Walker 2017), and Walsh in fact invited one of its curators, Jean-Hubert Martin, to host his *Theatre of the World* exhibition at MONA in 2013. The exhibition saw the coffin of Iretheruru (Twenty-Sixth Dynasty, 600–525 BC) and Giacometti's elongated bronze sculpture *Femme Leoni* (1947) set on opposing ends of a gallery hung with Pacific barkcloths. Unmoored from traditional museum classifications, such pieces were rendered up purely for subjective engagement. An aesthetic and sensorial experience with material culture as orchestrated through a balance of ancient and contemporary is not in itself problematic. It can be just as valid an encounter as other forms of knowing and being. What can be ethically problematic in these conditions is the complete exclusion of other more discursive practices that tether these objects to other histories and other places. As noted by Jay Sanders (cited in Marstine 2017, 7), 'aesthetics – the canon – ignored the social and economic conditions of works and euthanized its production and reception … [and] distances us from the ethical'. Any dialogue between past and present is conditioned by the practices around it, and in the art market that equates to wealth and status, however much other attributes are lauded.

The above examples are ethically problematic, but they involve very particular types of institution and platform that have ongoing, regular interactions with the art market. Their foundations in wealthy, private individuals' personal collections and collecting tastes mean that their operations diverge from the ethical concerns of public museums, usually by being more centred around the 'authentic' rather than provenance and in seeking out works already considered of high commercial worth. The types of partnership that museums establish with artists as part of interventions (as opposed to insertions) are not necessarily just about the singularity of the artwork or the fame of the artist. Rather, they often prioritise how the art production process itself functions within the institution and in discursive space in ways that are of mutual benefit to museum and artist. As former Weltkulturen Museum Frankfurt director Clémentine Deliss has maintained, artworks produced in relation to collections exist outside of an artist's market evaluation (Deliss and Sokołowska 2014). The increasing recognition that buying from the contemporary antiquities market is problematic may be precisely the reason that curators see contemporary art interventions as a way to introduce fresh elements to a collection, given an inability to substantially expand their holdings or to change permanent displays.

Ethical practice is not merely about relying on professional codes of conduct, but also about a dynamic engagement with issues (Marstine 2013), which artists and museum staff might prioritise in their initial and ongoing discussions. Installations of the type produced by Sallam, for example, less readily circulate in the market than sculptures or paintings, but rather speak to many of the complex moral and ethical problems that museums are grappling with. They are not produced primarily for high commercial gain or for sale but are research products in their own right, outputs of time, effort and discourse – just like any other academic production or curatorial effort, for which scholars earn a livelihood, peer acknowledgement and career recognition. The same is true for many artists with whom museums or scholars might collaborate. Nonetheless, while site-specific artworks might defy commercialisation due to their immobility, the itinerant cost of the artists themselves may not: the 'mobilization of the artist radically redefines the commodity status of the art work, the nature of artistic authorship, and the art-site relationship' (Kwon 2002, 31). Sallam's invitation to multiple institutions perhaps points in this direction whereby she becomes the commodity 'with a special purchase on criticality' (Kwon 2002, 47).

There is a second concern about how the art world commoditises contemporary artworks, and that is the way in which it mutes the political and social efficacy of art (Krauss 2000). Egyptian artist Khaled Hafez, for instance, has voiced unease as the market for Egyptian contemporary art has flourished, suggesting that it is being commoditised by a Western neocolonial fashion for the politics and heritage of the Middle East (Tully 2010, 302). Certainly, after the 2011 Egyptian revolution, activist and protest street graffiti became a lucrative proposition, appropriated by non-Egyptian institutions 'through the growing interference and agendas of international funds, organizations, cultural centres, curators and the so-called "gate keepers" of the art world' (Abaza 2013). Museums are included here, and several have sought to commission street artists to recontextualise their Egyptian collections (e.g. Figure 6.1).

Alaa Awad's acclaimed murals, which were displayed in Munich's Staatliches Museum Ägyptischer Kunst (SMÄK) exhibition hall in 2022–3 (Chapter 5), are an example. His images draw extensively from ancient Egyptian iconography, as in *Al-Naaehaat*, a mourning scene depicting ancient Egyptian women accompanying a sarcophagus symbolising the deaths of the Port Said Stadium massacre in 2012. But as Abaza (2013) has observed, these scenes are not easily understood by local lay people,

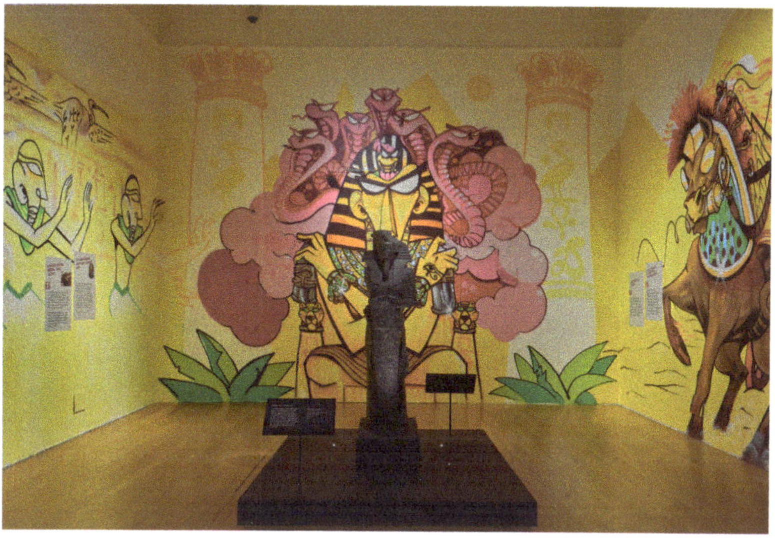

Figure 6.1 Commissioned work by Egyptian graffiti artist Nofal O in the British Museum's *Tutankhamun Reimagined* exhibition, 2022.

and she confessed that she might not have made the connections between ancient Egyptian funeral rites and the massacre had she not interviewed the artist. Could it be, she speculated, that the overemphasis on ancient Egyptian themes in Awad's work is what has allowed it to fit with the trend of commodification in the international market and be so readily co-opted into the safe space of the foreign museum? Notably in that museum space, the affective and grounded significance of place that produced the work amongst a wider assemblage of mural art – the intensity of political crises, violence and loss of Cairo's Mohammed Mahmoud Street – is nowhere to be seen, similarly to the absence of context for the antiquities on display. There is, Abaza concedes, an unresolved tension between the lived embodied interactions with the walls in Cairo, depicting highly moving themes, and the international art world's celebration of the artists. The SMÄK presentation was fundamentally about design, focusing on the biography of authorship and the formal aesthetics of the paintings rather than an exploration of the works as still alive and having agency. In considering, then, what contemporary art does in these museum spaces, we should not forget what the museum does to contemporary art.

Motivations for inviting artists

A 2020 report on mapping contemporary art in UK heritage organisations documented that the core motivators for the institutional commissioning of artists were audience diversification; extending traditional approaches to heritage interpretation; and deepening visitors' sensory, emotional and critical engagement, especially with hidden or untold stories (Black et al. 2020, 69). These aims are ones that were largely shared in the case studies and examples explored in the previous chapters, such as Bonn's Ägyptische Museum where museum staff saw artists as a means to expand and change their audience or SMÄK's embrace of the *Adam, wo bist du?* exhibition as a method to engage the public debate on the difficult history of National Socialism – *Vergangenheitsbewältigung* (Chapter 5). Twentieth-century geopolitics, national priorities and local economies have all had a part to play in opening older institutions to new modes of interpretation. The embrace of contemporary art has thus often reflected museum responses to current realities and the institutional need to redefine their relevance – whether on account of economic decline, political reform or cultural development – rather than just a more narrowly defined intellectual pursuit. The interplay between 'new' and 'old' is therefore not simply about juxtaposing antiquity and contemporary material culture in a hermetically sealed dialogue, but is rather a broader prompt, challenging old ways of doing things.

Ultimately, museums holding Egyptology collections have largely employed insertion or intervention modalities of artistic display as an adaptive and public engagement strategy. For the British Museum, embracing *Time Machine* was a key part of an attempt to shift away from its profile of elitism in the 1990s towards being more relevant and engaging at a time of considerable economic and political pressure. At the Museo Egizio, the needs of urban regeneration and the influence of the wider city's museum ecosystem facilitated many of the early incursions of contemporary art into their galleries. These pressures were less acute in Munich, although a move towards more contemporaneous modes of presentation was part of the city's broader cultural policy to be seen as more dynamic. Here, museum builders and curators were already predisposed to modernist practices of art presentation, following particularly strong German art-historical traditions. Nevertheless, an expanded audience, along with wider relevance for the Egyptian collection, has been a primary motivation for the SMÄK's embrace of contemporary art. A cynical reading might accuse such institutions of using commissions to 'become extensions of the museum's own self-promotional apparatus'

(Kwon 2002, 47) rather than as true experiments in challenging interpretations or addressing institutional biases. However, diversification of audience is just one of the multilayered effects, including unintentional ones, that come with these intercessions.

While each case study reflects local concerns, all the exhibitions form part of, and are shaped by, a global capitalist museum assemblage that shares approaches (Levitt 2015, 134). Definitions of contemporary art produced in world centres – metropoles such as London and New York – are reinscribed through itinerant curators who are parachuted in to bring something novel to galleries worldwide. *Moth to the Flame* in Turin, for instance, was curated by artist Liam Gillick (a British citizen living in New York), curator Tom Eccles (an American college professor at Bard College) and *ArtReview* editor-in-chief Mark Rappolt (a British citizen working for an international contemporary art magazine based in London); and two decades earlier, *Time Machine* brought principally London-based artists to Italy. Meanwhile, *Tea with Nefertiti*'s curators were at that time based in New York and they invited high-profile artists who had already displayed their work internationally at various biennials and large contemporary art galleries. This global museum assemblage homogenises artist participation and it is notable that several of the same names recur in exhibitions intent on combining antiquity and contemporary art, such as Marc Quinn, Damien Hirst and Grayson Perry.

Today, contemporary art continues to be tacked on to projects and exhibitions where it is hoped that it might bring in new audiences, provide an authentic voice exterior to the museum, or provoke an emotional response to challenge sterile traditional presentations or narratives (Stearn 2016). This can be a particularly appealing strategy for inflexible permanent galleries where change can be difficult to instigate or logistically complicated by the unwieldy nature of the displays, as is the case for Egyptian statue galleries. However, in such instances, artists can feel a sense of vulnerability in being co-opted into a tokenistic strategy of diversification. Several authors have drawn critical attention to the overly celebratory way in which contemporary art is introduced into museums, especially where it is to address colonial histories (Geismar 2015, 185; Kennedy 2021; Theuri 2021). Claims that artists' interventions bring in a wider audience have also been challenged, as the subtext may often be that museums are actually seeking to attract a different, younger audience of art cognoscenti (Robins 2013, 10) or else assume a level of visual literacy and cultural capital that is ultimately exclusionary. Contemporary art, like Egyptology or archaeology, is itself a form of culturally situated production that is neither ahistorical nor self-explanatory. Furthermore, most of the artists brought in to engage with Egyptian collections have preconceived ideas profoundly shaped by prior encounters with museums, as the artist interviews recounted in Chapters 3 to 5 attest. Meaning-making is always contingent and requires an acknowledgement of positionality within projects as well as within disciplines.

The curators interviewed for this study spoke of contemporary art and modernist works as means to 'make ancient arts contemporary' or to make them 'accessible with our visual references'. Yet, ancient Egypt, as profoundly Western domesticated museum culture and 'chronotope' (Stevenson 2022a), is also readily familiar to publics today through the production and reproduction of visual clichés, as well as to curators and scholars through the practices of classifying, describing and interpreting. This ongoing process of cultural meaning, recursively oscillating between the unknown and the familiar, is, as Clifford (1988, 146) describes, part of what defines self and other. 'This process', he further suggests, is characteristic of global modernity, a 'permanent ironic play of similarity and difference, the familiar and the strange'. In this context, contemporary art can be utilised as a challenge to that easy acquaintance we have in modern society with ancient Egypt by bringing in the unexpected. Such a possibility was expressed by one white middle-aged female visitor whose reaction upon visiting *Time Machine* at the British Museum was captured in the museum's education department film:

> The Egyptian stuff is so familiar, over one's lifetime one has looked at it over and over again in various places and somehow looking at it again and comparing it and understanding what the modern artists have got from it, you look at it completely newly.[6]

Articulated here is what historian Susan Crane has identified as memory disruption. She has posited that when visitors enter the museum, they do so with preconceived ideas and expectations from previous museum encounters – 'an excess of memory from other times, other museums' (Crane 1997, 47). Thus, when institutions present alternative modalities of collections' representation and the histories they attend to, visitors experience a memory disruption. Crane argues that it is in these moments that previously bounded interpretive possibilities are opened.

This does not mean, of course, that the invitation is warmly accepted. Most of the curators and artists interviewed for this study spoke of those who were wholly resistant to changing long-held views on Egypt or the role of museums in scientific communication, with some publics, scholars and curators uncomfortable with art and its role in rethinking assumptions. Historian of museums Tony Bennett pushes us to think about such resistance. He acknowledges that while there is vigorous academic debate over issues of representation, how this is translated into museum practice is problematic since it may be 'at the price of decline in the ability to connect with the ways in which socially majoritarian behaviors and values are routinely reshaped and transformed' (Bennett 2006, 66). He goes on to postulate that any programme of social change must contend with the extraordinary inertia that results from decades of certain forms of social learning in museums, meaning that behaviour cannot be altered simply by the raising of consciousness. Instead, paraphrasing Bourdieu, Bennett contends that there must be 'a thoroughgoing process of countertraining, involving repeated exercises'. With each iteration of contemporary art practice amongst permanent displays and as they become more commonplace, those expectations that Crane refers to will be recalibrated, perhaps leading to the wider acceptance, amongst curators and publics, of artistic intervention. This has arguably been the case in Germany, where following the regular artist installations in the Neues Museum and SMÄK, numerous other museums in the country have welcomed contemporary artworks into their displays of ancient Egypt, such as the Ägyptisches Museum of the Rheinische Friedrich-Wilhelms-Universität Bonn, Museum für Byzantinische Kunst in Bode (Chapter 2) and Reiss-Engelhorn-Museen in Mannheim, with the inclusion of artists such as Ugo Dossi who had previously been given a platform in Munich (Chapter 5). A similar situation also appears to be taking shape in Italy (Chapter 4), with the transformation of what were previously very traditional museums.

Dialogues between past and present

Many of the exhibitions in this study were accompanied by overtures claiming that they would 'encourage us to look afresh at both modern and ancient art ... to remind ourselves of the perennial power of sculpture' (*Statuephilia* curators, cited in Squire 2012, 468), that 'contemporary art can give a new life to the works of the past, demonstrate how the culture of the Egyptian world is still vital today' (Raveri, cited in Paglieri 1995) and can 'spark new dialogues and discussions' (Squire et al. 2018, xiii). Given the preponderance of such statements, the question is, why do our views on the past need refreshing? Perhaps it betrays a tacit acknowledgement of the disciplinary traps in which we find ourselves?

For instance, regarding *Time Machine* at the British Museum in 1994, Putnam observed:

> I noticed with a lot of colleagues that BM was by the time – they got to that sort of a system keeper level or whatever – they were almost like bureaucrats; they were no longer even interested in this subject … I didn't have any background in Egyptology. But I think I was far more inspired by Egyptology than they were, you know. I think they'd lost that.

Our disciplinary constraints and working practices can conspire to dull those aspects of our subject that originally drew us to them. Arguably, our specialist perspectives might be refreshed by working with artists to assist in the interpretation of the source material itself. Thus, although the focus is frequently upon external audiences in museum partnerships with artists, museum staff are equally themselves an audience that can experience a transformation of perspectives through these activities, as was documented for the Museo Egizio (Chapter 4). A further example is Egyptologist and curator Andreas Dorn, who, on account of Anja Schindler's questioning of the Egyptian collection at the University of Bonn for *Death is Sky Blue* (Chapter 2), acknowledged that he 'began to take a closer look at the light blue objects, began to learn to see in a new way, asked myself questions, passed questions on to Anja Schindler and kept discovering the unknown alongside the familiar'.[7] Because she asked different questions about Egyptian imagery than he as an Egyptologist did, this triggered processes of thought, although not necessarily answers to specific questions.

These sentiments resonate with the arguments of historian of science Chiara Ambrosio (2014, 364). She has challenged the assumption that artists' work merely adds a dimension to visualisation that renders science more communicable. Instead, she appeals for a more serious consideration of the critical mission of artists, arguing that scientific practice itself can benefit from artists through their questioning of the assumptions and modes of working that scientists often take for granted. Here, contemporary art can potentially offer a disruptive fissure, a deliberate pause in discourse, creating a space in which other possibilities might exist. And this includes rethinking our own positionality and what points of reference we reach for in discursive practices.

Bertola and Rich (2020, 161), meanwhile, have suggested that the role of the 'contemporary artist, informed by history, is to create, either fleetingly or more permanently, some commentary on how the past informs the present'. However, as Chapter 1 demonstrated, contemporary artists have long informed how the ancient Egyptian past is interpreted – the language used to describe and visualise past material culture. Can the role of artists in shaping the presentations and language of Egyptology be traced to more recent times? Passing gestures towards contemporary art have been made in Egyptological literature, providing an opening for discourse, although mostly these remain interesting asides or anecdotes – a narrative device and point of inspiration rather than an adoption of new methodological approaches (e.g. Versluys 2018; Junge 1990). The very word 'dialogue' presupposes that there is a two-way exchange of ideas. However, it is more usual for Egyptologists to respond to contemporary artistic expression by considering how it compares with the 'real' interpretation of Egyptian visual culture (e.g. Spencer 2015). In these instances, contemporary art simply serves as a creative foundation for the communication of historical facts and the performance of Egyptological expertise, rather than also being seen as an opportunity for interdisciplinarity and to speak back to how we understand the past.

This is not to say that Egyptologists have necessarily been closed to in-depth conversations with artists. But there is a perception that an artist's vision is sacrosanct or that artists are very difficult and demanding, and that is just the way it is. One curator noted in interview that 'if you invite people – you don't get in the way', another commented that 'some of them were quite difficult – they want what they want and they have their preconceived vision' and a third remarked that a lot of the artists they had worked with had 'a big ego but you leave them to it'. Such predispositions can translate into an overreliance on the artist or invited curator to take all the agency in providing an alternative perspective, rather than generating concepts or narratives in partnership with museum or academic staff. Interdisciplinary conversations are also a valuable way to mitigate the concern expressed amongst several Egyptology curators that inviting contemporary artists is risky as 'you never quite know what you're going to get'.

Assumptions about the nature of artistic practice might also explain the lack of impact such projects have had on museum structures, interpretation or documentation in the longer term. Yet this is also due to differences in professional experience and expertise. Egyptologists and curators are used to dealing with artefacts – with their manipulation, interpretation and systems of presentation. They typically have far more limited experience of working with living artists, especially those who work in a complex range of media, have more involved technical requirements or need lengthy installation procedures in which the artistic process itself may experiment with multiple iterations. The 2023 *Expéditions d'Égypte* exhibition team in Brussels, for instance, had to contend with several time-lapse video projections. For Sallam's *A Tourist Handbook for Egypt Outside of Egypt*, five framed black and white photographs of Parisian streets were hung on the wall, onto which a set of projections were made, to sequentially light up picture by picture, overlaying coloured collaged images of Napoleon's battles in Egypt, intermittently interspersed with text between the frames. Getting this right took time and patience.

Equally, Sallam's video installation *If I Can Be Heard in the Place Where You Are* required a very particular type of cube television monitor on a stand as part of its gallery impact. While the Brussels museum had its own television set and suggested that a flat-screen format would be a suitable interface, the use of the specified arrangement, typical by contemporary art conventions, distinguished Sallam's audio-visuals as a sculptural exhibit in its own right – not a supplementary set of background visuals hung on the wall, but an integral part of the exhibition narrative and embodied experience of the displays. Thus, while some members of staff initially regarded the artist's requirements as archetypally difficult, these concerns reflected the museum staff's unfamiliarity with standard codes of contemporary art practice and installation. Fortunately, a key member of the exhibition team was a gallerist with 12 years' experience of exhibiting contemporary art, and was able to mediate between the museum's permanent staff and the artist, liaising diplomatically with art handlers and curators, on the one hand, and the artist, on the other, thus producing an exhibition that staff were proud of.

Some of the most successful disruptions – the ones that are most accessible and potentially relevant to museum curators and Egyptologists – are those that rely on historical research themselves. Such an approach is seen in the art-making practices of Rita Keegan (Chapter 3), Sara Sallam (Chapters 2 and 4) and Ala Younis (Chapter 5), which have many commonalities with academic and curatorial methodologies. This challenges assumptions that the artistic process lacks rigour in contrast to an institution's intellectual integrity (Barrett and Millner 2014, 5). Might it be possible, then, to draw a distinction in significance between artists of two different kinds – those whose work is derivative, reproducing forms of aesthetic appeal (as characterised several of the SMÄK's installations based on a philosophy of 'art for art's sake'), compared to those who have engaged in the production of knowledge about the past and a deeper questioning of the worlds in which these things were made to have meaning?

There has been scepticism and caution expressed as to the extent to which artistic means can be integrated into investigations of the past. Archaeologist (and former Slade student artist) Steven Mithen (2004) has argued that although there is overlap between the activities that constitute 'archaeology' and 'art', there remains an essential difference. For Mithen, the archaeologist's goal is to reconstruct as closely as possible what happened in the past. That might never be objectively feasible, but the attempt to do so within theoretical historical contexts remains a central tenet, a responsibility 'to make statements that go beyond one's own personal experiences and subjective beliefs' (Mithen 2004, 166). For artists, he asserts, there are no constraints upon the nature of their interpretations and no responsibility to go beyond their self-expression. A slightly different sentiment was articulated in a review of Renfrew's book *Figuring it Out*, noting the 'absolute scission between premodern and postmodern art' in that the latter lacks 'the embedded spiritual sense that had been integral to the art of all other periods … there is now no complex system of meaning in which art plays a role' (Weingarten 2005, 288). Merriman (2004), meanwhile, has queried the use of artists, holding that they overly emphasise the aesthetic at the expense of contextualisation and interpretation. He has suggested instead 'informed imagination', which he defines as

> an approach to interpretation which is based on the knowledge of the archaeological and historical context of the material provided by the expertise of the curators, but which acknowledges diversity of views, the contingency of archaeological interpretations, and encourages imagination and enjoyment in the visitors' own constructions of the past (Merriman 2004, 102).

Aesthetic engagement, however, can be just as valid a route to knowledge as other means and is never without its own complex system in which meaning is produced. There is a long-standing tension in art history between the aesthetic and semiotic appraisal of images, the former foregrounding artworks as the active agents in the relationship between object and viewer, the latter prioritising artworks' meaning in the context of the time at which they were produced. But it is the tension itself that is generative. In their review of contemporary art interventions in Australian museums, Barrett and Millner (2014, 100) note a trend in the 2010s towards artists deploying beauty in works created with museums as a key strategy of both artists and professionals to change a museum's didactic voice.

Most productively of all for archaeology, contemporary art can be a reminder that analytical, disembodied approaches to interpreting the past are limited unless room is given to understanding other, intangible elements of human experience. Curator Anastasia Christophilopoulou, for instance, has argued that certain artworks can act as a bridge to interpreting the past not just with archaeological data but through an 'experimental and sensory process' (Christophilopoulou 2023). Pieces like Issam Kourbaj's *Dark Water, Burning Worlds* (Chapter 3), she contends, are not quite artworks and not quite artefacts, implying that they are hybrid objects that exist between the ancient world and contemporary art. It is here that experiments with artistic practice and interventions can offer a personally and socially engaged approach to Egyptology, calling attention to multisensorial, affective and experiential modes of encountering the world.

The artist Porras-Kim, for instance, brought auditory elements into her 2022 Gasworks show (Chapter 3) in the form of *Recital of the Granodiorite Stela of Hor and Suty*, which comprised a life-sized graphite representation on paper of the stela now in the British Museum, together with a four-minute-long piece of music composed and interpreted by Egyptologist Heidi Köpp-Junk. Sallam's work (Chapters 2 and 4) also often includes verbal recitations from ancient Egyptian sources. The use of spoken word has been a lauded element in the institutional critique of artists such as Fred Wilson, either to make objects speak back or to disrupt the traditional, familiar silence of museum and galleries: a 'strategic, ghosting effect … constructing a subject position with which, or against which, the visitor is asked to identify' (González 2011, 331). Yet the tensions between the intellectual and practical dimensions of these works are rarely evaluated in art criticism. The imposition of sound into gallery space is often contested. For instance, in the Sainsbury Centre, although Sallam's voice initially freely carried across the galleries from her *Come to Your House* installation (Chapter 2), she noticed on later visits that the volume had been conspicuously turned down despite her intention that visitors be aware that there was a 'funeral' taking place and be guided by the sound to join the ceremony. In these instances, the museum's authority in maintaining the norms of display is clear. Similarly, decisions on whether to use headphones or open sound can change visitors' relationships to artworks and gallery space. The former potentially offers an intimate engagement, but also one that is easily ignored in comparison to open sound, which can more directly affect other artefacts in the gallery. How the physical space of the museum affects the acoustics of an artwork and its interactions with other sensory elements needs explicit debate amongst exhibition producers.

Creating olfactory atmospheres is another aspect of sensorial enhancement that artists have brought into Egyptian galleries, as in the works of Marilyn Arsem and Anja Schindler (Chapter 2), as well as Rita Keegan (Chapter 3). The sensorial field, artists remind us, is embedded in matter, permitting archaeologists to find material evidential traces of lived worlds. It is this sensory archaeology that deserves greater attention as a counterpoint to a modernist archaeology that is especially pervasive in museums where it has rendered objects legible and visible, 'on a pedestal, admired from a distance, and enframed through various representational devices' (Hamilakis 2014, 56). Both Keegan and Sallam spoke in interview of the need to 'create new ways of relating' and humanising the material displayed. These artists, however, also privilege the process of research as much as the products, which may take a wide variety of forms. Aesthetic, contextual and interpretive approaches need not be as mutually exclusive as Merriman (2004) proposed.

Even with productive fissures and departure points for the interpretation of the past, we should nevertheless remain cautious about exaggerated claims that pairings of ancient material culture and contemporary art put past and present into direct dialogue. If artistic practices are to be utilised as a mode of archaeological interpretation, then some form of institutional critique can be valuable for revealing the frame that mediates these dialogues – both physical and intellectual. Throughout the case studies, architectural structures, display materials and the spatial syntaxes of exhibition halls affected engagements. Exhibitions often work more to draw art further into the present through modernist settings and design-led interpretive solutions than they do to speak back to the ancient past. At the British Museum a subtle modernist aesthetic frames encounters, inspired by Henry Moore and realised using concrete pedestals, while at the SMÄK the modernist aesthetic is stark, appealing to contemporary artists and often overpowering the ancient objects themselves despite the claim to minimalism. The framing of the Museo Egizio's collection, amidst the old-fashioned cases that were in use prior to the twenty-first century redevelopments, attracted the artists who exhibited there; they often responded more to that interior aesthetic than to the material contained there, as has also been the case for the Petrie Museum in London. Many of the interviews with artists and curators reaffirmed this significance of place for their practice. Thus, site visits for artists should be an essential part of the curatorial process if intervention rather than mere insertion is sought.

The question of whether a dialogue is really created between past and present artefacts is itself one that may be too generalising. What artists have been asking in the 2020s is not how to put the past and present into dialogue, but *whose* pasts and *which* presents are being created and represented. In April 2023 the Egyptian-Honduran, US-based artist Jackie Milad opened her commission at the Baltimore Museum of Art's *Histories Collide* alongside Fred Wilson's Egyptian-themed sculpture *Artemis/Bast* (1992). The show included two examples of her bright and lively mixed-media abstract paintings and collages, *Shabti Emerge* and *Unwrapping, Unrolling* (Figure 6.2). Both address history, myth and the dispersal of Egyptian heritage in an attempt to connect ancient and contemporary Egypt, and also to provide meaningful links between collections and diasporic communities. Milad, like Sallam, has found herself searching museum collections for resonances and fragments of her own family connections to Egypt. Her Baltimore commission was based on a grant from the Baltimore Municipal Art Society allowing

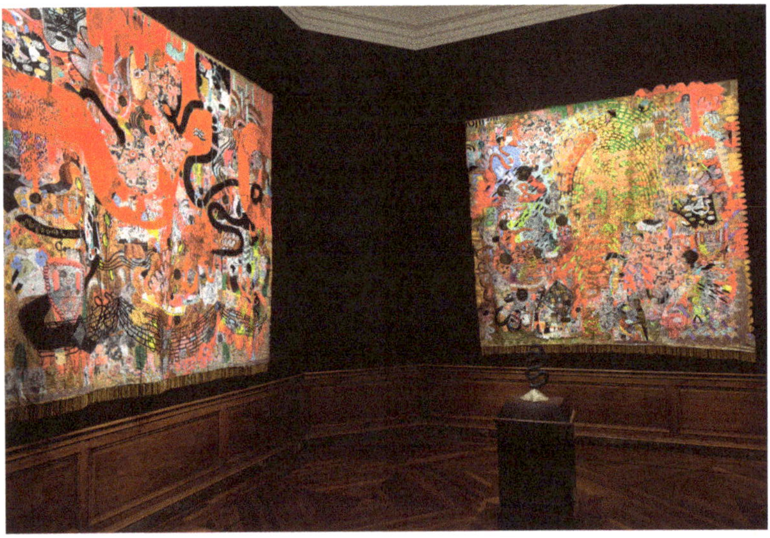

Figure 6.2 Two of Jackie Milad's collages at the Baltimore Museum of Art in 2023: *Unwrapping, Unrolling*, 2023, mixed media on hand-dyed with tea canvas, acrylic, gel medium, paint marker, flashe paint, plastic beads, brass, mixed textile and paper collage, 128 × 133.25 in.; and *Shabti Emerge*, 2023, mixed media on hand-dyed with tea canvas, acrylic, gel medium, paint marker, flashe paint, plastic beads, brass, mixed textile and paper collage, 128.5 × 133.25 in. Courtesy of the artist and Baltimore Museum. Photograph by Mitro Hood.

her to visit the British Museum to study the Egyptian collection. But the museum did not reveal the full story she was looking for. There was, she said, an 'abyss of information' despite ancient Egypt being so heavily researched. The museums had it wrong because 'Egypt wasn't there'.[8] In this regard, both Sallam and Milad have found inspiration not in the collections per se but from what is missing from those collections: contemporary Egyptians and the land that is home.

Modernist approaches to art, developed between the art market, museums and Egyptology, brought Egypt into a sterilised present of twentieth-century Europe and America. They have singularised artefacts, severing them not just from the landscape in which they were made meaningful, but also from the communities that live amongst them and continue to draw meaning from them (Abd el-Gawad and Stevenson 2023). Consequently, that cliché that ancient Egyptian art is 'timeless', which surfaces continuously in all manner of writing on antiquity, is not necessarily a transcendent value. It is an artifice produced through the decontextualisation of artworks across modernist ideology, art market strategies and the new museum idea charted in Chapter 1. What is left unsaid in this praise of timelessness is placelessness – the implication that these artworks can belong anywhere. Those modernist practices are themselves now being challenged by today's artists in works such as Sallam's *Home Outside of Home*, bringing knowledge and the power of place back into the frame of dispersed heritage. This imperative was also present in Liliane Karnouk's 1994 *Time Machine* creation in which she used miniature palm stems around the sarcophagus of Nesisut. These, she recalled, 'brought Egypt to the British Museum' (Wattie 2019). Contemporary art can therefore inject that vital jolt to dislodge decontextualised material from a museum-habituated gaze, relocating it not just in time but in place, from which alternative meanings, evocations and insights may emerge. Other attempts, such as *Statues Also Die* in Turin, while not repositioning Egypt in the contexts of its communities, do draw into relief the institutional power and authority that encase them.

These pieces can also far better speak to those Egyptological interpretations that have explicitly confronted long-held assumptions about famous museum objects by recognising the role of institution, place and landscape in meaning-making and human experience (e.g. Richards 2002). The corporeal experience of three-dimensional space is something that artists are often particularly well attuned to, as are many museum curators, who together might provide alternative approaches to the reductive replication of Egyptological objects on the printed page, which is the medium most familiar to scholars. Museums too, as they start to undertake more urgent research on provenance, as they recognise the value of their photographic, archival and replica collections, and as they broaden the range of communities they work with, are equally well placed to engage in dialogue with artists. Certainly, within more recent visual arts practice there have been shifts away from the individual agency of artists (who create singular installations) towards artistic practice that is collective and open. In this context, artists and non-artists collaborate as an intellectual community working towards a common goal of addressing a specific issue (NCCPE 2021). For these reasons, it is becoming more difficult today to differentiate between the artist and curator (Groys 2009). The preparatory exchange between Sara Sallam and curator Elisabeth Van Caelenberge at the Brussels Art and History Museum's *Expéditions d'Égypte* is one example. Although several of the works installed as part of the intervention had been used in previous exhibitions, such as *The Fourth Pyramid Belongs to Her*, artist and curator worked together to realise fresh materialities that would work more effectively in the unfolding scenography of the exhibition, such as photographs realised as fluttering banners or the animation of colourful elements in a projected scene.

Interdisciplinarity?

If artists can provide a counterpoint to the seeming fixity of Egyptological interpretation and offer a more inquisitive positionality, this is a more realistic mode of intellectual enquiry than that presented by museums, as it uses evidence to contest knowledge, engages in debate and puts forward alternative readings. The possibilities for interdisciplinarity between academics and artists acted as a point of reflection for several artists and curators interviewed. Till Fellrath, for example, when I asked if, looking back, there was anything he might change about the 2014 *Tea with Nefertiti* exhibition, suggested that it would have been beneficial to host an academic symposium alongside the exhibition, 'creating more of a discourse of people', and to maintain the dialogue that the show had started. Building in time for reflexivity is therefore one recommendation to emerge from discussions with curators and artists, not just at the end of a project but throughout (Theuri 2021, 47). Similarly, long-term visitor evaluation is an important element of recursive reflection on what contemporary art does in these instances, so that these initiatives are not just self-serving outreach projects or, in the case of invited institutional critique, assumed to be inherently morally righteous (Fredheim

2020). This can help to establish if the public are active agents in art consumption, as has been claimed for true 'interventions' (La 2017), and how they might be embedded within institutional commitments (Stevenson 2022b, 19). And if exhibitions really are to be experiments (Macdonald and Basu 2007; Hansen et al. 2019; Bjerregaard 2019), evaluation is an essential part of the testing process.

Open-ended debate is rarely something that museums enable in their displays, and the uncertainties surrounding the fragmentary records and materials that constitute archaeological resources are not usually made apparent. Instead, most interpretive museum labels are assertive, seemingly offering certainty. This is perhaps a hangover from the predominance of a discourse established last century between dealers, curators and artists on the significance of style that, with training, can be read off an object in the evaluation of 'high art'. It is this form of knowledge that museum audiences are most used to, with research consistently showing that, across different types of museums and countries, the public retains a very high level of trust in museums (American Alliance of Museums 2021; Crooke 2021, 114–15; Dilenschneider 2023). Moreover, it seems that part of this trust derives from the perceived neutrality of such institutions (Adams 2013). Therefore, leaving all the work of questioning to artists may not be the most effective means of challenging histories, since their work is more likely to be seen as simply subjective alternatives that 'do not impinge on the authoritative' (Riggs 2023). The reception of the Belgian exhibition *Expéditions d'Égypte*, discussed in Chapter 2, underscores this point. That exhibition presented two separate narrative registers – the anonymous institutional voice and the artist's first-person account. The former was the one most frequently reported by reviewers, the latter ignored. The issue of how museums can best provide interpretation of pairings between the ancient and the contemporary is not an easy one to tackle. Artists might be reluctant to interpret their work at all, others reticent to permit museums to do that interpretation work themselves. Conversation, negotiation and experimentation are inherent in these endeavours.

There may be particular exhibitionary contexts in which artists, curators and scholars would have a more equal footing and share the narrative space more holistically. However these partnerships are construed, subtle power imbalances between artist and curator remain a challenge for interdisciplinary goals, as Sallam recounts:

> I'm an Egyptian artist who has been invited to intervene in Western institutions, so there is always pull and push … it was never the

> case that I felt unable to express myself but it is also internalised these power dynamics so it doesn't need to be with the exact people you are working with, it is just the institution and all the baggage and the history it still has a way of affecting collaborations.[9]

As Sallam touches upon here, collaborations with individual members of museum staff are frequently very positive – and the majority of curators and artists interviewed for this study reiterated this sentiment – but scaling up to the whole institution often leaves such projects peripheral to central budgeting, policy-making and routinised practice. There can, moreover, be challenges due to the academic understanding of 'interdisciplinarity' whereby it is generally thought to involve two or more cognate disciplines (Bertola and Rich 2020, 159), in contrast to work with non-academic partners which is regarded variously as 'knowledge exchange' or 'partnerships' rather than 'interdisciplinarity'. The politics over authorship may equally complicate relations. As one of the interviewed curators reflected, while the potential for interdisciplinarity between artists and curators is 'immense', breaking free from standard disciplinary frames of reference itself is extremely difficult given the years of training to get to the stage where one is in a position to have these conversations in museums or universities. But interdisciplinarity, as defined in the Introduction, acknowledges and respects disciplinary boundaries. Renfrew (2003, 95), for instance, concluded that artists and archaeologists have their own distinct ways of knowing the past – they have parallel visions – but there are opportunities to learn from each other. There is perhaps, too, a misplaced assumption of homogeneity within disciplines, when in fact there exists diversity within and not just between disciplines. In Egyptology there are schisms between those who identify as art historians, as in the case of Wildung and Schoske, and those who consider themselves archaeologists who emphasise more contextual approaches to the past, as has been the case at the Museo Egizio.

Legacies

Despite the bold statements made around contemporary art – the spectacle, the flurry of events programming and associated conferences – the institutional memory is often limited. Few of the exhibitions in this study have left much of an archival trace in their host institutions or have had a significant impact on long-term curatorial strategies, with perhaps the exception of Sallam's work in Turin in 2022. As a form of intervention in how museums interpret and approach their collections, the power of institutional critique has long been queried (e.g. Foster 1996; Krauss 2000). Fred Wilson's 1997 time in the British Museum (Chapter 3) is perhaps most telling. Despite Wilson's high profile as a major purveyor of institutional critique, his *In the Course of Arrangement* is little known and barely ever referenced in the literature. It had no major marketing campaign to bring attention to it and no visibility at the higher levels of British Museum management. On the one hand, this would seem to allow the more 'critical distance' that art scholars such as Foster (1996) have advocated if institutional critique is to retain its credibility without being co-opted or neutralised by the institution itself. But in this instance, the artwork alone did not bring about change or dialogue as it was not supported by a wider conversation and integration within other museum activities or responsibilities that legitimised its status and visibility.

If there really is to be a dialogue, should it not be documented – be it in hard copy as part of 'related document files' or a notation on the records of artefacts that artworks were associated with – to avoid truncation of that dialogue? In some instances, this lack of institutional memory is a correlate of the exhibition's goal to diversify audiences rather than challenge existing interpretations per se, as noted above. In other cases, the idiosyncratic and novel nature of interventions may make them challenging to document, especially for performance pieces or works situated generically within a gallery, and museums may not have an effective vocabulary for discipline-specific collections management systems. This is where prioritising time for interdisciplinary dialogues is even more important.

Absences from formal documentation can, however, also be a product of where responsibility for an exhibition lies. The museum reformers of the early twentieth century, discussed in Chapter 1, who sought to divide display for the public from specialist collections for scholars, also underwrote new professional divisions as the tasks of mounting exhibitions fell to new teams of designers, audience engagers, visitor services personnel and educationalists. Meanwhile the curator's role in traditional museums remained focused 'behind the scenes' in the reserve collection or on research more generally, as tends to be the case for most museum-based Egyptologists. Where the primary instigation for artist interventions has been from education, exhibition or learning teams (and especially where responsibility lies primarily with temporary members of staff) – as in the examples at the British Museum, Brussel's Art and History Museum, the Petrie Museum and the Saffron Walden Museum – it is less likely that a formal record will be kept or that concerted programmes of work with artists will be maintained. Exhibition-making is hugely time-consuming. The administrative paperwork, logistical planning and ongoing events programming that runs alongside the show are all labour-intensive.

There is also the matter of exhibition catalogues, those glossy tomes which are so highly regarded in the art and museum world as the formal record of temporary periods of display. As curators both in Bonn and Brussels commented in interview, the published catalogue was considered to be the final archive, with no further documentation of the interventions held in collections management systems or any other formal institutional records. The scholarship and photographic labour that go into the production of these catalogues leave archival processing as a peripheral concern, quickly abandoned or easily forgotten as exhibitions are deinstalled and new priorities take centre stage. Yet the catalogues for *Expéditions d'Égypte* and *Statues Also Die* are not representative of the exhibition, with the juxtapositions ignored as artefacts and artworks are isolated, individualised and decontextualised.[10]

With the exception of Munich, where a stability of vision instantiated by individual directors for almost 40 years has materialised a contemporary space and philosophy towards contemporary art, most of the examples explored have been singular events rather than part of a committed programme that is integral to the museum's mission or purpose. Sometimes this is due to projects being reactive, responding to external initiatives rather than being strategically planned. This oversight is not specific to Egyptian collections. It is a shortcoming associated with most interventions at heritage sites (Black et al. 2020), and calls have been made for artistic practice and exhibition design to be embedded more systematically within museum work (e.g. Marshall 2012). Too often museums are treated simply as venues for social commentary and critique, muting the capacity of time-limited interventions to transform practice in meaningful ways. Rather, it is more usually in the day-to-day work of museums that change happens at an institutional level. Similarly, evaluation of exhibitions is usually made in time-limited, project-centric assessments or in generalised, synoptic reports rather than long-term studies of the contribution of such work to museum missions, interpretive processes or visitor engagement. Archival traces of contemporary works might remain online, making this itself a potential space for intervention and interdisciplinary experiment.

Nevertheless, does the very significance of many interventions lie in their transgressive power, one that refuses to be collected lest it be institutionalised or instrumentalised? Whether site-specific installations are as effective in other locations or other times can also be questioned, with living artists sometimes critical of how their works are subsequently reinterpreted or used. Several of the institutions examined have acquired works that were initially only temporary interlocutors. In Munich, the architectural framing proved to be a strong pull for artists, who were happy to donate their works for long-term display, with Frepoli's *Purple*, for example, finding a comfortable niche in the scenography of the permanent displays. The museum also benefited from the donation of a dozen of Bassem Yousri's disruptive figurines, which still 'break out' from storage from time to time to interrupt the gallery narrative. At the Museo Egizio, Sallam's presence in the galleries in 2022 proved to be a pivotal intercession not just physically but strategically, prompting a change in acquisition policy and forward planning on the part of the institution. Ultimately, acquisition needs to be accompanied by institutional strategy with a strong sense of how the work fits with the museum's identity and development. In the 1990s this was not well articulated for the British Museum. The acquisition of Mitoraj's *Moonlight* and its later removal to storage by the institution highlight the transient values that can be ascribed to pieces whose long-term place in collections beyond an exhibition-specific role is not underpinned by a strong sense of purpose.

Nevertheless, even accepting that productive interdisciplinary artistic projects are process-driven rather than object-driven may mean that what remains from 'wilfully temporary' (Meyers 2000) installations is the documentation. The 'archival impulse' (Foster 2004) in contemporary art goes two ways. Not only does it draw on archives, it can also produce them, thereby becoming part of existing collections through citation and juxtaposition, setting the ground for ongoing or future conversations. And those conversations themselves contribute to an iterative, wider dialogue potentially challenging any simplistic division between site- and non-site-specific interventions.

Putnam, reflecting on the legacies of curating interventions in galleries, questioned whether we are expecting too much of individual exhibitions in looking for them to have a permanent legacy.[11] If we take them on their own, perhaps that is so, but Bennett's (2006) observations noted above on the importance of countertraining and repeat exercises can push us to reconsider. While individually each of the interventions examined may not have substantially altered the institutional structures in which they were accommodated nor had a significant impact upon Egyptological knowledge production, collectively they offer a body of material that provides a panorama of possibilities. They may present an invitation to think about a wider range of activities and frames of reference for seeing ancient Egyptian collections. Incrementally, change might follow.

Sallam, for instance, is hopeful about the longer-term effects of her work. Citing a motivating aspiration for Egyptian archaeologists to reframe and reclaim the Egyptological field, she queried in our interview whether 'we need to follow the same approaches that we learned from the colonial practice'. But, she noted with regret, there is 'a lot of pressure to measure up to the Western standards ... there is no space to reflect critically about the practices when you are all the time trying to reach the Western standard.' In this context, she feels that by addressing the non-Egyptian museum visitor, there may be the power to reshape museum practices, challenge displays and change terminology in the West, which could have positive 'ripple effects' for transformations elsewhere. For this reason, oral narrations of her works have been in English, although Sallam herself acutely recognises the tensions of giving voice to ancient Egyptian works in colonial languages and remains conflicted about doing so. Such tensions and conflicts are part of ongoing conversations and an iterative approach to artistic production, in which artist, curator and scholar engage in experiment and reflection.

*

As I was completing this text in September 2023, I received an enquiry from a small local authority museum in northern England asking whether I could recommend an Egyptian artist whom they might commission as part of their gallery redisplay. The desire for such alternative presentations will continue in numerous forms for a variety of purposes, but there is a risk that institutions fall into a repetitive pattern. By the early 2000s the harnessing of contemporary artistic works in site-specific locales like museums had become an automatic signifier of criticality or progressive programming (Kwon 2002). However, many of the examples in this study suggest that the potential for reflexive engagement requires more than insertion of recent works. Whatever the motivations are for inviting contemporary artists to display work together with ancient material, what I do at least hope to encourage is a sensitivity to the wider contexts, purposes and implications of artistic work with and in collections, rather than just a reiteration of tired soundbites that past and present will somehow 'be in dialogue' as a result. Archaeological context is a restless project of tacking back and forth between artefacts, archives and ideas, with curators navigating multiple histories and facilitating divergent conversations. In that dynamic, there can be space for incorporating artists more directly in discourse than has been the case previously, so as to produce more fluid and complex relationships. Rather than just asking how the ancient informs the modern, or vice versa, it is more relevant to ask how they influence each other, given the mutually constituting frameworks and societal conditions that shape world views. Such experiments may not necessarily give immediate insight into the past and, like any trial, they may not succeed. By the same token, they might elicit new questions, provoke fresh approaches to staid interpretive strategies and release a more flexible space within which to think, reflect and act. But this needs time, respect and communication.

Institutional critique is an important, but blunt tool. While it can expose the frame that has produced how we know art and archaeology, for museums to be serious about inviting contemporary artists for a fresh perspective on collections – and to better stimulate a lasting legacy – there should be investment and support throughout the institution. This requires working across different types of expertise and meaningfully involving permanent members of staff. Museums need, therefore, to consider their capabilities to support artists. Conversations around ethics may be relevant too if commercialisation is to be avoided in favour of a sensitivity to current political situations. Artworks can not only be present in the gallery, but also explored further in allied event programmes, visitor evaluation and documentation.

What is abundantly clear from this review of contemporary art interventions in galleries of ancient Egypt is the continuation of the long-standing Euro-American dominance of international art that Winegar (2006) recognised in the late 1990s and early 2000s Egyptian art scene, and which upholds structures of judgement underpinned by neocolonial framings of non-Western art. However these collaborations are approached, then, institutions need to be mindful not to overstate what artists and interventions can achieve, and to be cognisant of how Egyptian communities and Egyptian artists are engaged, considered or represented. This all requires establishing trust, being open to and giving time to new ways of working, as well as building in reflexivity. In so doing, that much-lauded 'dialogue' between static antiquities and fresh art might become a more animated, nuanced conversation amongst museum professionals, artists and publics from conception to installation, and beyond.

Notes

1 See https://cahncontemporary.com/category/projects-artists/ [Accessed 7 September 2023].

2 Held at the Getty Villa, it showcased the modern works of these artists 'alongside ancient art, continuing a dialogue between the modern and the antique that is still alive today'. https://www.getty.edu/art/exhibitions/modern_antiquity/ [Accessed 11 July 2023].

3 https://www.frieze.com/article/revealing-galleries-and-curators-frieze-london-and-frieze-masters-2023 [Accessed 5 July 2023].

4 https://www.turpsbanana.com/mass-mag [Accessed 2 August 2023].

5 https://issuu.com/drcypher/docs/a130 [Accessed 3 March 2023].

6 British Museum Education Services video (VHS) from 1995, filmed in the gallery during the opening of *Time Machine*. Copy in the possession of James Putnam.

7 https://anja-schindler.com/en/work/der-tod-ist-himmelblau/ [Accessed 18 August 2023].

8 Gantt Center 2022. *Open Air: Artist talk with Jackie Milad.* 13 December 2022. Available at: https://www.youtube.com/watch?v=UFNIbO1ZkJA [Accessed 17 June 2023].

9 Comments by Sara Sallam during a discussion panel for the Egypt Exploration Society, 23 June 2023: https://www.youtube.com/watch?v=RmFRAB2shH4 from 52:24 [Accessed 4 July 2024].

10 Although, in the case of the Museo Egizio, every Egyptian antiquity involved in the exhibition did have its associated record updated to reflect its involvement. This was largely for the needs of location control and it has yet to be tested whether a similar record would be made if the object was not moved from its standard display spot but a contemporary artwork brought to that spot to pair with it.

11 Comments by Putnam during a discussion panel for the Egypt Exploration Society, 23 June 2023: https://www.youtube.com/watch?v=RmFRAB2shH4 from 1:35 [Accessed 4 July 2024].

Appendix
List of interventions discussed in the text

The table that follows is not a comprehensive list of art interventions in ancient Egyptian museum displays, but rather provides a summary of those referenced in the preceding text.

Venue	Exhibition title	Date	Exhibiting artists
Ägyptisches Museum of the Rheinische Friedrich-Wilhelms-Universität Bonn	Der Tod ist Himmelblau	2016	Anja Schindler
Ägyptisches Museum of the Rheinische Friedrich-Wilhelms-Universität Bonn	Re:animation – Aegyptiaca im Dialog mit Zeichnungen und Skulpturen von Ruth Tauchert	2017	Ruth Tauchert
Ashmolean Museum	Unravelled	2017 to present	Angela Palmer
Archaeology Museum of Bologna	Faïence-Faenza: From Ancient Egypt to Contemporary Art	2021–2	Luigi Ontani
Bolton Museum and Art Gallery	From a Modern Land. Ancient Egyptian Textiles: Contemporary Paintings	2007	Ros Ford
Boston Museum of Fine Arts	Odd Spaces	2013	Marilyn Arsem
British Museum	Time Machine: Ancient Egypt and Contemporary Art	1994–5	Stephen Cox, Andy Goldsworthy, David Hiscock, Rita Keegan, Liliane Karnouk, Jiří Kolář, Alexander Mihaylovich, Igor Mitoraj, Marc Quinn, Peter Randall-Page, Martin Riches, Kate Whiteford
British Museum	Collected	1997	Richard Wentworth, Fred Wilson
British Museum	A Sense of Form – Henry Moore at the British Museum	1998	Henry Moore
British Museum	Statuephilia: Contemporary Sculptors at the British Museum	2008–9	Noble and Webster
British Museum	Tutankhamun Reimagined	2022	Nofal O

Egyptian Museum Cairo	Eternal Light: Something Old, Something New	2017	Adam Henein, Adel El-Siwi, Ahmed Morsi, Esmat Dawestashy, Farouk Hosny, Farouk Wahba, Ghada Amer, Hany Rashed, Huda Lutfi, Khaled Hafez, Mohamed Abla, Nazir Tanbouli, Said Badr, Sarwat Al-Bahr, Youssef Nabil, Effat Nagi
Louvre	Contrepoint: l'Art contemporain	2010	William Kentridge
Manchester Museum	Divers Memories: The Company of Things	1996	Katie Maverick McNeel
Manchester Museum	Shabtis: Suspended Truth	2017	Zahed Taj-Eddin
Museum für Byzantinische Kunst	Think Big!	2022–3	Gail Rothschild
Musées royaux d'art et d'histoire	Expéditions d'Égypte	2023	Sara Sallam
Museo Egizio	Les Egyptes Bleues	1987	Henri Maccheroni
Museo Egizio	Time Machine: antico Egitto e arte contemporanea	1995	Francesco Clemente, Stephen Cox, Brian Eno, Andy Goldsworthy, David Hiscock, Jiří Kolář, Igor Mitoraj, Marc Quinn, Mimmo Paladino, Peter Randall-Page and Martin Riches, Kiki Smith, Kan Yasuda
Museo Egizio	Ostrakon: The Memory of Times	2003	Enrico Colombotto Rosso, Camillo Fancia, Riccardo Licata, Giovanni Bonardi
Museo Egizio	Like a Moth to a Flame	2017	Gianni Colombo
Museo Egizio	#EnjoyEternity	2018	Sharon Ritossa
Museo Egizio	Anche le Statue Muoiono (Statues also Die)	2018	Jananne Al-Ani, Morehshin Allahyari Kader Attia, Ali Cherri, Mimmo Jodice, Liz Glynn, Iman Issa, Walid Raad and Simon Wachsmuth
Museo Egizio	Through Tutankhamun's Eyes: Alternative Perspectives on Egyptology	2022	Sara Sallam

Venue	Exhibition title	Date	Exhibiting artists
Petrie Museum	Our Inheritance in the Great Pyramid – God's Cubit	2001	James Putnam/David Wilson
Petrie Museum	Collective Traces	2006	Christie Brown
Petrie Museum	A Storm is Blowing	2013	Cathy Haynes
Petrie Museum	Shabtis: Suspended Truth	2013	Zahed Taj-Eddin
Reiss-Engelhorn-Museen	Zeichen und Wunder	2023	Ugo Dossi
Rijksmuseum van Oudheden	Time and Again Kemet	2023	Wes Mapes, Sara Sallam, Mirjam Linschooten and Sameer Farooq
Saffron Walden Museum	Reimagining Egypt	2013	Khaled Hafez
Sainsbury Centre	Come to Your House	2022	Sara Sallam
Seattle Museum of Art	The Museum: Mixed Metaphors	1993	Fred Wilson
Staatliches Museum Ägyptischer Kunst (Residenz)	Sonnen und Skulpturen	1989	Burkhard Backe
Staatliches Museum Ägyptischer Kunst (Residenz)	Über Leben	1995	Marlies Poss
Staatliches Museum Ägyptischer Kunst (Residenz)	Out of Egypt	1996	James Reineking
Staatliches Museum Ägyptischer Kunst (Residenz)	Zeitzeichen	1997	Traude Linhardt

Staatliches Museum Ägyptischer Kunst	Tea with Nefertiti: The Making of the Artwork by the Artist, the Museum and the Public	2014	Ai Weiwei, Armand (b. Armenak Arzrouni), Mohamad-Said Baalbaki, Taha Belal, Adam Broomberg & Oliver Chanarin, Honoré Daumier, Fouad El Khoury, Mamduh Muhamad Fathallah, Hans-Peter Feldmann, Francis Frith, Georg Frey, Alberto Giacometti, Gilbert & George, Georges Henein, Candida Höfer, Iman Issa, J&K (Janne Schäfer & Kristine Agergaard), Emily Jacir, Brandt Junceau, Ida Kar, William Kentridge, Susanne Kriemann, Little Warsaw (Bálint Havas and András Galik), Maha Maamoun, Luigi Mayer, Lee Miller, Paula Modersohn-Becker, Amedeo Modigliani, Mahmoud Moukhtar, Vik Muniz, Youssef Nabil, Xenia Nikolskaya, Amy Nimr, Lorraine O'Grady, Grayson Perry, David Roberts, Nida Sinnokrot, Thomas Struth, David G. Tretiakoff, Kees van Dongen, Franz Lenbach, Van Leo (b. Alexander Boyadjian), Ala Younis, and Bassem Yousri
Staatliches Museum Ägyptischer Kunst	Begegnungen	2017	Isolde Frepoli
Staatliches Museum Ägyptischer Kunst	Rollenbibliothek	2018	Zygmunt Blazejewski
Staatliches Museum Ägyptischer Kunst	Adam, wo bist du?	2020	Ilana Lewitan
Staatliches Museum Ägyptischer Kunst	Zeichen und Wunder	2021	Ugo Dossi
Staatliches Museum Ägyptischer Kunst	An Egyptian Story	2023	Alaa Awad
Wadsworth Athenaeum	Transfer: The Maintenance of the Art Object	1973	Mierele Laderman Ukeles

References

Abaza, M. 2013. Mourning, narratives and interactions with the Martyrs through Cairo's graffiti. *E-International Relations* 7 October. Available at: http://www.e-ir.info/2013/10/07/mourning-narratives-and-interactions-with-the-martyrs-through-cairos-graffiti/ [Accessed 31 July 2023].

Abd el-Gawad, H. and Stevenson, A. 2023. Egyptian mummified remains: Communities of descent and practice. In Biers, T. and Clary, M. (eds) *Museums, Heritage, and Death*, pp. 238–58. London and New York: Routledge.

Adams, G. K. 2013. In museums they trust. *Museums Journal* 1 April. Available at: https://www.museumsassociation.org/museums-journal/news/2013/04/01042013-news-analysis/ [Accessed 8 July 2024].

Al-Azm, A. and Paul, K. A. 2019. *Facebook's Black Market in Antiquities: Trafficking, terrorism, and war crimes*. ATHAR Project. http://atharproject.org/wp-content/uploads/2019/06/ATHAR-FB-Report-June-2019-final.pdf [Accessed 1 July 2023].

Alberro, A. 2009. Institutions, critique, and institutional critique. In Alberro, A. and Stimson, B. (eds) *Institutional Critique: An anthology of artists' writings*, pp. 2–19. Cambridge: MIT Press.

Al-Maria, S. 2010. A history of Mathaf. In Ellis, A. (ed.) *Sajjil: A century of modern art*, pp. 43–9. Milan: Skira.

Alpers, S. 1991. The museum as a way of seeing. In Karp, I. and Lavin, S. D. (eds) *Exhibiting Cultures: The poetics and politics of museum display*, pp. 25–32. Washington, DC and London: Smithsonian Institution Press.

Ambrosio, C. 2014. Objectivity and visual practices in science and art. In Galavotti, M. C. et al. (eds) *New Directions in the Philosophy of Science*, pp. 353–68. New York: Springer.

American Alliance of Museums. 2021. *Museums and Trust 2021*. Available at: https://www.aam-us.org/2021/09/30/museums-and-trust-2021/#:~:text=Museums%20and%20Trust%202021%20confirms,and%20business%2C%20and%20social%20media [Accessed 13 July 2023].

Anon. 2017. Like a moth to a flame. *ArtReview* 16 May. Available at: https://artreview.com/preview-like-a-moth-to-a-flame-2017-turin/ [Accessed 11 May 2023].

Apollinaire, G. and Guillaume, P. 1972 [1917]. *Sculptures nègres*. New York: Hacker Art Books.

Appiah, K. A. and Wilson, F. 2006. *Fred Wilson: A conversation with K. Anthony Appiah*. New York: Pace Wildenstein.

ArchDaily. 2016. The State Museum of Egyptian Art and The University of Film and Television/Peter Böhm Architekten. *ArchDaily* 7 December. Available at: https://www.archdaily.com/800882/the-state-museum-of-egyptian-art-peter-bohm-architekten [Accessed 27 March 2023].

Arrowsmith, R. R. 2010. *Modernism and the Museum: Asian, African, and Pacific art and the London avant-garde*. Oxford: Oxford University Press.

Artnet News 2017. In Turin for Artissima? Here's what you should see and do while you're there. *ArtNet News* 3 November. Available at: https://news.artnet.com/market/insiders-guide-to-turin-1138403 [Accessed 30 May 2023].

Austin, S. forthcoming. *Tut on Tour: Thirty years of demand creation through exhibition*. PhD thesis, UCL.

Avanzo, D. and Mimmo, S. 2014. *Ommagio a Tutankhamon: L'arte egizia incontra l'arte contemporanea*. Venice: Grafiche Biesse.

Bahrani, Z. 2003. *The Graven Image: Representation in Babylonia and Assyria*. Philadelphia: University of Pennsylvania Press.

Bailey, D. 2017. Disarticulate – repurpose – disrupt: Art/Archaeology. *Cambridge Archaeological Journal* 27(4): 691–701.

Baines, J. 1985. Theories and universals of representation: Heinrich Schäfer and Egyptian art. *Art History* 8(1): 1–25.

Barbero, G. 2003. *Ostrakon: La memoria dei tempi*. Rome: Verso l'Arte Edizioni.
Bardaouil, S. and Fellrath, T. 2014. *Tea with Nefertiti: The making of the artwork by the artist, the museum and the public*. Milan: Skira.
Barrett, J. and Millner, J. 2014. *Australian Artists in the Contemporary Museum*. Farnham: Ashgate.
Belting, H. 2012. Contemporary art and the museum in the global age. *Disputatio: Philosophical Research Bulletin* 1(2):16–30.
Bencard, A., Whiteley, L. and Thon, C. H. 2019. Curating experimental entanglements. In Hansen, M. V., Henningsen, A. F. and Gregersen, A. (eds) *Curatorial Challenges: Interdisciplinary perspectives on contemporary curating*, pp. 133–46. London and New York: Routledge.
Bender, B., Hamilton, S. and Tilley, C. 2007. *Stone Worlds: Narrative and reflexivity in landscape archaeology*. Walnut Creek: Left Coast Press.
Bennett, T. 2006. Exhibition, difference, and the logic of culture. In Karp, I., Kratz, C. A., Szwaja, L. and Ybarra-Frausto, T. (eds) *Museum Frictions: Public cultures/global transformations*, pp. 46–69. Durham, NC: Duke University Press.
Bernal, M. 1987. *Black Athena. The Afroasiatic roots of classical civilization: The fabrication of Ancient Greece 1785–1985*. New Brunswick: Rutgers University Press.
Bertola, C. and Rich, R. 2020. Practising history: Art, archives, and footnotes. In Cass, N., Park, G. and Powell, A. (eds) *Contemporary Art in Heritage Spaces*, pp. 149–65. London and New York: Routledge.
Bestock, L. 2008. The Early Dynastic funerary enclosures of Abydos. *Archéo-Nil* 18: 43–59.
Bevan, R. 1994. A snake in the British Museum. *The Art Newspaper* December.
Bierbrier, M. 2019. *Who Was Who in Egyptology*. Fifth Edition. London: Egypt Exploration Society.
Biro, Y. 2015. African arts between curios, antiquities, and avant-garde at the *Maison Brummer*, Paris (1908–14). *Journal of Art Historiography* 12: 1–15.
Biro, Y. 2023. Innate taste of construction of the gaze: Joseph Brummer and the promotion of the African object as art. In Biro, Y., Brennan, C. E. and Force, C. H. (eds) *The Brummer Galleries, Paris and New York: Defining taste from antiquities to the avant-garde*, pp. 157–85. Leiden: Brill.
Biro, Y., Brennan, C. E. and Force, C. H. (eds) 2023. *The Brummer Galleries, Paris and New York: Defining taste from antiquities to the avant-garde*. Leiden: Brill.
Bjerregaard, P. (ed.) 2019. *Exhibitions as Research: Experimental methods in museums*. London and New York: Routledge.
Black, N., Burton, A., Cass, N., Farley, R., King, J. Newman, A. and Pollock, V. 2020. *Mapping Contemporary Art in the Heritage Experience*. Newcastle: University of Newcastle.
Bodenstein, F. 2011. National museums in Belgium. In Aronsson, P. and Elgenius, G. (eds) *Building National Museums in Europe 1750–2010: Conference proceedings from EuNaMus, European National Museums: Identity politics, the uses of the past and the European citizen, Bologna 28–30 April 2011*, pp. 47–68. EuNaMus Report No 1. Linköping: Linköping University Electronic Press.
Bothmer, B. V. 1978. On photographing Egyptian art. *Studien zur Altägyptischen Kultur* 6: 51–3.
Bracewell, M. 1996. Past, but not gone. *The Independent* 9 April.
Bragg, M. 2013. My friend Francis Bacon, possessed by devils. *The Telegraph* 15 November.
Breger, C. 2006. The 'Berlin' Nefertiti bust: Imperial fantasies in twentieth-century German archaeological discourse. In Schulte, R. (ed.) *The Body of the Queen: Gender and rule in the courtly world 1500–2000*, pp. 281–305. New York: Berghahn Books.
Brown, C. 2006. Collective traces. *Ceramics Technical* 23: 3–10.
Brown, N. 2022. The use of ancient Egypt in contemporary art. In Candelora, D., Ben-Marzouk, N. and Cooney, K. M. (eds) *Ancient Egyptian Society: Challenging assumptions, exploring approaches*, pp. 210–22. London and New York: Routledge.
Bru, S. 2024. Avant-garde Egypt: Introducing the avant-garde in the longue durée. *Journal of Avant-Garde Studies* 4(1): 1–12.
Buchloh, B. 1990. Conceptual art 1962–1969: From the aesthetic of administration of the critique of institutions. *October* 55: 105–43.
Buck, L. 2016. The buck stopped here: Too much nostalgia on Sir Norman's watch. *Evening Standard* 21 January. Available at: https://www.theartnewspaper.com/2016/01/21/the-buck-stopped-here-too-much-nostalgia-on-sir-normans-watch [Accessed 2 February 2023].
Burney, B. and Underwood, L. 1932. *Sculpture Considered Apart from Time and Place*. London: Sydney Burney Gallery.

Calderoni, I. 2018. Anche le statue muoiono. In Ciccopiedi, C., Del Vesco, P. and Greco, C. (eds) *Statues Also Die: Destruction and preservation in ancient and modern times*, pp. 64–71. Turin: Museo Egizio.

Callahan, S. 2022. *Art + Archive: Understanding the archival turn in contemporary art*. Manchester: Manchester University Press.

Capart, J. 1905. *Primitive Art in Egypt*. London: Grevel & Co.

Carruthers, W. 2015. What we are talking about when we talk about Tutankhamun's beard. *The Max Weber Programme Blog*. Available at: https://blogs.eui.eu/maxweberprogramme/what-we-are-talking-about-when-we-talk-about-tutankhamuns-beard/ [Accessed 11 April 2023].

Carruthers, W. 2022. On Egyptological anniversaries. Available at: https://williamcarruthers.wordpress.com/2023/01/05/on-egyptological-anniversaries/#comments [Accessed 10 May 2023].

Cass, N., Park, G. and Powell, A. 2020. Introduction. In Cass, N., Park, G. and Powell, A. (eds) *Contemporary Art in Heritage Spaces*, pp. 1–11. London and New York: Routledge.

Challis, D. 2013. Creating typecasts: Exhibiting eugenic ideas from the past today. *Museum Management and Curatorship* 28(1): 15–33.

Challis, D. and Romain, G. 2014. Ancient Egypt: Culture and 'barbarism'. In Challis, D. and Romain, G. *A Fusion of Worlds*. Available at: https://www.ucl.ac.uk/equiano-centre/educational-resources/fusion-worlds/context/ancient-egypt-culture-and-barbarism [Accessed 25 August 2022].

Charles, F. 2023. Expéditions d'Égypte: Deux siècles d'aventure égyptologie belge au Musée d'art et d'histoire. *Culturius Magazine* 4 April.

Childs, S. T. 2022. Finding space to store archaeological collections: Challenges and progress in the United States. In Stevenson, A. (ed.) *The Oxford Handbook of Museum Archaeology*, pp. 221–46. Oxford: Oxford University Press.

Christophilopoulou, A. 2023. On *Dark Water, Burning World*: A collaboration with artist Issam Kourbaj. In Macmillan, L. (ed.) *Dark Water, Burning World: Issam Kourbaj*. Llandysul: Gomer Press.

Ciccopiedi, C. and Del Vesco, P. 2021. Reflecting on the exhibition Anche le Statue Muoiono. In Ciccopiedi, C., Del Vesco, P. and Greco, C. (eds) *Anche le Statue Muoiono: Conflitto e patrimonio tra antico e contemporaneo*, pp. 26–44. Turin: Museo Egizio.

Ciccopiedi, C., Del Vesco, P. and Greco, C. (eds) 2021. *Anche le Statue Muoiono: Conflitto e patrimonio tra antico e contemporaneo*. Turin: Museo Egizio.

Clifford, J. 1988. *The Predicament of Culture: Twentieth-century ethnography, literature, and art*. Cambridge, MA: Harvard University Press.

Close, C. 1994. Kiki Smith. *Bomb Magazine* 49. Available at https://bombmagazine.org/articles/kiki-smith-1/ [Accessed 4 July 2023].

Coblence, E. and Sabatier, V. 2014. Articulating growth and cultural innovation in art museums: The Louvre's business model revision. *International Studies of Management and Organization* 44(4): 9–25.

Cochrane, A. and Russell, I. 2007. Visualizing archaeologies: A manifesto. *Cambridge Archaeological Journal* 17(1): 3–19.

Cohen, D. 1994. A bridge across the centuries. *The Daily Telegraph* 3 December: 16.

Cook, M. and van Riemsdijk, M. 2014. Agents of memorialization: Gunter Demnig's *Stolpersteine* and the individual (re-)creation of a Holocaust landscape in Berlin. *Journal of Historical Geography* 43: 138–47.

Coolidge, C. 2016. Mixing modern art with antiquities. *PENTA* 26 March. https://www.barrons.com/articles/mixing-modern-art-with-antiquities-1458967055 [Accessed 5 January 2022].

Corrin, L. 1993. Mining the Museum: An installation confronting history. *Curator* 36(4): 302–13.

Crane, S. A. 1997. Memory, distortion, and history in the museum. *History and Theory* 36(4): 44–63.

Crane, S. A. 2000. Introduction: Of museums and memory. In Crane, S. A. (ed.) *Museums and Memory*, pp. 1–17. Palo Alto: Stanford University Press.

Crooke, E. 2021. Participation, trust, and telling difficult histories in museums. In Black, G. (ed.) *Museums and the Challenge of Change: Old institutions in a new world*, pp. 113–22. London and New York: Routledge.

Cummings, E. 2016. A curatorial dilemma: An examination of temporary exhibitions combining African and Egyptian visual culture. *Journal of Ancient Egyptian Interconnections* 8: 21–5.
Deliss, C. (ed.) 2012. *Object Atlas: Fieldwork in the museum*. Bielefeld, Germany: Kerber.
Deliss, C. 2020. Against the monodisciplinarity of ethnographic museums. In von Oswald, M. and Tinius, J. (eds) *Across Anthropology: Troubling colonial legacies, museums, and the curatorial*, pp. 130–41. Leuven: Leuven University Press.
Deliss, C. 2021. Recasting the civic imperative of the museum. *Museum* November–December: 26–31.
Deliss, C. and Sokołowska, J. 2014. Postcolonial Museum Laboratory: Clémentine Deliss in conversation with Joanna Sokołowska. *View: Theories and Practices of Visual Culture* 7. https://doi.org/10.36854/widok/2014.7.1431.
Delley, G. and Schlanger, N. 2022. Recovering the history of archaeology in museums. In Stevenson, A. (ed.) *The Oxford Handbook of Museum Archaeology*, pp. 29–44. Oxford: Oxford University Press.
Delvaux, L. and Van Caelenberge, E. 2023. *Expéditions d'Egypte: Histoires d'une collection*. Bruxelles: Ludion and Musées royaux d'art et d'histoire.
Del Vesco, P. 2016. Museo Egizio: Framing archaeological context. *Egyptian Archaeology* 48: 14–19.
Dercon, C., Bardaouil, S., Fellrath, T., Schoske, S. and Wildung, D. 2014. Nofretete – tête-à-tête: An inquiry into the rethink of exhibitions. In Bardouil, S. and Fellrath, T. (eds) *Tea with Nefertiti: The making of the artwork by the artist, the museum and the public*, pp. 21–45. Milan: Skira.
Desai, D. 2002. The ethnographic move in contemporary art: What does it mean for art education? *Studies in Art Education* 43(4): 307–23.
Devey, R. 2007. Art and ancient artefacts bring Egypt to life. *The Bolton News* 2 March. Available at: https://www.theboltonnews.co.uk/news/1232595.art-and-ancient-artefacts-bring-egypt-to-life/ [Accessed 19 January 2023].
Die Werft. n.d. State Museum of Egyptian Art. Die Werft website. Available at: http://www.diewerft.com/en/projects/state-museum-of-egyptian-art.html [Accessed 6 April 2023].
Dilenschneider, C. 2023. More people trust museums now than before the pandemic (data). Available at: https://www.colleendilen.com/2023/03/01/more-people-trust-museums-now-than-before-the-pandemic-data/#:~:text=The%20rate%20at%20which%20museums,compared%20to%20before%20the%20pandemic [Accessed 3 December 2023].
Dittgen, N. 2022. Museale Interventionen als Aktualitätsbeschleuniger – Am Beispiel des Badischen Landesmuseums. *Kulturelle Bildung Online*. Available at: https://www.kubi-online.de/artikel/museale-interventionen-aktualitaetsbeschleuniger-beispiel-des-badischen-landesmuseums [Accessed 28 June 2023].
Donadoni, A. M. 2006. Anna Maria Donadoni and the Egyptian Museum. *Archaeologia* 30 February. Available at: http://www.antikitera.net/news.asp?ID=7396&TAG=Antico%20Egitto&page=44 [Accessed 12 September 2023].
Dorsett, C. 1995. Clues on an artistic trail. *Museums Journal* May: 32–3.
Drower, M. 1985. *Flinders Petrie: A life in archaeology*. London: Victor Gollancz.
Dubrovsky, N. and Graeber, D. 2019. Another art word. Part 1: Art communism and artificial scarcity. *E-Flux Journal* 102: September. Available at: https://www.e-flux.com/journal/102/284624/another-art-world-part-1-art-communism-and-artificial-scarcity/ [Accessed 3 March 2024].
Elias, C. 2019. Whose digital heritage? Contemporary art, 3D printing and limits of cultural property. *Third Text* 33(6): 687–707.
Elnozahy, M. 2021. Forever is now, on the art of Art D'Égypte. *Mada Masr* 20 October. Available at: https://www.madamasr.com/en/2021/10/20/feature/culture/forever-is-now-on-the-art-of-art-degypte/ [Accessed 21 April 2024].
Ess, X. 2023. 'Expéditions d'Égypte', un flas-back au pays des Pharaons à voir au Musée Art & Histoire. *RTBF* 17 April. Available at: https://www.rtbf.be/article/expeditions-degypte-un-flash-back-au-pays-des-pharaons-a-voirau-musee-art-histoire-11183704 [Accessed 7 July 2023].
Étienne, M. 2021. Giacometti and the art of ancient Egypt: The facets of a gaze. In Pautot, T., Perrin, R. and Étienne, M. (eds) *Alberto Giacometti et L'Égypte Antique*, pp. 31–52. Paris: FAGE Édition.
Evans, C. 2004. Unearthing displacement: Surrealism and the 'archaeology' of Paul Nash. In Renfrew, C., Gosden, C. and DeMarrais, E. (eds) *Substance, Memory, Display: Archaeology and art*, pp. 103–18. Cambridge: McDonald Institute of Archaeology.

Evans, J. M. 2012. *The Lives of Sumerian Sculpture: An archaeology of the Early Dynastic temple*. Cambridge: Cambridge University Press.

Falk, J. H. and Dierking, L. D. 2013. *The Museum Experience Revisited*. Walnut Creek, CA: Left Coast Press.

Feaver, W. 1994. Art. *The Observer* 18 December.

Feist, A. and Hutchinson, R. (eds) 1989. *Cultural Trends 1989*. London: Policy Studies Institute.

Ferrari, A. 2022. Modernism and ancient Egypt: Harlem, Paris and London. In Ferrari, A. and Hinson, B. (eds) *Visions of Ancient Egypt*, pp. 112–23. Norwich: Sainsbury Centre for Visual Arts.

Ferrari, A. and Hinson, B. (eds) 2022. *Visions of Ancient Egypt*. Norwich: Sainsbury Centre for Visual Arts.

Ferri, M. 2021. L'arte contemporanea nei musei 'classici', Strinati: 'Modernità e antico non sono in antitesi, ma possono generare potenti suggestioni'. *FQ magazine* 25 July. Available at: https://www.ilfattoquotidiano.it/2021/07/25/larte-contemporanea-nei-musei-classici-strinati-modernita-e-antico-non-sono-in-antitesi-ma-possono-generare-potenti-suggestioni/6270655/#:~:text=Diciamo%20che%20l'idea%20della,contemporanea%20di%20arti%20e%20filosofia.%20 [Accessed 5 June 2023].

Fisher, J. (ed.) 1994. *Global Visions: Towards a new internationalism in the visual arts*. London: Kala Press.

Force, C. H. 2023. Picassos at 'Brummer Frères – curiosités' and beyond: From Frank Burty Haviland's collection to John Quinn's. In Biro, Y., Brennan, C. E. and Force, C. H. (eds) *The Brummer Galleries, Paris and New York: Defining taste from antiquities to the avant-garde*, pp. 186–231. Leiden: Brill.

Förster, F. 2017a. Anja Schindler: Der Tod is Himmelblau: Moderne Kunst in den Sammlungen des Ägyptischen Museums 26 Oktober 2016 bis 23 April 2017. *Amun: Magazin für die Freunde Ägyptischer Museen und Sammlungen* 54: 41–64.

Förster, F. 2017b. *Re:animation: Aegyptiaca im Dialog mit Zeichnungen und Skulpturen von Ruth Tauchert: Ägyptisches Museum Bonn*. Bonn: Universität Bonn.

Foster, H. 1996. *The Return of the Real: The avant-garde at the end of the century* (An October Book). Cambridge: MIT Press.

Foster, H. 2004. An archival impulse. *October* 110: 3–22.

Frankfort, H. 1932. On Egyptian art. *Journal of Egyptian Archaeology* 18: 33–48.

Frankfort, H. 1935. New works by Barbara Hepworth. *Axis: A Quarterly Review of Contemporary 'Abstract' Painting and Sculpture* 3: 14–18.

Franklin, A, 2019. *Anti-Museum*. London and New York: Routledge.

Fraser, A. 2005. From the critique of institutions to an institution of critique. *Artforum* 44(1): 154–60.

Fredheim, L. H. 2020. Decoupling 'open' and 'ethical' archaeologies: Rethinking deficits and expertise for ethical public participation in archaeology and heritage. *Norwegian Archaeological Review* 53(1): 5–22.

Frost, S. 2019. A bastion of colonialism. *Third Text* 33: 4–5, 487–99.

Fry, R. 1920. Modern paintings in a collection of ancient art. *The Burlington Magazine for Connoisseurs* 37(213): 303–9.

Gallo, F. and Storini, M. C. 2018. *Antico e contemporaneo: Sguardi, prospettive, riflessioni nterdisciplinari all fine della modernità*. Rome: Sapienza University Press.

Gange, D. 2015. The ruins of preservation: Conserving ancient Egypt 1880–1914. *Past Present* 226(10): 78–99.

Gardner, A. and Kleinitz, C. 2000. Interview with Dr Robert Anderson, Director of the British Museum. *Papers from the Institute of Archaeology* 11: 7–16.

Garnett, A. 2021. The Petries and the Pre-Raphaelites: Hilda Urlin and Henry Holiday. *Papers from the Institute of Archaeology* 30(1): 1–30.

Geismar, H. 2015. The art of anthropology: Questioning contemporary art in ethnographic display. In Witcomb, A. and Message, K. (eds) *The International Handbooks of Museum Studies. Volume 1: Museum Theory*, pp. 183–210. Chichester: Wiley and Sons.

Geismar, H. 2018. *Museum Object Lessons for the Digital Age*. London: UCL Press.

Gell, A. 1996. Vogel's net: Traps as artworks and artworks as traps. *Journal of Material Culture* 1(1): 15–38.

Gell, A. 1998. *Art and Agency*. Oxford: Oxford University Press.

Gheorghiu, D. 2009. *Artchaeology: A sensorial approach to the materiality of the past*. Bucharest: UNArte.

Giannini, F. 2022. Quando l'arte contemporanea invade gli spazi antichi. *Finestre sull'Arte* 11 August. Available at: https://www.finestresullarte.info/opinioni/quando-l-arte-contemporanea-invade-gli-spazi-antichi [Accessed 5 June 2023].

Gilli, M. 2015. From 'industrial Turin' to 'touristic Turin': Strategies for urban repositioning. In Ineson, E., Smith, M. and Nita, V. (eds) *International Case Studies for Hospitality, Tourism and Event Management Students and Trainees*, pp. 100–6. Iaşi: Editura Technopress.

Giraud, C. 2018. Egizio, Fondazione Sandretto, Musei Reali: A Torino grande mostra diffusa sul patrimonio in rovina. *Artribue* 17 March. Available at: https://www.artribune.com/arti-visive/archeologia-arte-antica/2018/03/egizio-fondazione-sandretto-musei-reali-a-torino-grande-mostra-diffusa-sul-patrimonio-in-rovina/ [Accessed 12 May 2023].

Globus, D. (ed.) 2011. *Fred Wilson: A critical reader*. London: Ridinghouse.

Godfrey, M. 2007. The artist as historian. *October* 120: 140–72.

González, J. 2001. Against the grain: The artist as conceptual materialist. In Berger, M. (ed.) *Fred Wilson: Objects and installations 1979–2000*, pp. 22–31. Baltimore: University of Maryland.

González, J. 2011. Fred Wilson: Material museology. In Globus, J. (ed.) *Fred Wilson: A critical reader*, pp. 326–73. London: Ridinghouse.

Griffiths, R. 1993. The politics of cultural policy in urban regeneration strategies. *Policy and Politics* 21(1): 39–46.

Groys, B. 2009. Politics of installation. *e-flux Journal* 2. Available at https://www.e-flux.com/journal/02/68504/politics-of-installation/ [Accessed 21 June 2023].

Guerra, M. 2021. Feeling home, promoting home: Cultural heritage, community building and participatory tourism in Barriera di Milano (Turin, Italy). In Condevaux, A., Gravari-Barbas, M. and Guinand, S. (eds) *Tourism Dynamics in Everyday Places*, pp. 98–115. London: Routledge.

Habsburg-Lothringen, B. 2015. From object to environment: The recent history of exhibitions in Germany and Austria. In Message, K. (ed.) *The International Handbook of Museum Studies: Media*, pp. 327–47. Chichester: John Wiley & Sons.

Hall, J. 1994. About time. *The Guardian* 5 December: 5–6.

Hamilakis, Y. 2014. *Archaeology and the Senses: Human experience, memory, and affect*. Cambridge: Cambridge University Press.

Hanna, M. 2013. What has happened to Egyptian heritage after the 2011 unfinished revolution? *Journal of Eastern Mediterranean Archaeology & Heritage Studies* 1(4): 371–5.

Hansen, M. V., Henningsen, A. F. and Gregersen, A. 2019. Introduction: Thinking and doing exhibitions. In Hansen, M. V., Henningsen, A. F. and Gregersen, A. (eds) *Curatorial Challenges: Interdisciplinary perspectives on contemporary curating*, pp. 1–5. London and New York: Routledge.

Hardwick, T. 2011. Five months before Tut: Purchasers and prices at the MacGregor sale, 1922. *Journal of the History of Collections* 32(1): 179–92.

Hardwick, T. 2023. Pioneers or followers? The Brummer brothers and Egyptian art, 1910–1922. In Biro, Y., Brennan, C. E. and Force, C. H. (eds) *The Brummer Galleries, Paris and New York: Defining taste from antiquities to the avant-garde*, pp. 265–98. Leiden: Brill.

Hawkins, H. 2011. Dialogues and doings: Sketching the relationships between geography and art. *Geography Compass* 5(7): 464–78.

Hegenbart, S. 2024. Introduction: Collaborating cultures, negotiating identities. In Hegenbart, S. (ed.) *Curating Transcultural Spaces: Perspectives on postcolonial conflicts in museum culture*, pp. 1–24. London: Bloomsbury.

Herzer, H., Schocke, S., Wedewer, R. and Wildung, D. 1986. *Ägyptische und moderne Skulptur*. Munich: Lipp.

Heylen, E. 2023. Histoire: Quand l'ancien cotoie le contemporain. *Marie Claire* April: 100.

Hilton, T. 1994. The British Museum has persuaded 12 artists to come up with modern responses to ancient Egyptian sculpture: Why? *The Independent on Sunday* 11 December.

Ho, K. 2023. Tracey Emin becomes first woman artist appointed British Museum trustee. *Art News* 15 November. Available at: https://www.artnews.com/art-news/news/tracey-emin-becomes-first-woman-artist-appointed-british-museum-trustee-1234686940/ [Accessed 17 November 2023].

Hockney, D. and Stangos, N. (eds) 1993. *That's the Way I See It: David Hockney*. London: Thames and Hudson.

Holbraad, M. and Pedersen, M. 2017. *The Ontological Turn: An anthropological exposition*. Cambridge: Cambridge University Press.

Howley, K. 2020. The materiality of shabtis: Figurines over four millennia. *Cambridge Archaeological Journal* 30(1): 123–40.

Humbert, J-M., Pantazzi, M. and Ziegler, C. 1994. *Egyptomania: Egypt in Western art, 1730–1930*. Ottowa: National Gallery of Canada.

James, P. 1992. *Henry Moore on Sculpture*. New York: Da Capo. First Edition 1967.

James, T. G. H. 1985. *Egyptian Painting and Drawing*. London: British Museum.

Janik, L. 2020. *The Archaeology of Seeing: Science and interpretation, the past and contemporary visual art*. London and New York: Routledge.

Johns, R. 2022. Riley in Cairo: British art and Egypt in the 1980s. *Art History* 45(3): 650–72.

Jones, A. and MacGregor, G. 2002. Introduction: Wonderful things – colour studies in archaeology from Munsell to materiality. In Jones, A. and MacGregor, G. (eds) *Colouring the Past*, pp. 1–22. Oxford: Berg.

Jung, P. and Wildung, D. (eds) 2008. *5000 Jahre Afrika, Ägypten, Afrika: Sammlung W. und U. Horstmann und Staatliche Museen zu Berlin*. Berlin: Kettler Verlag.

Junge, F. 1990. Anhang: Harmonie und Dissonanz: Überlegungen zu den materialen Zügen ägyptischer Ästhetik und zur Vergleichbarkeit ägyptischer mit moderner Skulptur. In Eaton-Krauss, M. and Graefe, E. (eds) *Studien zur ägyptischen Kunstgeschichte*, pp. 26–38. Hildesheim: Gerstenberg Verlag.

Kapur, G. 1994. A new inter nationalism: The missing hyphen. In Fisher, J. (ed.) *Global Visions: Towards a new internationalism in the visual arts*, pp. 39–49. London: Kala Press.

Karnouk, L. 2005. *Modern Egyptian Art 1910–2003*. Cairo: The American University Press in Cairo.

Kennedy, L. 2021. Who and what narratives are on display? In Dalal-Clayton, A. and Puri Purini, I. (eds) *Doing the Work: Embedding anti-racism and decolonisation into museum practice*, pp. 22–41. London: University of the Arts London.

Kent, S. 1995. Art preview: A show in ruins. *Time Out* 18–25 January.

Kentridge, W. 2010. *Carnets d'Égypte*. Paris: Éditions Dilecta.

Kester, G. 2005. Conversation pieces: The role of dialogue in socially-engaged art. In Kucor, Z. and Leung, S. (eds) *Theory in Contemporary Art Since 1985*, pp. 76–100. Oxford: Blackwell.

Khalil, M. 2020. André Lhote and Egypt. In Kuban, Z. and Wille, S. (eds) *André Lhote and his International Students*, pp. 171–88. Innsbruck: Innsbruck University Press.

Khan, N. 1976. *The Arts Britain Ignores: The arts of ethnic minorities in Britain*. London: Arts Council of Great Britain.

Kholeif, O. 2014. Walk like an Egyptian? *Art Monthly* November: 5–8.

Kiilerich, B. 2021. The classical in contemporary art and visual culture. *Classical Art and Archaeology* 8: 1–12.

Klemm, C. and Wildung, D. 2008. *Giacometti, der Ägypter: Ausstellung der Staatlichen Museen zu Berlin, Altes Museum und Ägyptisches Museum und Papyrussammlung vom 29. Oktober 2008 bis 31. Dezember*. Munich: Deutscher Kunstverlag.

Knappett, C. 2006. Beyond skin: Layering and networking in art and archaeology. *Cambridge Archaeological Journa*l 16(2): 239–51.

Konijn, F. 1993. A universal language of art: Two exhibitions of non-Western art in Dutch museums of modern art. In Leyten, H. and Damen, B. (eds) *Art, Anthropology and the Modes of Representation*, pp. 23–30. Amsterdam: Royal Tropical Institute.

Kosmadaki, P. 2017. The archaic. In Holmes, B. and Joannou, D. (eds) *Liquid Antiquity*, pp. 100–3. Athens: Koenig Books.

Kosmadaki, P. 2021. The past is present: Curating multi-temporality: Contemporary art and the classical. *Classical Art and Archaeology* 8: 1–32.

Krauss, R. 1979. Sculpture in the expanding field. *October* 8: 30–44.

Krauss, R. 2000. *A Voyage on the North Sea: Art in the age of the post-medium condition*. New York: Thames & Hudson.

Küster, B. 2022. Aspekte der Positioniertheit Interventionen zeitgenössischer Künstler*innen in ethnologischen Sammlungen aus kunstwissenschaftlicher Sicht. *21: Inquiries into Art, History, and the Visual* 3(1): 127–56.

Kwon, M. 2002. *One Place after Another: Site-specific art and locational identity*. Cambridge, MA: MIT Press.

La, K. C. 2017. Object to project: Artists' interventions in museum collections. In Marshall, C. R. (ed.) *Sculpture and the Museum*, pp. 217–39. London and New York: Routledge.
La Nasa, J., Degano, I., Modugno, F., Guerrini, C., Facchetti, F., Turina, V., Carretta, A., Greco, C., Ferraris, E., Colombini, M. P. and Ribechini, E. 2022. Archaeology of the invisible: The scent of Kha and Merit. *Journal of Archaeological Science* 141: 1–14.
La Rue, H. 1995. Listening to the dialogue. *Museums Journal* May: 33.
Lancaster, P. 1995. A 20th century time machine. *The Middle East* 1 February.
Larceneux, F., Caro, F. and Krebs, A. 2016. The reaction of visitors to contemporary art in a classical art institution: A Louvre Museum case study. *International Journal of Arts Management* 18(2): 4–13.
Lee, D. 1995. Interview with Andy Goldsworthy. *Art Review* February.
Lehrer, E. 2020. Material kin: 'Communities of implication' in post-colonial, post-Holocaust Polish ethnographic collections. In von Oswald, M. and Tinius, J. (eds) *Across Anthropology: Troubling colonial legacies, museums, and the curatorial*, pp. 289–323. Leuven: Leuven University Press.
Levitt, P. 2015. *Artifacts and Allegiances: How museums put the nation and the world on display*. Berkeley: University of California Press.
Lichtenberg, L. 2023. De Egyptische topcollectie van Brussel. *Archaeologie Magazine* 6 June: 22–7.
Lonetree, A. 2012. *Decolonizing Museums: Representing Native America in national and tribal museums*. Chapel Hill: University of North Carolina Press.
Lorente, J. P. 2011. *The Museums of Contemporary Art*. Farnham: Ashgate.
Lucie-Smith, E. 1964. The functional art of tribal Africa. *The Times* 17 November: 5.
Lytton, C. 2023. Should the ancient Egyptian mummies in our museums really be on display? *The Telegraph* 5 February.
Macaluso, S. 2018. Antico e contemporaneo: Ricostruzione e salvaguardia della memoria. 'Anche le statue muoiono'. *Arte e Arti* 27 March. Available at: https://www.artearti.net/mostre/anche-le-statue-muoiono [Accessed 12 May 2024].
Macdonald, S. 2002. *Behind the Scenes at the Science Museum*. Oxford: Berg.
Macdonald, S. 2005. Accessing audiences: Visiting visitor books. *Museum and Society* 3(3): 119–36.
Macdonald, S. and Basu, P. (eds) 2007. *Exhibition Experiments*. Oxford: Blackwell.
MacGregor, N. 2010. *A History of the World in 100 Objects*. London: Penguin.
MacRitchie, L. 1994. Artists respond to ancient Egypt. *Financial Times* 6 December: 17.
Mahler, L. 2019. Fechheimer, Hedwig Jenny (born Brühl; also Hedwig Simon). *The Modern Art Index Project* (June), Leonard A. Lauder Research Center for Modern Art, The Metropolitan Museum of Art. https://doi.org/10.57011/YPXY9648.
Malbert, R. 1995. Artists as curators. *Museums Journal* May: 25–6.
Málek, J. 1999. *Egyptian Art*. London: Phaidon.
Malraux, A. 1947. *Le Musée l'art pour l'art*. Geneva: Skira.
Marsching, J. D. and Polli, A. (eds) 2012. *Far Field: Digital culture, climate change, and the Poles*. Chicago: Chicago University Press.
Marshall, C. 2005. When worlds collide: The contemporary museum as art gallery. In MacLeod, S. (ed.) *Reshaping Museum Space: Architecture, design, exhibition*, pp. 170–84. London and New York: Routledge.
Marshall, C. 2012. Ghosts in the machine: The artistic intervention as a site of museum collaboration-accommodation in recent curatorial practice. *The International Journal of the Inclusive Museum* 4(2): 65–80.
Marstine, J. 2013. Situated revelations: Radical transparency in the museum. In Marstine, J., Bauer, A. A. and Haines, C. (eds) *New Directions in Museum Ethics*, pp. 1–23. London and New York: Routledge.
Marstine, J. 2017. *Critical Practice: Artists, museums, ethics*. London and New York: Routledge.
McGavran, S. A. 2013. *Modernist Orientalisms: Klee, Matisse, and North Africa, c. 1906–1930*. PhD thesis, Washington University in St Louis.
McLeod, M. (ed.) 1985. *Lost Magic Kingdoms*. London: British Museum.
McShine, K. L. 1999. *The Museum as Muse: Artists reflect*. New York: Museum of Modern Art.
Mellor, D. 1995. *David Hiscock*. London: Zelda Cheatle.
Merriman, N. 2004. Involving the public in museum archaeology. In Merriman, N. (ed.) *Public Archaeology*, pp. 85–108. London: Routledge.

Meskell, L. 2005. *Object Worlds in Ancient Egypt: Material biographies past and present*. Oxford and New York: Berg.
Meyers, J. 2000. The functional site; or, The transformation of site specificity. In Suderburg, E. (ed.) *Space, Site, Intervention: Situating installation art*, pp. 23–37. Minneapolis: University of Minnesota Press.
Mithen, S. 2004. Contemporary Western art and archaeology. In Renfrew, C., Gosden, C. and DeMarrais, E. (eds) *Substance, Memory, Display: Archaeology and art*, pp. 153–62. Cambridge: McDonald Institute of Archaeology.
Moiso, B. 2016. *La storia del Museo Egizio*. Modena: Franco Cosimo Panini.
Monroe, J.W. 2018. The market as 'artist': The French origins of the obsession with provenance in historical African art. *Critical Interventions* 12(1): 52–70.
Montserrat, D. 2000. *Akhenaten: History, fantasy and ancient Egypt*. London and New York: Routledge.
Moore, H. 1982. *Henry Moore at the British Museum*. London: H. N. Abrams.
Moreno García, J. 2015. The cursed discipline? The peculiarities of Egyptology at the turn of the twenty-first century. In Carruthers, W. (ed.) *Histories of Egyptology: Interdisciplinary measures*, pp. 50–63. London: Routledge.
Moriarty, C. and Weight, A. 2008. The legacy of interaction: Artists at the Imperial War Museum 1981–2007. *Tate Papers* Spring. Available at: https://cris.brighton.ac.uk/ws/files/213570/MoriartyTatePaper.pdf [Accessed 3 September 2023].
Morris, J. 2023. What does the future hold for the antiquities trade? *Apollo* March. Available at: https://www.apollo-magazine.com/antiquities-collectors-art-market-provenance/ [Accessed 11 July 2023].
Morris Hargreaves McIntyre 2009. *'Where We Are Now, Where Have We Come From': Visitor responses to Statuephilia: Contemporary sculptors at the British Museum*. Manchester: Morris Hargreaves McIntyre.
Moser, S. 2006. *Wondrous Curiosities: Ancient Egypt at the British Museum*. London and Chicago: University of Chicago Press.
Moser, S. 2010. The devil is in the detail. *Museum Anthropology* 33(1): 22–32.
Moser, S. 2015a. Reconstructing ancient worlds: Reception studies, archaeological representation and the interpretation of ancient Egypt. *Journal of Archaeological Method and Theory* 22: 1263–308.
Moser, S. 2015b. Legacies of engagement. In Carruthers, W. (ed.) *Histories of Egyptology*, pp. 19–32. Abingdon and New York: Routledge.
Moser, S. 2020. *Painting Antiquity: Ancient Egypt and the art of Lawrence Alma-Tadema, Edward Poynter and Edwin Long*. Oxford: Oxford University Press.
Mossetto, G. and Vecco, M. 2001. Modelli di musei e la loro evoluzione. In Mossetto, G. and Valentino, P. A. (eds) *Museo contro museo: Le strategie, gli strumenti, i risultati*, pp. 3–14. Milan: Giunti Editore.
NCCPE 2021. *What Works: Artist and researcher collaborations*. Bristol: National Co-ordinating Centre for Public Engagement.
Niemojewski, R. 2021. *Biennials: The exhibitions we love to hate*. London: Lund Humphries Publishers.
Noordegraaf, J. 2004. *Strategies of Display: Museum presentation in nineteenth- and twentieth-century visual culture*. Rotterdam: NAi Publishers Rotterdam.
Nyord, R. 2018. Taking ancient Egyptian mortuary religion seriously: Why would we, and how could we? *Journal of Ancient Egyptian Interconnections* 17: 73–87.
O'Doherty, B. 1986. *Inside the White Cube*. San Francisco: Lapis Press.
Ovenden, C. A. 2003. *Towards Understanding the Experiential Meanings of Primary School Children's Encounters with Ancient Egyptian Objects*. PhD thesis, UCL.
Paglieri, M. 1995. Artisti di oggi pazzi dell Egitto. *La Repubblica* 11 December.
Palmer, A. 2008. *Angela Palmer: Unravelled – The Journey of an Egyptian Child Mummy and Other Portraits*. London: Waterhouse & Dodd.
Parcak, S., Gathings, D., Childs, C., Mumford, G. and Cline, E. 2016. Satellite evidence of archaeological site looting in Egypt: 2002–2013. *Antiquity* 90: 188–205.
Pautot, T. et al. 2021. *Alberto Giacometti et l'Égypte antique*. Paris: FAGE Éditions.
Pearce, S. 1999. Presenting archaeology. In Merriman, N. (ed.) *Making Early Histories in Museums*, pp. 12–27. London: Leicester University Press.
Penzel, A. 2022. Versteckte / Verdeckte Geschichten Interventionen im Museum. *Museum Heute* 61: 30–1.

Petrie, W. M. F. 1904. *Methods and Aims in Archaeology*. London: MacMillan and Co.
Petrie, W. M. F. 1910. The lighting of picture galleries. *The Museums Journal* 10(8): 54–5.
Petrie, W. M. F. 1911. *The Revolutions of Civilisation*. Goring-by-Sea: Harper and Brothers.
Petrie, W. M. F. 1931. History in art. *Antiquity* 5: 277–90.
Peuckert, S. 2014. *Hedwig Fechheimer und die ägyptische Kunst: Leben und Werk einer jüdischen Kunstwissenschaftlerin in Deutschland*. Berlin: De Gruyter.
Piggot, R. J. 2017. *Murmur: The house as vehicle for artistic and curatorial intervention*. PhD thesis, Monash University.
Pine, B. J. and Gilmore, J. H. 1999. *The Experience Economy*. Brighton, MA: Harvard Business Review Press.
Pipe, F. 2020. Eric Allden's diary. In Pipe, F., Harrison, M., Bucklow, C., Whitfield, S., Townsend, J. H. and Pretorius, S. (eds) *Inside Francis Bacon*, pp. 12–61. London: Thames and Hudson.
Plaza, B. 2000. The Bilbao effect (Guggenheim Museum Bilbao). *Museum News. American Association of Museums* 86(5): 13–15.
Pollard, J. 2004. The art of decay and the transformation of substance. In Renfrew, C., Gosden, C. and DeMarrais, E. (eds) *Substance, Memory, Display: Archaeology and art*, pp. 47–62. Cambridge: McDonald Institute of Archaeology.
Porras-Kim, G. 2022. *Out of an Instance of Expiration Comes a Perennial Showing*. London: Gasworks.
Poss, M. 1995. *Über Leben: Skulpturen und Installation im Dialog mit Ägypten*. Munich: Staatliches Sammlung Ägypt Kunst.
Proctor, R. A. 2022. A multimillion-dollar museum and star-powered installations are arriving in Egypt. But its art scene remains desperate and disenfranchised. *Art News* 25 October. Available at: https://news.artnet.com/art-world/egyptian-art-degypte-2197437 [Accessed 3 May 2023].
Pujol, E. 2001. The artist as educator: Challenges in museum-based residences. *Art Journal* 60(3): 4–6.
Putnam, J. 1993. Exhibition brief. Unpublished British Museum internal paper.
Putnam, J. 1994. Introduction. In Putnam, J. and Davies, W. V. 1994. *Time Machine: Ancient Egypt and contemporary art*, p. 8. London: British Museum.
Putnam, J. 1995a. Ancient Egypt and contemporary art. *Visual Arts and Galleries Association (VAGA) Newsletter* October: 6 7.
Putnam, J. 1995b. *Time Machine: Antico Egitto e arte contemporanea*. Torino: Museo Egizio.
Putnam, J. 2009. *Art and Artifact: The museum as medium*. Second Edition. New York: Thames and Hudson.
Putnam, J. and Davies, W. V. 1994. *Time Machine: Ancient Egypt and Contemporary Art*. London: British Museum.
Quirke, S. 2021. Middle Kingdom birth tusks, and an enigmatic coffin in Turin. *Museo Egizio YouTube Channel*. Available at: https://www.youtube.com/watch?v=Skx2rNiXHtg&t=615s [Accessed 19 August 2022].
Rabbat, N. 2013. Egyptomania: Nasser Rabbat on 'Tea with Nefertiti'. *Artforum International* 51(7): 99–100.
Rafii, R. 2019. Destruction on display: The politics of preservation. *The Revealer* 9 August. Available at: https://therevealer.org/destruction-on-display-the-politics-of-preservation/ [Accessed 31 July 2023].
Rancière, J. 2013. *Aisthesis: Scenes from the aesthetic regime of art*. London: Verso.
Raunig, G. and Ray, G. (eds) 2009. *Art and Contemporary Critical Practice: Institutional critique*. London: Mayfly.
Reid, N. 2016. The university art museum and institutional critique: A platform for contemporary practices. *International Journal of the Inclusive Museum* 9(4): 1–15.
Renfrew, C. 2003. *Figuring it Out: The parallel visions of artists and archaeologists*. New York: Thames and Hudson.
Renfrew, C. 2004. Art for archaeology. In Renfrew, C., Gosden, C. and DeMarrais, E. (eds) *Substance, Memory, Display: Archaeology and art*, pp. 7–34. Cambridge: McDonald Institute of Archaeology.
Renfrew, C., Gosden, C. and DeMarrais, E. (eds) 2004. *Substance, Memory, Display: Archaeology and art*. Cambridge: McDonald Institute of Archaeology.

Richards, J. 2002. Text and context in late Old Kingdom Egypt: The archaeology and historiography of Weni the Elder. *Journal of the American Research Center in Egypt* 39: 79–102.
Rico, T. 2017. Heritage Studies and Islam: A crisis of representation. *Review of Middle East Studies* 51(2): 183–7.
Riggs, C. 2014a. *Ancient Egyptian Art and Architecture*. Oxford: Oxford University Press.
Riggs, C. 2014b. *Unwrapping Ancient Egypt: The shroud, the secret and the sacred*. London: Bloomsbury.
Riggs, C. 2017. In the shadows: The study of ancient Egyptian art (Review of Hartwig, Melinda K. (Hg.): *A Companion to Ancient Egyptian Art*. Chichester: John Wiley & Sons Ltd. 2015). *Orientalistische Literaturzeitung* 112(4–5): 293–300.
Riggs, C. 2019. *Photographing Tutankhamun: Archaeology, ancient Egypt, and the archive*. London and New York: Routledge.
Riggs, C. 2021. *Treasured: How Tutankhamun shaped a century*. London: Atlantic Books.
Riggs, C. 2023. Modern myths: Christina Riggs encounters ancient Egypt in Turin. *Apollo* February: 24–5.
Roberts, L. A. 2013. The role of sculpture in communicating archaeology in museums. *Papers from the Institute of Archaeology* 23(1): 1–21.
Robert Wade Design Associates. 1981. *The British Museum: Redesign and reorganisation of the Egyptian Sculpture Gallery*. London: Museums and Galleries Group.
Robins, C. 2013. *Curious Lessons in the Museum: The pedagogic potential of artists' interventions*. Farnham: Ashgate.
Roelstraete, D. (ed.) 2013. *The Way of the Shovel: On the archaeological imaginary in art*. Chicago: Chicago University Press.
Rubinstein, D. 2021. When worlds collide: Sean Kelly and Charis Tyndall on creating conversation between the contemporary and the ancient. *TEFAF* 8 September. Available at: https://www.tefaf.com/stories/when-worlds-collide-sean-kelly-and-charis-tyndall-on-creating-conversation-between-the-contemporary-and-the-ancient [Accessed 5 January 2022].
Russell, I. A. and Cochrane, A. 2013. Introduction. In Russell, I. A. and Cochrane, A. (eds) *Art and Archaeology: Collaborations, conversations, criticism*, pp. 1–8. New York: Springer.
Russmann, E. R. 2001. *Eternal Egypt: Masterworks of ancient art from the British Museum*. London: British Museum Press.
Salice, S. M. 2016. Creative revitalization of the urban space: The residual area project in Turin. In Salice, S. M. (ed.) *The Urban Gaze: Exploring urbanity through art, architecture, music, fashion, film and media*, pp. 119–27. Leiden: Brill.
Sallam, S. 2019. *They Were Also Humans: On the dehumanising nature of photographic and filmic portrayals of Egyptian mummies*. MA thesis, Universiteit Leiden.
Sallam, S. 2022. Decolonising my gaze. In Ferrari, A. and Hinson, B. (eds) *Visions of Ancient Egypt*, pp. 60–3. Norwich: Sainsbury Centre for Visual Arts.
Savoy, B. and Wildung, D. 2011. Neue Impulse aus Berlin? Ägyptische Museen vor und nach der Eröffnung des Neuen Museums in Berlin. In Bergvelt, E. and Gardner, D. (eds) *Museale Spezialisierung und Nationalisierung ab 1830: Das Neue Museum in Berlin im internationalen Kontext*, pp. 51–68. Berlin: G+H Verlag.
Schaefer, S. 2020. With the others. In Klein, J. and Loveless, N. (eds) *Responding to the Site: The performance work of Marilyn Arsem*, pp. 66–8. Bristol and Chicago: Intellect Ltd.
Schäfer, H. 1928. *Ägyptische und heutige Kunst und Weltgebäude der alten Ägypter*. Berlin and Leipzig: De Gruyter.
Schelstraete, I. 2023. Hoe het oude Egypte naar Brussel kwam. *De Standaard* 3 April: 2–3. Available at: https://www.standaard.be/cnt/dmf20230402_95612293 [Accessed 5 September 2023].
Schneider, A. 2006. Appropriations. In Schneider, A. and Wright, C. (eds) *Contemporary Art and Anthropology*, pp. 29–52. Oxford: Berg.
Schoske, S. 2018. Tiefblick: Die Skulptur 'Present Continuous' von Henk Visch. *MAAT: Nachrichten aus dem Staatlichen Museum Ägyptischer Kunst München* 7: 4–6.
Schoske, S. 2019. Mumien-Tabu. *MAAT: Nachrichten aus dem Staatlichen Museum Ägyptischer Kunst München* 12: 26–9.
Schoske, S. and Wildung, D. 2020. Objekte: Moderne Kunst. *MAAT: Nachrichten aus dem Staatlichen Museum Ägyptischer Kunst München* 16: 57–62.

Settis, S. 2018. Resurrezioni. In Ciccopiedi, C., Del Vesco, P. and Greco, C. (eds) *Anche le Statue Muoiono: Conflitto e patrimonio tra antico e contemporaneo*, pp. 9–19. Turin: Museo Egizio.

Shanks, M. 1992. *Experiencing the Past: On the character of archaeology*. London and New York: Routledge.

Shatanawi, M. 2011. Contemporary art in ethnographic museums. In Buddensieg, A. and Belting, H. (eds) *The Global Art World: Audiences, markets, and museums*, pp. 368–84. Berlin: Hatje Cantz.

Shaya, J. 2021. Lingering tropes and noteworthy narratives in recent archaeology exhibitions. *American Journal of Archaeology* 125(4): 639–55.

Sheehan, J. J. 2000. *Museums in the German Art World: From the end of the old regime to the rise of modernism*. Oxford: Oxford University Press.

Shelton, A. 2001. The recontextualization of culture in UK museums. *Anthropology Today* 8(5): 11–16.

Shelton, A. 2013. Critical museology: A manifesto. *Museum Worlds* 1(1): 7–23.

Sieg, K. 2021. *Decolonizing German and European History at the Museum*. Ann Arbor: University of Michigan Press.

Simon, N. 2010. *The Participatory Museum*. Santa Cruz: Museum 2.0.

Small, Z. 2017. Keith Haring and ancient Egypt connect at Frieze Masters. *Hyperallergic* 6 October. Available at: https://hyperallergic.com/404478/keith-haring-ancient-egypt-frieze-masters/ [Accessed 5 July 2023].

Smith, C. 2016. Beyond metaphor: Archaeology as a social and artistic practice. *Journal of Visual Art Practice* 15(2–3): 270–85.

Smith, T. 2006. Contemporary art and contemporaneity. *Critical Inquiry* 32(4): 681–707.

Smith, T. 2011. Contemporaneity in the history of art: A Clark Workshop 2009, Summary of the papers and discussions. *Contemporaneity: Historical Presence in the History of Art* 1: 3–34.

Spalding, J. 2023. *Art Exposed*. Melton Woodbridge: ACC Art Books.

Spanier, S. 2004. The Louvre, the great bastion of comme il faut art history, has succumbed to contemporary art. *Apollo* 160: 39.

Spence, R. 2017. *Like a Moth to a Flame*: Historic meets contemporary art in Turin. *Financial Times* 3 November. Available at: https://www.ft.com/content/67e60b38-baf7-11e7-bff8-f9946607a6ba [Accessed 9 May 2023].

Spencer, N. 2015. Ancient Egyptian sources. In The Singer *exhibited 1889 and* Applause *1893 by Edward Onslow Ford*. London: Tate Research Publication. Available at: https://www.tate.org.uk/research/in-focus/the-singer-and-applause-edward-onslow-ford/ancient-egyptian-sources [Accessed 3 May 2024].

Spencer, N. 2016. Modern Egypt project. *Newsletter Egypt and Sudan, British Museum Newsletter* 3: 32.

Squire, M. 2012. Classical archaeology and the contexts of art history. In Alcock, S. E. and Osborne, R. (eds) *Classical Archaeology*, pp. 468–500. Chichester: Wiley-Blackwell.

Squire, M., Cahill, J. and Allen, R. (eds) 2018. *The Classical Now*. London: Kings College London.

Staatliche Kunstsammlungen Dresden. 2014. *Paul Klee: Die Reisen ach Ägypten 1928/29*. Dresden: Sandstein Kommunikation.

Stallabrass, J. 2020. *Contemporary Art: A very short introduction*. Oxford: Oxford University Press.

Stearn, M. 2016. Contemporary challenges: Artist interventions in museums and galleries dealing with challenging histories. In Kidd, J., Cairns, S., Drago, A., Ryall, A. and Stearn, M. (eds) *Challenging History in the Museum: International perspectives*, pp. 101–14. London and New York: Routledge.

Stephens, K. 2001. Artists in residence in England and the experience of the year of the artist. *Cultural Trends* 11(42): 41–76.

Stephens, S. 2012. Artistic merits. *Museums Journal* 112: 22–7.

Stevenson, A. 2019. *Scattered Finds: Archaeology, Egyptology and museums*. London: UCL Press.

Stevenson, A. 2022a. *Egyptian Archaeology and the Twenty-First-Century Museum*. Cambridge: Cambridge University Press.

Stevenson, A. 2022b. Introduction. In Stevenson, A. (ed.) *The Oxford Handbook of Museum Archaeology*, pp. 1–26. Oxford: Oxford University Press.

Stevenson, A. and Del Vesco, P. 2024. Displaying Egypt in the world and in Turin in the nineteenth and early twentieth centuries. In Greco, C. and Ciccopiedi, C. (eds) *Memory is Our Future: Two hundred years of Museo Egizio*, pp. 165–82. Moden: Franco Cosimo Panini Editore.

Stevenson, R. J. 2014. The forgotten sense: Using olfaction in a museum context. In Levent, N. S. and Pascual-Leone, A. (eds) *The Multisensory Museum: Cross-disciplinary perspectives on touch, sound, smell, memory*, pp. 151–65. Lanham: Rowman and Littlefield.

Strong, M. 2015. Smelling fat and hearing flame: Sensory experience of artificial light in ancient Egypt. In Schellenberg, A. and Krüger, T. (eds) *Sounding Sensory Profiles in the Ancient Near East*, pp. 361–80. Atlanta: SBL Press.

Sullivan, E. 2020. Contemporary art in and out of the museum: AfricaMuseum reopening Tervuren, Belgium. *African Arts* 53(2): 80–3.

Tate, n.d. https://www.tate.org.uk/art/art-terms/h/history-painting [Accessed 3 May 2024].

Taylor, J. R. 1994. Museums: Time Machine. *The Times* 18 December.

Theuri, S. 2021. From institutional racism to duties of care. In Dalal-Clayton, A. and Puri Purini, I. (eds) *Doing the Work: Embedding anti-racism and decolonisation into museum practice*, pp. 42–55. London: University of the Arts London.

Tully, G. 2010. *'Answering the Calls of the Living': Collaborative practice in archaeology and ancient Egyptian daily life exhibitions in Western museums*. PhD thesis, University of Southampton.

Tully, G. 2017. Re-imagining Egypt: Artefacts, contemporary art and community engagement in the museum. In Onciul, B., Hawke, S. and Stefano, M. (eds) *Engaging Heritage, Engaging Communities*, pp. 91–106. Martlesham: Boydell & Brewer.

Tychy. 2023. Arts Review: 'Come to your house' by Sara Sallam. *Tychy Blog* 4 January. Available at https://tychy.wordpress.com/2023/01/04/arts-review-come-to-your-house-by-sara-sallam/ [Accessed 26 June 2023].

Tythacott, L. 2003. *Surrealism and the Exotic*. London: Routledge.

Valdez-Tullet, J. and Chittock, H. (eds) 2016. *Archaeology with Art*. Oxford: Archaeopress.

Vallaster, C., Wallpach, S. and Zenker, S. 2018. The interplay between urban policies and grassroots city brand co-creation and co-destruction during the refugee crisis: Insights from the city brand Munich (Germany). *Cities* 80: 53–60.

Vallora, M. 1995. Ritorno al futuro con I Faraoni. *La Stampa* 18 December.

Van Bockhaven, V. 2019. Decolonising the Royal Museum for Central Africa in Belgium's Second Museum Age. *Antiquity* 93(370):1082–7.

Van de Weyer, M. 2023. Kunst. *Plus (He Belang van Limburg)* 29 April: 11.

Vecco, M. and Piazzi, M. 2015. Deaccessioning of museum collections: What do we know and where do we stand in Europe? *Journal of Cultural Heritage* 16(2): 221–7.

Vergo, P. (ed.) 1989. *The New Museology*. London: Reaktion.

Versluys, M. J. 2018. 'Une géographie intérieure': The perpetual presence of Egypt. *Aegyptiaca: History and Reception of Ancient Egypt* 3: 159–66.

Vilches, F. 2007. The art of archaeology: Mark Dion and his dig projects. *Journal of Social Archaeology* 7(2): 199–223.

Vogel, S. B. 2013. Kunst am Golf: Ausstellungen in Doha, Dubai und Sharjah. *Kunstforum* 221: 244–59.

Walker, A. 2019. Exhibit review. *Studies in Late Antiquity* 3(2): 313–29.

Walker, G. 2017. A twenty-first-century Wunderkammer: Museum of Old and New Art (MONA) Hobart, Tasmania, Australia. *The International Journal of the Inclusive Museum* 9(2): 1–17.

Walker, M. and Frood, E. 2023. Marianne Walker and Elizabeth Frood in conversation. *Mass Sculpture Magazine* 2: 12–21.

Walsh, C. 2021. From Thebes to Philadelphia: Tracing the provenance of an Egyptian relief. *Barnes Foundation Research Notes*. Available at: https://www.barnesfoundation.org/whats-on/research-notes-may-2021 [Accessed 8 March 2023].

Wang, S. 2021. Museum coloniality: Displaying Asian art in the whitened context. *International Journal of Cultural Policy* 27(6): 720–37.

Warnod, A. 1911. Arts décoratifs et curiosités artistiques. *Comœdia* 20 June: 3.

Watson, A. and Keating, D. 1999. Architecture and sound: An acoustic analysis of megalithic monuments in prehistoric Britain. *Antiquity* 73(280): 325–36.

Wattie, A. 2019. Meet the artist: Liliane Karnouk. *Yomimiyo* 1 January. Available at: https://yomimiyo.com/2019/01/01/meet-the-artist-liliane-karnouk/ [Accessed 9 August 2023].

Weibel, P. and Buddensieg, A. 2007. Editorial. In Weibel, P. and Buddensieg, A. (eds) *Contemporary Art and the Museum: A global perspective*. Ostfildern: Hatje Cantz.

Weingarten, J. 2005. Review: Colin Renfrew, 'Figuring it Out, What Are We? Where Do We Come From? The Parallel Visions of Artists and Archaeologists'. *American Journal of Archaeology* 109(2): 287–9.
Welchman, J. (ed.) 2006. *Institutional Critique and After*. Zurich: JRP/Ringier.
Westgarth, M. 2020. *The Emergence of the Antique and Curiosity Dealer in Britain, 1815–1850: The commodification of historical objects*. Abingdon and New York: Routledge.
Wetzel, J. 2020. Umstrittenes Gedenken an Nazi-opfer. *Süddeutsche Zeitung* 23 October. Available at: https://www.sueddeutsche.de/muenchen/muenchen-stolpersteine-aegyptisches-museum-1.5091221 [Accessed 21 July 2023].
Widmaier, K. 2017. *Bilderwelten: Ägyptische Bilder und ägyptologische Kunst*. Leiden: Brill.
Wildung, D. 1988. *Die Kunst des alten Ägypten*. Freiburg im Breisgau: Herder.
Wildung, D. 2004. Strahlendes Rot. *Amun* 2: 32f.
Wildung, D. 2021. Auf Distanz: Altägypten und die Kunst der Modern. In Dossi, U. *Zeichen und Wunder*, pp. 1–3. München: The Staatliches Museum Ägyptischer Kunst.
Wilkinson, R. H. 1993. *Egyptian Echoes: Contemporary art inspired by ancient monuments. Exhibition catalogue*. Arizona: Sun City Art Museum.
Wilson, F. 1994. The silent message of the museum. In Fisher, J. (ed.) *Global Visions: Towards a new internationalism in the visual arts*, pp. 152–60. London: Kala Press.
Winegar, J. 2006. *Creative Reckonings: The politics of art and culture in contemporary Egypt*. Stanford: Stanford University Press.
Winter, I. 1996. Exhibit/Inhibit: Archaeology, value, history in the work of Fred Wilson. In Gangitano, L. and Nelson, S. (eds) *New Histories*, pp. 182–91. Boston: Institute of Contemporary Art.
Wolf, L. 2005. L'art contemporain au Louvre. *Etudes* 402: 108–11.
Wonsich, R. 2018. *Ethnologische Museen dekolonisieren: Kunst als Ausweg aus der Krise der Repräsentation?* Stuttgart: ifa (Institut für Auslandsbeziehungen). Available at: https://doi.org/10.17901/AKBP2.01.2018 [Accessed 3 May 2024].
Yates, D. and Smith, E. 2022. Museums and the market: Passive facilitation of the illicit trade in antiquities. In Stevenson, A. (ed.) *The Oxford Handbook of Museum Archaeology*, pp. 87–97. Oxford: Oxford University Press.
Younis, A. 2019. Nefertiti in a museum: On memory and its artefacts. *M+ Magazine*. Available at: https://www.mplus.org.hk/en/magazine/nefertiti-in-a-museum-on-memory-and-its-artefacts/#footnote-source-3 [Accessed 17 April 2023].
Zinn, K. 2019. The *Museum of Lies*: Incorrect facts or advancing knowledge of ancient Egypt? *Journal of History and Cultures* 10: 165–90.

Index

Page references in *italics* are to illustrations

www.ingramcontent.com/pod-product-compliance
Lightning Source LLC
LaVergne TN
LVHW051131260826
846232LV00020B/64
* 9 7 8 1 8 0 0 0 8 7 5 6 9 *